THE SUPER CADRES

ANC MISRULE IN THE AGE OF DEPLOYMENT

PIETER DU TOIT

Jonathan Ball Publishers
JOHANNESBURG ▪ CAPE TOWN

First published in South Africa in 2024 by
JONATHAN BALL PUBLISHERS
A division of Media24 (Pty) Ltd
PO Box 33977
Jeppestown
2043

ISBN 978-1-77619-299-1
ebook ISBN 978-1-77619-300-4
audiobook ISBN 978-1-77619-444-5

*Every effort has been made to trace the copyright holders and
to obtain their permission for the use of copyright material.
The publishers apologise for any errors or omissions and would be
grateful to be notified of any corrections that should be incorporated
in future editions of this book.*

jonathanball.co.za
x.com/JonathanBallPub
facebook.com/JonathanBallPublishers

Cover by Sean Robertson
Design and typesetting by Martine Barker
Printed and bound by CTP Printers, Cape Town
Set in Adobe Caslon Pro and Acumin Pro

For Janetha, Schalk and Lukas

And there is another feeling that is a great consolation in poverty.
I believe everyone who has been hard up has experienced it. It is a
feeling of relief, almost of pleasure, at knowing yourself at last genuinely
down and out. You have so often talked about going to the dogs – and
well, here are the dogs, and you have reached them, and you can stand
it. It takes off a lot of anxiety.

George Orwell, Down and Out in Paris and London, *1933*

And all around them sat the Russia that the slumbering puritan
in Barley had long hated but never seen: the not-so-secret czars of
capitalism, the industrial parvenus and conspicuous consumers, the
Party fat-cats and racketeers, their jewelled women reeking of Western
perfumes and Russian deodorant, the waiters doting the richest tables.

John le Carré, The Russia House, *1989*

According to Mr Mantashe, the strategic deployment of comrades
is an important part of the ANC's strategy to control the levers of
power in the state. The party seeks to exercise control over the public
administration, including the public service and the state-owned
enterprises.

Chief Justice Raymond Zondo,
Report by the Judicial Commission of Inquiry into Allegations of
State Capture, Corruption and Fraud in the Public Sector,
including State Organs, Part 6, Volume 2

Contents

PART THREE: EXPANSION

PART FOUR: DESTRUCTION

Key turning points, 1994 – present day

1994	10 May	Nelson Mandela becomes head of state
1996	October	*Sarafina 2* becomes the first post-apartheid corruption scandal
	14 June	Gear is adopted as South Africa's macroeconomic policy framework
1997	18 December	Thabo Mbeki becomes ANC president, and cadre deployment is adopted
1998	December	The Department of Energy publishes a White Paper on future energy constraints
	8 December	Jacob Zuma becomes the first chairperson of the deployment committee
	18 December	Cabinet adopts the Strategic Defence Procurement Package – the arms deal
1999	14 June	Thabo Mbeki becomes the second democratic president
2001	January	The Scorpions are established; investigation into the arms deal continues
	November	An investigation clears government of wrongdoing related to the arms deal
2002	November	Deputy President Jacob Zuma is investigated by the Scorpions
2003	23 August	Bulelani Ngcuka, national prosecutions head, declines to prosecute Zuma
2005	2 June	Schabir Shaik found guilty on corruption charges, Mbeki fires Zuma
	20 June	The National Prosecuting Authority charges Zuma

2006	20 September	Charges against Zuma are dropped
2007	October	Load-shedding starts as Eskom struggles to supply electricity
	18 December	Zuma is elected president of the ANC at Polokwane
	28 December	The NPA again charges Zuma with corruption, fraud and racketeering
2008	21 May	Amendment bills introduced to dissolve the Scorpions
	12 September	Judge Chris Nicholson finds that Mbeki interfered in the case against Zuma
	20 September	Mbeki is removed as president by the ANC, replaced by Kgalema Motlanthe
2009	30 January	The Scorpions are officially dissolved by caretaker president Motlanthe
	6 April	The NPA drops charges against Zuma
	9 June	Zuma is elected president and inaugurated at the Union Buildings
2010	June, July	South Africa hosts the FIFA World Cup.
2012	January	The Public Protector launches an investigation into Zuma's Nkandla home
	18 December	Zuma is re-elected ANC president, with Cyril Ramaphosa his deputy
	18 December	Ramaphosa becomes chairperson of the ANC's deployment committee
2013	30 April	The Gupta wedding party plane lands at Waterkloof Air Force Base
2014	19 March	The Public Protector finds that Zuma must reimburse the state for Nkandla
	24 May	Zuma is inaugurated for his second term, Ramaphosa becomes his deputy
	25 May	Ramaphosa becomes leader of government business in Parliament, and chairperson of the Eskom war room
	23 September	Tom Moyane is deployed to SARS
	December	The boards of Eskom, Transnet, Prasa and others are reconfigured
2015	9 December	Zuma fires Nhlanhla Nene as finance minister
	14 December	Pravin Gordhan is appointed finance minister after the markets crash

	11 October	Gordhan is charged by the Hawks, the NPA says it will prosecute
2016	14 October	The Public Protector releases her report into state capture
	3 November	Mcebisi Jonas, deputy finance minister, says the Guptas tried to bribe him
2017	30 March	Zuma fires Gordhan and Jonas, inserts Malusi Gigaba at finance
	18 December	Ramaphosa defeats Nkosazana Dlamini-Zuma and becomes ANC president
2018	15 February	Ramaphosa is sworn in as president after engineering Zuma's removal
	23 May	Commission of inquiry into SARS is launched; investigations into the NPA and the Public Investment Corporation followed
	20 August	The Zondo commission into allegations of state capture commences
2019	25 May	Ramaphosa is inaugurated as president after the election
	15 July	Zuma testifies at the Zondo commission, but refuses to return
2021	29 June	After a lengthy legal process, Zuma is sent to prison by the Constitutional Court
	8 July	Zuma enters prison at the Estcourt Correctional Centre
	9–17 July	Violence erupts in KwaZulu-Natal, Gauteng, fuelled by Zuma's incarceration
	21 September	Zuma is released early on medical parole by Arthur Fraser, corrections head
2022	September	Load-shedding at its worst as Eskom starts to crumble
2023	11 August	After lengthy court battles, Ramaphosa grants Zuma special remission
2024	29 May	The ANC loses its majority, Ramaphosa takes the party into a coalition
2025	14 April	Zuma corruption trial scheduled to commence in the Pietermaritzburg High Court

Key terminology

arms deal: Umbrella term for the 1999 Strategic Defence Procurement Package, aimed at re-equipping South Africa's armed forces but which became associated with widespread corruption within the ANC.

cadre deployment: The placement of party members in key positions at all levels of government and the public service, including state-owned enterprises.

democratic centralism: Political ideology, derived from Leninism, in which the decisions of top party structures are binding on all members.

deployment committee: ANC structure, created in 1998, that oversees all appointments to government and the public service, including state-owned enterprises

government of national unity: The multi-party coalition government (1994–1996) mandated by the interim constitution.

lawfare: Use of the legal system and legal means to attack political opponents or bring about policy change.

load-shedding: Periodic scheduled electricity blackouts necessitated by shortfalls in Eskom's generating capacity.

macroeconomic framework: Outline of government economic policy, setting out its broad goals, for example Gear (1996).

National Democratic Revolution: The basis of the ideology of the ANC, aimed at the building of a socialist society through a two-stage revolution.

neoliberalism: Economic thinking based around private enterprise, markets and limited state involvement in the economy.

rent-seeking: The practice of individuals attempting to profit financially from their positions in government and the public service.

Scorpions: Law enforcement agency (full name: Directorate of Special Operations) set up within the NPA to combat corruption. After the ANC's Polokwane conference, the unit was dissolved and its functions transferred to the Hawks, part of the SAPS.

spy tapes: Clandestine recordings used to advance the thesis that the prosecution of Jacob Zuma for corruption was politically manipulated.

'Stalingrad strategy': The array of legal manoeuvres used by Jacob Zuma's legal team to delay or halt his prosecution on corruption charges. The name is derived from the Soviet defence of Stalingrad in 1942–1943.

state capture: Penetration of government departments and agencies, including state-owned enterprises, by individuals (for example, the Gupta brothers) and criminal syndicates seeking to extract state resources and control policy and appointments.

Strategy and Tactics: ANC political document, updated at each party conference, setting out the route to the National Democratic Revolution and the achievement of a socialist society.

transformation: The remaking of key institutions and the economy in line with the ANC's objective of creating a socialist society.

Abbreviations

ANC	African National Congress
ANCYL	ANC Youth League
ARVs	antiretrovirals
BEE	black economic empowerment
Codesa	Convention for a Democratic South Africa
Cosatu	Congress of South African Trade Unions
DA	Democratic Alliance
DG	director general
DP	Democratic Party
DSO	Directorate of Special Operations (Scorpions)
EFF	Economic Freedom Fighters
GCIS	Government Communication and Information System
GDP	gross domestic product
Gear	Growth, Employment and Redistribution
GNU	government of national unity
HIV/Aids	Human immunodeficiency virus/ Acquired immunodeficiency syndrome
ICC	International Criminal Court
IFP	Inkatha Freedom Party
MCC	Medicines Control Council
MDC	Movement for Democratic Change (Zimbabwe)
MEC	member of the executive council (provincial cabinet)
NPA	National Prosecuting Authority
NPC	National Planning Commission

NUM	National Union of Mineworkers
NWC	national working committee
OSEO	Office for Serious Economic Offences
PCAS	Policy Coordination and Advisory Services
Prasa	Passenger Rail Agency of South Africa
RDP	Reconstruction and Development Programme
SABC	South African Broadcasting Corporation
SACP	South African Communist Party
SADC	Southern African Development Community
SADF	South African Defence Force
Sadtu	South African Democratic Teachers' Union
SAMRC	South African Medical Research Council
Sanac	South African National Aids Council
SANDF	South African National Defence Force
SAPS	South African Police Service
SARB	South African Reserve Bank
SARS	South African Revenue Service
Scopa	standing committee on public accounts
SDPP	Strategic Defence Procurement Package
SIU	Special Investigating Unit
SOEs	state-owned enterprises
SSA	State Security Agency
UDF	United Democratic Front
UDM	United Democratic Movement

Prologue

ON THE AFTERNOON OF THURSDAY, 30 MAY 2024, Gwede Mantashe stood alone in front of the giant electronic results board at the Independent Electoral Commission results centre at Gallagher Estate in Midrand.

It had been a catastrophic day for the African National Congress (ANC), with its support projected to implode. The advent of sophisticated polling ahead of the country's seventh general election meant the public had access to real-time data on sentiment as voting day approached. And in the weeks and months leading up to election day on 29 May, it had become clear the ANC was on a precipice.

Mantashe, the ANC's hidebound chairman, stood on the far right of the electronic board, staring at the Western Cape provincial numbers. The polls had been closed for 18 hours, results were trickling in and projections had already revealed the harsh truth: the ANC had been rejected by an electorate that had given the party successive overall majorities since the dismantling of apartheid. It was happening rapidly and it was happening across the country.

Over the previous months, the ANC had dismissed all questions about the possibility of losing its parliamentary majority. The party's conceit was on full display and everyone – apart from the party itself – could see it. During the election campaign, when ANC leaders were dispatched to townships, suburbs and cities across the country, they were dismissive of the portents. In Cape Town, President Cyril Ramaphosa swatted away questions about his party's performance: 'We know what is going to happen, and the people of South Africa know in their own hearts of hearts what they are going to do in terms of giving the ANC an overwhelming majority.'[1]

Fikile Mbalula, the secretary general, went to ask residents of a township north of Durban for their votes, arriving in a multimillion-rand Mercedes-AMG G63 owned by a fraud and corruption accused, Anwar 'Dogg' Khan. Mbalula's entourage flung ANC T-shirts from car windows as they cruised in and out of the township.[2] On Gauteng's East Rand, where an ANC-EFF government had been delivering misery and misrule, Mantashe berated a journalist and bluntly said, 'There will be no coalition, okay? Why do you imagine a coalition? There will be no coalition. We are working for a majority.'[3]

Two weeks before the election, polls showed that the ANC was headed for disaster. Its national support was tracking below 40 per cent and declining rapidly.[4] The party had been buoyed by two months of stable Eskom electricity supply but it seemed the effect was tapering off. The ANC needed something else, and fast. On 13 May, Ramaphosa announced that he would sign the contentious National Health Insurance Bill into law. Enacted, it could destroy private health care and the economy but it was considered a handy bargaining tool to shore up electoral support.

Despite an initial uptick, ANC support continued to decline,[5] and the following week Ramaphosa scrambled his second big and unimaginative announcement: a new ANC government would implement a basic income grant.[6] And on Sunday 26 May, three days before the election, he decided to abuse his office and demand prime airtime from the public broadcaster, the South African Broadcasting Corporation (SABC), and private news channels, to deliver an 'address to the nation'. Disguised as a statesmanlike address to commend the Independent Electoral Commission and encourage people to vote, it was nothing more than an ANC stump speech, urging the voting public to return the ANC to office. It was one of many low points during the Ramaphosa era.

At the ANC's final election rally, Ramaphosa showed all the swagger that party leaders have become known for. 'All those who say the ANC is going to be below 50 per cent will really get to see who we are on 29 May. You haven't seen anything. You hear about us in newspaper reports and you see us on TV, but you will see who the real top dog is,' he told the massive crowd at FNB Stadium in Johannesburg.[7]

Panyaza Lesufi, the ANC premier in the economic heartland of Gauteng, was equally boisterous – and utterly naive. If Ramaphosa ended the election campaign as a populist, Lesufi was the instigator. He shamelessly repurposed the province's budget to launch various 'job creation' programmes before the election, with government marketing material in the ANC's colours and his face emblazoned on posters, flyers and newspaper advertisements. 'We didn't contest these elections with only political parties. We contested these elections against talk show hosts, television stations, analysts and businesses that supported our opponents, but we remained resolute and focused. The ANC is unstoppable and victory is certain. We will win on 29 May,' Lesufi declared.[8]

At the Gallagher Estate results centre, wearing his ANC tracksuit, Mantashe slowly walked along the electronic results board, scrutinising every province's numbers. No one spoke to him and no one bothered him. He had overseen the ANC's operations and internal machinations since 2007, when he was elected alongside Jacob Zuma to the party's leadership. He had overseen the implementation of the Zuma agenda after the party's Polokwane conference and had helped to elect Zuma as head of state in 2009. During Zuma's years as president, it was Mantashe who kept the party in check and whipped the parliamentary caucus whenever there was the slightest sign of revolt. And when Ramaphosa took over, he transferred his loyalty to the new president.

Mantashe is the complete party man. He believes the ANC is the driving force in society, that the interests of the party trump everything else, including the national interest. This meant that Mantashe, like Ramaphosa and almost every other ANC leader in government, acted solely to advance the interests of the party.

As he slowly returned to the ANC desk, he stopped for casual chats with representatives of other parties, journalists and observers. Then he walked to Helen Zille, chair of the Democratic Alliance (DA) federal council. 'I didn't want to come here,' he told her in Xhosa, 'because I knew it was going to be difficult. But I also couldn't stay away.'

It was appropriate that Mantashe was there to witness the ANC's hegemony crumbling after 30 years. As the party's secretary general during its most destructive decade, its chair since 2017 and one of the most enthusiastic defenders of its ruinous cadre deployment policy, he bears more responsibility than most for its fate in the 2024 elections.

Mantashe represents a refusal to reform. And the downfall of the ANC.

Introduction

OVER THE PAST CENTURY AND MORE, South Africa has been shaped by two nationalisms: Afrikaner and African. Both were born out of strife and trauma. For Afrikaner nationalists, the motivation was the loss of their Boer republics and subjugation by the British in the Anglo-Boer War. The bitterness caused by the war – loss of political power and independence, and suppression of culture and language – never left Afrikaners. The National Party was established in 1914 as their primary political tool, and what followed was a people's project that sought to achieve two goals: the economic upliftment and emancipation of Afrikaners; and the attainment of political power to establish Afrikaner control of South Africa.

The project was driven with religious fervour. It included the establishment of enterprises such as Nasionale Pers, Rembrandt and Sanlam, the development of language and the creation of a shared historical narrative that placed the Afrikaner atop society. The ousting of Jan Smuts in 1948 signalled the final victory of Afrikaners. In control of the state, they moved to implement policies and enact bills not only to entrench their power but to rearrange society. The state was the primary tool to achieve this.

Although the Afrikaner nationalists achieved much success in their efforts to put a growing number of Afrikaners through school and university, the so-called 'poor white problem' remained a concern, so after 1948 parastatals became a primary employment agency. Employees at the railways, steelworks and harbours became increasingly

Afrikaans as the National Party government used its position to advance its constituents' interests.

The civil service was also repurposed in service of the nationalist project. The pre-1948 civil service was built on the British tradition, staffed by professional bureaucrats. While not quite leading a purge, the National Party encouraged a change of the guard. One exception was the Union Defence Force, loyal to Smuts and led by mostly English-speaking professional soldiers. The nationalists moved decisively to clean house and replace the military leadership with Afrikaners.

In 1978, *Sunday Times* journalists Ivor Wilkins and Hans Strydom wrote *The Super-Afrikaners*, published by Jonathan Ball Publishers. The book ripped open the veil of secrecy surrounding the Broederbond, revealing the depth and breadth of its involvement in the Afrikaner nationalist government and its influence over Christian nationalist society. It showed how the Bond influenced government policy, how deeply it was embedded in the cabinet and how its members were elevated to the highest positions in the state. Every head of government or state between 1948 and 1994 was a member of the Bond and its highest body, the executive council.

The book detailed how the Bond directed the affairs of the Dutch Reformed Church (known as 'the National Party at prayer'), how it controlled the mass media through the SABC and Afrikaans newspapers, and how it wielded influence over universities and education. The Bond was the network behind the apartheid state. 'Often, non-members suspected that some key issues had already been resolved in Bond divisions, making open discussion a mere formality. The question arose: did the Bond, as the organisation's leaders liked to claim, recruit people because they had leadership potential, or did, as critics argue, people get promoted and become leaders because of their Bond membership?' wrote historian Hermann Giliomee, quoted by Max du Preez in the 2012 reissue of *The Super-Afrikaners*.

Established in 1912 in response to the South Africa Act of 1910, which created a unitary South African state out of four disparate British colonies and excluded the black majority, the ANC was the standard bearer for the aspirations of black people. Its leaders – educated, articulate and determined – pleaded their case at Versailles and in London following the Great War. And in later years they tried to reason with the Afrikaner nationalists when they replaced the United Party in 1948.

The ANC has always been a dynamic organisation, and when its senior figures grew tired and docile in the 1940s, a new kind of leader emerged. Under Nelson Mandela, Walter Sisulu and Oliver Tambo, the ANC became much more strident in its attempt to liberate the black majority from the brutality and excesses of apartheid. It directly challenged the violent and repressive apartheid state, first by trying to reason with apartheid premier Hendrik Verwoerd, then by resorting to an armed struggle. In 1960 it was banned, and during 30 years of exile it enjoyed the support and patronage of much of the free world. Upon its return, in 1990, Mandela led an organisation with unmatched moral authority and in command of a cohort of leaders who sought to fundamentally change a country constructed on discrimination and exploitation.

In 1994, the ANC – the former representative of black grievances, an erstwhile underground resistance organisation and eventually a liberation movement – finally became a political party with an electoral majority. It formed a government, with Mandela as the head of state, and enjoyed wide support. Mandela's successor, Thabo Mbeki, embarked on a reorganisation of society after the elder statesman's primary job of reconciliation had been shelved following his retirement. With Mbeki modern, democratic South Africa under ANC hegemony started to take shape.

This book shows that Mbeki's plan was dependent on ANC mastery across state and society. He was an advocate of African nationalism, seeking to obtain power and maintain control of society based on the fundamental belief that his organisation was anointed to rule until, in the words of Jacob Zuma, 'Jesus comes'.

National trauma was the basis for Afrikaner and African nationalisms. Both believed in the superiority of their beliefs and sought to maintain power and control at all costs. Afrikaner nationalism entrenched a system of racial segregation, discrimination and suppression. African nationalism entrenched a closed system of patronage politics and resource extraction, delineated by race and party affiliation.

Like the Afrikaner nationalists, the ANC identified the state as the primary vehicle to fulfil its aspirations. In 1997, at its national conference in Mafikeng (today Mahikeng), the party formalised a policy known as cadre deployment. Three years after becoming the country's first fully democratically elected government, it sought to create a mechanism that would ensure its complete dominance over all levers of state power.

The argument at the time was rational enough: after the role apartheid's bureaucracy played in subjugating millions of black South Africans, the democratic state needed to replace large sections of it with new people so that the new government's reform agenda was not sabotaged or stopped. To that end, the party had to implement a system that ensured the appointment (later, deployment) of civil servants amenable to directives and policies formulated by the government.

The policy, however, went much further than advertised. It represented the fusion of the ANC with the state and sought to make it impossible to eject the ANC from the marrow of the government. In 1998, the party's deployment committee was established and placed under Zuma's leadership. Its mandate was to ensure that ANC 'cadres' (a word that references party operatives in Soviet Russia and communist China) were placed in all strategic positions in the state: the cabinet, the civil service, at the head of institutions and agencies such as the National Prosecuting Authority (NPA), in the leadership of parastatals such as Eskom and Transnet, in senior positions in the mass media, including the SABC. The goal of the cadre deployment policy was complete and irreversible ANC leadership.

The system introduced at the end of Mandela's presidency (before he left office, he assented to legislation that would make cadre deployment easier) but formulated and implemented by Mbeki ensured that the ANC's culture of patronage politics and rent-seeking would flourish. Mbeki's intention with cadre deployment was to ensure the supremacy of African nationalism and party control. But what it eventually led to was the severe weakening of the state, institutionalised corruption and the rise of a predatory class of ANC deployee focused on large-scale resource extraction.

❖

How different is the ANC's policy of cadre deployment from the Broederbond's efforts to flood National Party and government ranks with like-minded Afrikaner nationalists? During the commission of inquiry into state capture it was Barbara Hogan, a former cabinet minister, who gave the clearest insight until then on how cadre deployment distorted and destroyed good governance and accountability. She told the commission that ANC leaders, including Zuma when he was president and Gwede Mantashe when he was secretary general, saw it as their right to insist on specific appointments that were under her purview. She questioned the system of deployment, bluntly saying the system was untenable and open to manipulation and corruption.

This book explains how state capture exposed the depravity of cadre deployment. While it was abused by Mbeki to centralise control for his nationalist project, Zuma abused it to destroy the state and stay out of prison. ANC rent-seekers abused it to create elaborate and lucrative systems of patronage and extraction. And under Cyril Ramaphosa, cadre deployment became the last redoubt of party deployees as they sought to cart away as much treasure as possible before the party was voted out of power.

ANC records, released on the orders of the high court after an application by DA MP Leon Schreiber, reveal a formalised and complicated bureaucratic system at Luthuli House, where the deployment committee met to discuss almost every government appointment of significance. It had a formal secretariat, held regular meetings and kept minutes (seemingly destroying them when necessary and losing them when convenient). The records revealed how ministers had to beg to make senior appointments and were repeatedly sent away until they came with the 'right' candidates.

The deployment committee also tried to interfere with judicial appointments, and even Ramaphosa, as president, was made to apologise when he seemingly acted without the committee's input. Ramaphosa and Mantashe have spoken about the central role of the committee and how the party, and no one else, is the locus of power in the country.

Cadre deployment, the abuse of power and the politics of patronage and corruption lie at the heart of South Africa's failings under the ANC government of the last 30 years. The country has suffered from accelerated systems failure since Mandela presided over the ANC's 1997 conference and Mbeki formalised cadre deployment. Zuma helped create a mafia-like state, while Ramaphosa betrayed his lack of conviction in his pursuit of party unity over the national interest.

The net effect of the ANC's criminality and condonation of corruption, mediocrity and poor governance has been record unemployment, almost no economic growth, increased poverty, deteriorating development outcomes, high levels of crime and infrastructure collapse.

After the ANC's electoral decimation in May 2024, when it lost its majority after three decades in power, it was instructive to analyse where the party's campaign made mistakes and which actions cost it support. This book goes further and attempts to explain how the ANC's super cadres, a class of political power brokers and party headmen, consolidated their power and how the ANC squandered almost every opportunity to modernise South Africa after 1994. And it reveals how a closed crony system eventually destroyed the party of Mandela and brought South Africa to the brink.

Pieter du Toit
Johannesburg
1 June 2024

PART ONE
FOUNDATION

1

Better than the Nats?

NELSON MANDELA WAS ELECTED AS PRESIDENT at a sitting of the newly constituted National Assembly on Monday, 9 May 1994, in Cape Town. The election of the ANC leader as the South African head of state represented the culmination of the African people's conflict with colonialism and apartheid stretching over more than 300 years. Mandela's ascension to the presidency signalled victory and came with the goodwill of almost every government and political formation across the globe. With the exception of the small band of defeated white right-wingers, there was probably no one on Earth who did not want Mandela and his government to succeed.

Sitting beside Thabo Mbeki – the presumptive heir to the throne, the ANC's foremost intellectual and Oliver Tambo's de facto prime minister while the organisation was in exile – Mandela looked suitably impressed by the occasion. He wore a dark grey suit with a rose in his lapel. Every seat was filled by a Member of Parliament (MP), the ANC dominating with 252 out of 400. The country's old coat of arms remained embossed on the podium but the new republic's flag was in place by the speaker's chair. The procedure followed traditions and rules developed over more than a century of colonial and apartheid rule, but this time they were used to elect a Xhosa blueblood to lead the country, not an Afrikaner ideologue.

Mbeki, portly with a salt-and-pepper beard, vacated his seat next to Mandela as Albertina Sisulu, who once led the internal resistance against apartheid while her husband, Walter, was incarcerated, struggled with the microphone to nominate Mandela. Behind her, a young Trevor Manuel grinned. The nomination was seconded by a stern Cyril Ramaphosa, who had led the ANC negotiations team. Chief Justice Michael Corbett, appointed in 1989 (he was to serve for two more years in the democratic order), declared the nomination sound and Mandela was elected unopposed.

The short speech Mandela gave afterwards to thousands of supporters in front of the Cape Town City Hall is not regarded as one of his greatest, perhaps because his inauguration the following day in the amphitheatre at the Union Buildings in Pretoria overshadowed almost everything at the time. But after being introduced by Anglican Archbishop Desmond Tutu as 'our brand new president', he set out how he believed the new society and new country should look, function and live.

In the key passage, he tried to set a course not only for his government but for the governing party. After sketching the journey to democracy from the arrival of European settlers at the Cape of Good Hope through the ANC's policy positions and documents on constitutionalism and human rights, Mandela said this: 'They [the anchor documents] project a democracy in which the government, whomever that government may be, will be bound by a higher set of rules, embodied in a constitution, and will not govern the country as it pleases.'[1]

This was an important declaration of intent because it seemed Mandela truly believed liberal democracy could succeed only if the government bound itself to the rule of law and the supremacy of the Constitution. This implicitly and necessarily meant the democratic government would not have access to its predecessor's untrammelled and unfettered power – it would not be able to do what it liked. And Mandela declared that's how it should be.

Mandela also committed his government – which for the next two years would be one of national unity, incorporating representatives of smaller parties in terms of transitional arrangements – and future ANC governments to function at a higher ethical and moral level than the apartheid regimes. They would be 'bound by a higher set of rules', Mandela said, adding that he wanted his government to be responsive, to respect the law, uplift, build and govern for and on behalf of all South Africans. They were lofty aims.

Mandela hit the country 'like a crack of thunder', says journalist Tim du Plessis. 'After his release from prison and after he'd found his feet … when he said things like this, people thought he walked on water. Expectations of him were exaggerated but there was nothing of the image of a terrorist that the apartheid government created.'[2] Du Plessis was one of the most prominent journalists of the period, with deep contacts in the apartheid government and the vanquished Afrikaner political elite, and he had a good understanding of the inner workings of Afrikaner nationalist society. He started his career at *Beeld*, the Afrikaans daily in Johannesburg owned by Nasionale Pers, one of the biggest Afrikaner-owned corporations.

Naspers, as it was known, had historically been close to apartheid rulers, with the editor of its Cape Town daily, *Die Burger*, even known to attend National Party caucus meetings in Parliament. Du Plessis was one of its leading men, representing *Beeld* in the press gallery before being appointed its chief reporter covering the negotiating process. 'And if he [Mandela] then said, as he did, that they will hold themselves to a higher standard than the previous government, people believed him. The media believed him, I believed him because we were under the impression that this man had this incredible, globally respected moral authority. He leads the ANC and he is the ANC. The ANC is him. So, when he said this we believed it would happen.'[3]

The new president went further, saying that the new government would change people's lives and ensure dignity by helping to improve the environment in which people lived and worked so they could have a 'sense of self-esteem and confidence in the future'. Referring to the economy, he said his executive would 'encourage investors' to support job-creating projects, and the government would create a legal framework to 'assist, rather than impede, the awesome task of reconstruction and development of our battered society'. In what could be interpreted as a warning to his own party and reassurance to those who did not support the ANC, he concluded: 'We place our vision of a new constitutional order for South Africa on the table not as conquerors prescribing to the conquered. We speak as fellow citizens to heal the wounds of the past with the intent of constructing a new order based on justice for all.'[4]

There is no reason to doubt that Mandela truly believed those words, even though his successors and party brethren – or comrades – subsequently sullied and destroyed his vision and betrayed the commitment he gave. Decades after this speech, it is remarkable to think that a South African head of state or an ANC leader could deliver an address like that, for those who succeeded Mandela didn't merely stray from the path of constitutionalism, the rule of law, good governance, respect for human rights and responsive and responsible government; they abandoned it in favour of cronyism and corruption.

Du Plessis, who led *Beeld*'s political coverage of the transition period, says that even though his newspaper's position was by no means pro-ANC, it was convinced of the need for fundamental political change: 'In 1985, I was stationed in *Beeld*'s Pretoria office and the bureau chief, Piet Muller, met Thabo Mbeki in Maseru [Lesotho], arranged by a Quaker professor at the University of Pretoria, Gawie van der Merwe. Piet came back to Pretoria and told me, "Tim, these people aren't terrorists. They just want what you and I have." Well, I was this eager young political correspondent of a newspaper aligned to the National Party, owned by a company where PW Botha up until a few years before was a member of the board. So, I just listened to old Piet … but he was right, of course. And it became my position right through the period that this political transition wasn't just unavoidable, it was necessary.'[5]

Mandela's term of office was tumultuous. He took charge of a bankrupt state, a fragmented bureaucracy, a divided society and the apartheid statute books. He and his ministers had to craft a new government and state while navigating an alien and unknown legislature and a new constitutional system that still had to be tested. They had to normalise resource allocation, rebuild and reconstruct large swathes of society and establish a legal structure that ensured fairness and equality. Du Plessis and his media colleagues were convinced of the ANC's bona fides and reported as such. Mandela, Mbeki, Mac Maharaj, Pallo Jordan and other senior ANC leaders left an indelible impression on the media contingent.

The relationship between the ANC's luminaries and the leaders of the Fourth Estate was established at the Convention for a Democratic South Africa (Codesa) and the Multi-Party Negotiating Forum. 'They really were accessible. And they played the media game, or propaganda game if you will, much better than the National Party that had access to a whole department of information and publicity,' says Du Plessis. 'During the negotiations they were walking in the corridors among the rest of us ... and if you wanted to check something while writing your news report, you went looking for one of them and asked them whatever you wanted. They were enormously accessible. Chris Hani, for example, was as sweet as the sweetest honey from the Boland. He was the prime example of peace and negotiation and coexistence. He was refined, a cultured man, learned and sophisticated ... but he was a revolutionary.'[6]

The ANC had no experience of government and little management know-how. Mandela's first cabinet – 19 out of 29 government of national unity (GNU) members were from the ANC – was conspicuously devoid of executive or management experience. During the final decade and more of the ANC's exile, the organisation (it was not yet a political party) showed severe signs of strain, dysfunction and criminality. Its organisation structure was disparate, with the leadership mainly operating from Lusaka, Zambia, under Oliver Tambo as president and Mbeki, his loyal assistant.

The daily affairs were run by the national working committee (NWC), with the national executive committee (NEC) the highest structure and a revolutionary council executing the struggle. But with cadres scattered across southern Africa's frontline states – Angola, Botswana, Zimbabwe and Mozambique – as well as the UK and Eastern Europe, it was difficult for Tambo, Mbeki and others, such as Hani, to maintain discipline and more than a semblance of control.

The ANC during the late 1970s and throughout the 1980s was ragged, ill-disciplined, riven by conflict, paranoid, infiltrated by organised criminal networks, and at various times it disregarded human rights. The party's present-day malaise – poor and collapsed governance, lack of accountability, corruption and criminality – can easily be traced to that period, when reports started to emerge about malfeasance in the movement's ranks.

5

'Corruption was rampant,' one ANC cadre recalled, according to historian Stephen Ellis, who wrote the most comprehensive history of the organisation in exile and obliterated the myth of a disciplined, morally upright and ethically spotless revolutionary movement fighting for the greater good. 'Some leaders were using ANC personnel and facilities to indulge in illegal activities such as drug smuggling, car theft and illegal diamond mining.' Smuggling convoys were even protected by soldiers from the movement's military wing, uMkhonto weSizwe (MK).[7]

In 1980, Alan Brooks, a South African living in exile in London and a leader in the anti-apartheid movement, was asked to go to Lusaka to help set up a research department at ANC headquarters. What he found there shocked him and he wrote a scathing report to the organisation's leadership.[8] Beyond general observations about an 'unhealthy situation' and a 'crisis', he specifically referred to staffing problems, alcoholism, a 'lack of general discussion', a 'lack of leadership' and 'idleness and corruption'.[9] It seemed to be widespread. An internal ANC document from the time says corruption, racketeering, drug smuggling and sexual abuse of women were problems 'throughout our structures from the leadership to the last cadre in the section'.[10] Apart from general financial corruption – donor money from Scandinavian governments was said to have been stolen[11] – misuse of ANC property and cars was pervasive.

But the biggest issue seems to have been internal syndicates buying stolen cars from South Africa for personal use – or to be resold in Zambia for profit. As early as 1969, Hani warned about 'high-level corruption' and illicit moneymaking schemes, and by the late 1970s there were reports of commercial crime and smuggling.[12] According to Ellis, the car-smuggling racket seemed to have the tacit blessing of the ANC leadership, who believed it was a way to procure funds for the struggle. But by the 1980s criminality had become an enormous problem and Alfred Nzo, who was to become Mandela's first foreign affairs minister, wrote in an internal paper that 'it is clear to everybody that the evil of car smuggling is threatening our very healthy body in this region'.[13]

A list of names was provided to the leadership, but Ellis says nothing seems to have been done. Later, after it emerged that ANC members were abusing a Zambian concession to import cars duty-free, nothing was done to curb the practice. Thomas Nkobi, the ANC treasurer-general, also ignored a decree by Nzo that only vehicles in the ANC car pool were to be used.[14] Nkobi's name was later attached to the enterprise run by Jacob Zuma's benefactor Schabir Shaik, who used Nkobi Holdings as a front company for his crooked arms deal bribery scheme.

Ellis writes that ANC leaders in the late 1970s became involved in smuggling Mandrax. The organisation's links with authorities across southern Africa were the perfect foil for networks that operated in the area because they provided access to bent officials. The Mandrax networks even included new BMW and Mercedes-Benz cars, with cash and drugs hidden inside the panelling, being driven across borders. This became a massive problem and the ANC leadership listed it alongside 'violation of security', embezzlement and airline ticket fraud as a cause for concern.

In 1980, a subcommittee was established to look at the issue of corruption, with Joe Modise among its number. According to Ellis, this was ironic, given Modise's known involvement in criminality, including car smuggling. Before going into exile, he was involved in the 'Alexandra gang world' and had a penchant for good clothes and shoes, even mugging American tourists so he could commandeer a garment he liked. Nzo, the secretary general, and Nkobi, the treasurer-general, who were part of his networks, seem to have protected Modise despite his obvious criminal tendencies and his lack of organisational ability. As commander of MK since 1965, his job was to set up underground structures in South Africa and direct military action against the apartheid state.[15]

But as the years wore on and MK's lack of military prowess and success became clearer, the accusations against Modise piled up. In the 1980s, a group of ANC combatants complained to the leadership that 'for the last eight years nothing took place', referring to Modise's inability to turn Botswana into an active military zone.[16] And in Zimbabwe there was even less happening under Modise's military leadership – MK was less active there than in any other frontline state.[17]

Despite the ANC's acute lack of military success under Modise, he was able to preserve his position inside the organisation thanks to his 'control of strategic networks vital to the ANC's leadership … his propensity for violence and his skill as a political infighter … time and again Tambo defended him against criticism'.[18] There was even a charge that he used smuggling networks, intended to further the ANC's cause, for shopping in Johannesburg. 'He personally sent a comrade back home to buy Johnston and Murphy shoes,' his detractors charged, according to Ellis. Modise, who was to become the central figure in the strategic defence procurement package – the arms deal – also became Mandela's first minister of defence. And the arms deal was to be the ANC's first big ethical failure.

The ANC swept into government on a tidal wave of global goodwill. During a state visit to the United States, which saw the White House South Lawn packed with dignitaries, celebrities and a range of US military personnel and honour guards, President Bill Clinton welcomed Mandela: 'Now, all over the world, there are three words which, spoken together, express the triumph of freedom, democracy and hope for the future. They are, President Nelson Mandela.'[19]

Du Plessis says everyone – the public, the media and the business community – was completely won over not only by Mandela and his colleagues' charm but by their commitment to building a successful, functioning, democratic state. He believed the ANC leaders were absolutely committed to good government: 'Everyone believed it. And everyone bet on a successful transition, it just simply had to happen. Everyone said they were more or less convinced of the ANC's bona fides. The markets knew it and responded accordingly.'[20]

Journalists played a crucial role in preparing the ground for a peaceful transition and explaining to the public that South Africa had to become a democratic, constitutional state. Du Plessis says all editors subscribed to democracy, the transition – and the ANC leadership: 'The media corps were a diverse crowd, even though almost all of us in the mainstream were white. The English journalists were very sympathetic to the ANC … people like John Battersby, Shaun Johnson, Peter Sullivan, Allister Sparks … The Afrikaans journalists generally were more reserved. But the younger crowd, like us, when we saw the ANC were nothing like the caricature they were made out to be, bought into the whole thing much easier. Our whole being said this thing simply must happen.'[21]

There was no sign that the ANC would eventually turn out to be the organisation at the centre of state capture and corruption, of misrule, dysfunction, absolute control and statism. Says Du Plessis: 'The whole world bought into what was happening. The whole country did. So, if during that time … we were useful idiots, then the whole world were useful idiots.'[22]

But Pravin Gordhan, a celebrated ANC activist who became the founding commissioner of the South African Revenue Service (SARS), twice served as finance minister and was at the forefront of resistance against capture and corruption under Zuma, says in retrospect that signs of criminality were there. In the early days after the ANC's unbanning, with the normalisation of the political environment and the return of revolutionaries and exiles from abroad, some cadres quickly identified opportunities for enrichment. 'We had the first signs of obvious opportunism that became evident. I won't name names but in the Durban context, primarily the UDF [United Democratic Front] context, you found this streak beginning to develop. They were looking for money for themselves … guys who might have gone to Robben Island and came out, people from underground who were now repositioning themselves because they had a good instinct of what was going to come.'[23]

The streak Gordhan identified was to wreak havoc on South Africa.

2
Cadres take command

DEMOCRATIC SOUTH AFRICA'S FIRST EXECUTIVE was to be drawn from a range of political parties in accordance with the 1993 interim constitution and agreements reached at the preceding Multi-Party Negotiating Forum.

Pravin Gordhan, who was co-chairperson of the secretariat supporting the negotiations, says the ANC made 'serious compromises' in agreeing to the interim constitution because it bound a democratic government to a set of principles which the final constitution had to conform to before it could be certified by the court. But the process was principally driven forward, he says, because the ANC and the National Party were the main catalysts: 'There were 25 parties taking part [but] there were two champions for this process. They took responsibility for the country, and for shepherding it in a particular direction, and they were the National Party and the ANC. We had to make it look as if as many people as possible agreed ... but at the end of the day it was consensus [between those two parties] that counted.'[1]

Tim du Plessis, who covered the negotiations as a reporter and later edited *Beeld* and the mass-circulation Afrikaans Sunday newspaper *Rapport*, says the National Party was 'clueless' about what to do: 'The proposals they made at Kempton Park (where the negotiations were held) were cooked up by professors and the like: minority vetoes and rotating presidencies and stuff like that. And that's because they were under siege.'[2]

The ANC, as the majority party (it won 62 per cent of the vote in 1994), provided most ministers and deputy ministers in the GNU, with the National Party and Inkatha Freedom Party (IFP) seconding their leaders to the cabinet. Mandela consulted widely within the ANC before his inauguration, and although he had strong ideas about who should be his deputy, largely left the drawing up of a shortlist of potential ministers to Mbeki. 'Thabo had spent many years in exile and had also interacted with comrades inside the country; he had a better knowledge than me of people best qualified to serve in the cabinet.'[3]

Mbeki and Sydney Mufamadi – who would become police minister and later Cyril Ramaphosa's national security adviser – sat in the latter's flat and prepared a list that was forwarded to Mandela. He made two changes, introducing Derek Hanekom as minister of land affairs, despite criticism about a white person holding that portfolio, and Joe Slovo, the South African Communist Party (SACP) luminary, as minister of housing.[4]

The ANC leadership, or 'the officials' (who included Walter Sisulu, Jacob Zuma and Thomas Nkobi), accepted Mbeki's cabinet proposals. But debate ensued over whether Ramaphosa or Mbeki should take the second spot. 'He [Ramaphosa] is an impressive, adroit and persuasive individual and influenced both friend and foe [at the negotiations at Kempton Park]. He earned for himself a lot of respect and admiration and emerged as one of the most powerful figures among the constellation of eminent thinkers,' Mandela said, hailing him as 'the linchpin of the negotiations and one of the main architects of the new South Africa'.[5]

But Mandela was strongly influenced by ethnic considerations, arguing that throughout his political career he had been haunted by a perception that the ANC 'is a Xhosa organisation'. He believed the new national executive should reflect the country's ethnicities and that having Ramaphosa – whom he believed to be qualified for the job – from a smaller group (he is Venda) would assuage fears. 'Notwithstanding my argument, the officials were not convinced. They insisted that the general public would accept that, in choosing Thabo, the ANC was guided by merit and not tribal considerations. On the contrary, my concern was not based purely on merit, but on the false perception I felt it was our duty to correct,' Mandela said.[6]

On 6 May 1994, four days before Mandela's inauguration, he made his decision. Mbeki was surprised, having become used to losing out to Ramaphosa.[7] Mandela offered Ramaphosa the position of minister of foreign affairs, which he declined.[8] It set Mbeki on the path to the presidency as Mandela's inevitable successor, and this was confirmed later in 1994 when he was anointed as the ANC deputy president and Ramaphosa was re-elected unopposed as secretary general. But the harried and hurried internal ANC machinations before it succeeded the National Party in government in May 1994 sowed the seeds of a political conflict that was to direct the country's course for the next 30 years.

Mbeki, a skilled backroom operator, was the preferred choice of the ANC's exile elite and was able to manoeuvre himself into position, despite Ramaphosa's vaunted reputation thanks to the negotiations and his proximity to Mandela. But Mbeki's style of leadership – intransigent, cold – later led to bitter enmity in the ranks of the ANC leadership and helped foment the rise of Zuma, later to prove the single most destructive post-apartheid figure in South Africa.

The ANC members of the cabinet had talent, for sure, but they were all untested as executive managers in an organised system of government and governance, and they were schooled in disruption, destruction and revolution rather than reconstruction. Inevitably, they distrusted the bureaucracy and civil service they inherited – after all, civil servants administered apartheid's system of institutional racism. Add into the mix the culture of heightened paranoia, suspicion and distrust in which the organisation was marinaded over the last decades of exile – cadres were sent to camps, beaten, tortured and in some instances killed, based on nothing more than hunches[9] – and pervasive corruption, and Mandela's task became even more herculean.

Apart from the delinquent Joe Modise, the former MK commander who took charge of the armed forces, and Alfred Nzo, the ANC secretary general who became a nonentity as foreign minister, the cabinet also included Trevor Manuel (trade and industry, later a celebrated finance minister), Tito Mboweni (labour, later an accomplished Reserve Bank governor) and Hanekom (land affairs, later an ardent opponent of Zuma and state capture). Mandela also rewarded loyalty and seniority, appointing the SACP's Slovo to housing, law professor (and Manuel housemate) Kader Asmal to water affairs and struggle and UDF lawyer Dullah Omar to justice. Steve Tshwete became a popular sports minister and a young Mufamadi (later a leading ANC veteran opposing Zuma and Ramaphosa's national security adviser when he became president) took charge of the police.

Stella Sigcau, an ageing former homeland prime minister, made the cut at public enterprises (Mandela defended her when she was accused of corruption) and Nkosazana Dlamini-Zuma started her marathon cabinet stint when Mandela appointed her (then a 45-year old Medical Research Council researcher) as minister of health. She was to provide the ANC government's first foray into state corruption, but more about that (and Sigcau) later.

The only big-ticket ministries that did not go to the ANC were finance (Derek Keys was independent), energy (Pik Botha from the National Party reluctantly took that post) and home affairs (which went to IFP leader Mangosuthu Buthelezi). Mandela was aware that the incoming ANC government was an unknown quantity and that financial and economic decision-makers would be uncomfortable with 'a new entity with untested systems'.

Keys had served the outgoing government of FW de Klerk with aplomb and had the respect of the liberation movement, said Jay Naidoo, the firebrand Congress of South African Trade Unions (Cosatu) general secretary,[10] and regularly consulted with Mandela before he ascended to the presidency. 'There are certain positions we will not fight for now, because the country might not be ready for it,' Mandela told colleagues.[11] Some appointments did not work out: Naidoo became minister without portfolio in charge of the Reconstruction and Development Programme (RDP) and was later shuffled out of the executive. Pallo Jordan, the ANC's resident intellectual who went to posts and telecommunications, was also dropped.

Despite being head of state, Mandela seemed to believe himself to be above the fray, and in a sense that was the task he set himself. He did not want to be seen as the partisan political leader, solely focused on advancing the ANC agenda (refer to his 9 May speech, where he said a democratic government would not be able to govern as it pleases, nor did the ANC set the government's plan of action as 'conquerors'), but wanted to be a unifier.

Mandela had to make early choices about what his priorities would be and that necessarily extended to how his government would function. He 'genuinely felt that this principal task must be to continue the business of reassuring white society, all society, so that you do not have conflict', Mbeki said.[12] The new president didn't pay much attention to matters of state beyond peace and security, which meant 'the running of government shifted to the deputy president's office. Madiba didn't pay attention to what government was doing. We had to, because somebody has to,' Mbeki explained.[13] Mandela's focus in the first years of democracy was to prevent 'the unravelling or the deterioration of the transition project', said academic Mcebisi Ndletyana. 'He decided that stability was more important.'[14]

That doesn't mean Mandela wasn't a fierce champion of the ANC's extensive plans for social and economic transformation and societal reorganisation. He was a loyal cadre who readily submitted to decisions of the party's hierarchy. And some of the most significant policy formulations and implementations happened under his watch, including the system of cadre deployment, which would subsequently wreak such havoc at all levels of government.

Du Plessis says South Africans, in particular the media, should have paid more attention to how the ANC-in-government went about its business: 'We should have listened more carefully. We should have read everything they published and listened to every word they spoke, and we should have believed what they said. We should have tried harder to find out what was happening behind the scenes and in the bureaucracy. Because by then they were already starting to clean out the civil service. We did warn about it but what could you do? They were the duly elected government of the day, they were legitimate and were just doing what newly elected governments do across the world: putting their own people into key positions ...'[15]

Trevor Manuel, a spritely 38 years old when he became minister of trade and industry in 1994, had no qualms about changing personnel and changing attitudes in a department that was previously governed by apartheid statute. He started making changes on day one, including insisting on appointments that officials told him were not allowed.[16]

Did Mandela's age – he was 75 when he became president – play a role in his leadership style and his involvement in governance? It is difficult to say, because even though he had had health scares, including a prostate operation while in prison, he was remarkably healthy for a septuagenarian. His intellect was still sharp and intimidating and he had shown great skill and determination in steering the ANC through the negotiation period. But Mandela clearly was not a state-builder; he wasn't versed in statecraft and managing the complex affairs of government, never mind a government that was embarking on a massive integration and reconstruction project.

FW de Klerk was later asked who he thought was the better president: 'In terms of administration I was the better president, but as the leader of a nation he was the better one.' Tony Leon, the former Democratic Party (DP) and DA leader who had an amiable relationship with Mandela between 1994 and 1999 – and ready access to the president – says: 'Indeed Mandela, rather like Ronald Reagan across the Atlantic and some years earlier, had a brilliant ability to paint the broad canvas on which he wanted his administration to be portrayed and remembered by posterity, and he certainly omitted no colours or shades from his palette. Like Reagan, and except where some intense personal or political interest was involved, Mandela did not busy himself in too much detail, and ran a presidency of both famous intimacy and some detachment from the daily happenings in governance.'

Gordhan says the ANC achieved most of what it set out to do when the negotiations commenced. And once in government it was able to put its RDP into place, codifying it in the final constitution. 'Across the 30 years after 1994, some of the things we wanted to do would disappear and others were consolidated. But the principal issues related to poverty, inequality and the economy are contained in chapter two of the Constitution.'[17]

Du Plessis calls this period – the first couple of years after 1994 – the 'Pretoria Spring'. 'We thought these guys were finding their feet, that they were starting to get going and starting to govern. And it

15

was like spring rain: it was welcome, everything was open and we had access. Thinking back, I think this was actually a problem. We weren't critical enough; we were so flabbergasted because of the sudden openness, the transparency ... and this was perhaps one of the reasons we weren't critical enough. Previously, the system was closed. You didn't know how they thought. You had to get to know a minister very well before he would tell you what was discussed in cabinet. They actually never spoke about such things. But suddenly things were open and even ANC people outside cabinet gossiped with you about what was going on. It all contributed to the almost carnival atmosphere in the country.'[18]

The running of government, executing policy and ensuring accountability, fell to Mbeki, whose biographer, Mark Gevisser, writes that Mandela 'was an executive president who wished to lead, but had no particular interest in governing. As Mandela's first deputy president (De Klerk was second deputy president), Mbeki was South Africa's de facto prime minister.'[19] Leon recounts a colleague saying Mandela was like 'the lord mayor of Africa' while Mbeki was 'CEO'.[20]

Mbeki was tasked with setting up Mandela's presidential office,[21] which arguably enabled him to start building his own structures for command and control – a central and crucial feature of ANC governments. Joel Netshitenzhe, one of the ANC's most cerebral cadres – and an Mbeki loyalist – was seconded to the president's office as chief of communications, while other Mbeki confidants were also deployed in the Union Buildings' west wing, where the president's suite occupies offices on the second floor, under the clock tower.

Anthony Sampson writes in his authorised biography of Mandela that the new president quickly realised the limits of his powers, having been warned by De Klerk before he took office that it was 'comparatively easy' to win an election but exceedingly more difficult to govern.[22] Mandela delegated almost all executive functions to his deputies, who divided the responsibilities for cabinet committees between them.[23] He presided over fortnightly cabinet meetings 'with a light' hand, only intervening when necessary. 'He took it like a chief,' said Mac Maharaj.[24]

Discussions in cabinet were 'surprisingly non-partisan', devoid of ideology and with 'Afrikaner ministers genuinely committed to making the GNU work. You'd think they were part of the democratic movement,' one cabinet member said.[25] By and large, policy discussions reflected what the ANC leadership wanted, and De Klerk often had to mediate in disputes between ANC ministers.[26]

When De Klerk exited the GNU, Mbeki took sole responsibility, in addition to becoming the 'economics tsar', which meant he was responsible for coordinating economic policy across the government.[27] Setting up new offices, new teams and a new government proved a difficult challenge for the incoming administration. Mandela 'disarmingly' told Leon during a meeting about the dysfunction of Parliament that the ANC did not have the benefit of transition from struggle to power with an intervening period of preparation. 'The ANC went straight from the bush into power,' Mandela told Leon and his DP colleagues.[28] He then explained that the 1994 transition was the most dramatic political conversion since 1948, when the National Party was first elected. 'The NP,' Mandela said, 'had served a long period in opposition in Parliament before assuming power.'[29]

Du Plessis's optimism over the new government quickly started to wane: 'They had no idea about governance. They didn't know how a government worked. And that's why they were so wrong about how a governing party should relate to a government. They didn't know where the dividing line is. Even in the United States and Britain, where there are political appointments, there are certain lines that not even they cross. These guys just did it. And initially I don't think it was done in bad faith, it was out of pure ignorance. We didn't realise how they struggled [to govern].'[30]

When De Klerk became president in 1989, he dismantled large parts of the edifice constructed by PW Botha, who became known as the 'imperial president'. De Klerk stripped the Union Buildings 'down to its barest essentials', but with the change of guard it now had to cater for three outsized personalities: Mandela, Mbeki and De Klerk.[31] It simply wasn't equipped to do so and the new occupants were confronted by a lack of resources, infrastructure and staff. Naidoo, as minister in the Presidency in charge of the RDP, says that when he moved in, shortly after Mandela's inauguration, his office didn't even have a kettle.[32]

Mbeki badly managed the transition from struggle luminary to executive deputy head of state, with his office maintaining such an 'elastic notion of time' that meetings started late or were even cancelled.[33] This stood in stark contrast to Mandela, who was always painfully aware of other people's time. Mandela 'was strictly punctual' while Mbeki 'was more casual about appointments', Sampson wrote, explaining the bind Mbeki found himself in – and which Gevisser later wrote caused such great irritation for Mandela's successor: 'Mandela was given credit for triumphs, while Mbeki took the blame for mistakes.'[34]

In 1998, a commission chaired by academic Vincent Maphai recommended sweeping restructuring and reforms to address 'an absence of strong central leadership, vision and coordination from the office of the president'.[35] The ANC government, in the early years, was 'scattershot and inefficient'.[36]

3

Broederbond in the machine

THE MANDELA GOVERNMENT FACED three significant challenges: restructuring the public service to enable it to govern efficiently; crafting and implementing new policies; and taking charge of the economy. The ANC came into power determined to completely overhaul and restructure the state, changing departmental names and functions, altering the bureaucratic structure and shaping a new corporate governmental culture. It set out to redesign and rebuild the government and its institutions from the ground up. But for it to be able to achieve this, it needed full command and control of the apartheid civil service.

It almost immediately started with a restructuring process, including offering voluntary severance and early retirement packages (the so-called 'sunset clauses' gave job security to serving white civil servants and guaranteed their pensions, a source of great anger in the broader liberation movement). 'Care has been taken to ensure an orderly process of transition with due protection against the loss of key personnel.'[1] This was not only informed by the new government's 'developmental focus' but by 'a history of discriminatory provision of public services; and under-representation of blacks and women in much of the civil service ... and perceived non-delivery of public services and poor public administration in some areas,' according to the then Department of Finance (today the National Treasury).[2]

The reality, however, was that the next couple of years saw an exodus of teachers, health workers and skilled parastatal employees. This opened opportunities for transformation, a singular focus of the Mandela and later Mbeki governments – but it also severely curtailed service delivery, skills transfer and efficient government.

Mandela announced that he and senior government leaders would take a salary cut to set the tone before the civil service rationalisation started. The new government was extremely suspicious of the old guard, fearing that their latent antagonism towards their erstwhile political enemies could scupper any chance the GNU had of changing the country. It wanted to reconfigure and reorganise the civil service as a matter of urgency, seeing it as an opportunity to democratise the public service. Ideologically, it also believed a reconfigured bureaucracy, stacked with ANC loyalists and cadres, would entrench the party's support and make it almost impossible to eject it from power. It was to prove a political masterstroke for the ANC – but in later years became the bedrock on which the party's vast system of patronage was built and helped to hardwire networks of corruption and malfeasance into the state.

In the early years, though, the ANC just wanted civil servants who were amenable to the new dispensation. Mac Maharaj tells of his apprehension when he stepped into his ministerial office in May 1994,[3] while Mandela spoke of a wariness between him and presidential staff[4] and Trevor Manuel recalls the same when he went to his perch at the Department of Trade and Industry.[5]

'The key issue was how to get alignment in policy, and bear in mind, over the period I had come to understand who the Broederbonders were in the departments,' recalls Manuel. 'The human resources departments were the centre of their control. Some of them left government early on but some hung on with whitened knuckles. And it was the Public Service Commission that may have been the epicentre of Broederbond appointments. They controlled everything.'

While at the National Treasury, Manuel wanted to appoint Ismail Lagardien, then *Sowetan*'s parliamentary correspondent, as spokesperson, but the Public Service Commission, in charge of appointments to the public service, refused, saying Lagardien was not qualified. 'I had a run-in with the head of the Public Service Commission. And his brother at the time was the Auditor-General.

When you deal with this period, it's quite important to accept the starting points ...'[6]

He also recalls that there were 'all kinds of people' in government departments in the early days, many with doubtful credentials. One of them was a lawyer who went to Manuel's office and introduced himself as a former adviser to Adriaan Vlok, the notorious minister of law and order. He claimed Manuel's release from detention some years before was thanks to his intervention, and the minister started asking around. It turned out that the lawyer had been struck from the roll after he overcharged Vlok's department and had been quietly smuggled into the Department of Trade and Industry in another position. Manuel interpreted the lawyer's claim – that he had helped release him from prison – as a shot across the bow. 'If you're asking about hostility ... that he could tell me this ...'[7]

He offers a contextual explanation for what became known as cadre deployment – a party policy he later criticised: 'Just before we got into government, the deficit was 8.3 per cent in 1992, 1993, so you're not starting on zero. The South African Reserve Bank had also built up a net open forward position in trying to defend the rand with $47 billion, so the reserves at the SARB had a minus sign in front and that had to be worked up – not down, up! – to zero. Tax receipts were unbelievably low because the tax administration was very poor. In fact, there were so many loopholes in the tax system. Government borrowing was very, very expensive. There was no foreign borrowing, government could only borrow locally. There was the prescribed asset requirement, with every pension fund in the country required to put their money into government. So, it was quite a terrible situation in respect of public finances.'[8]

The incoming government, therefore, had to immediately make sweeping and urgent interventions, not only to give effect to the ANC's election promises and embark on a fundamental reorganisation of society but to prevent the country's finances and economy from deteriorating further. And Manuel argues that could not be done with some of the senior staff still in place at former apartheid government departments. Key executive positions had to be filled with officials and bureaucrats who were supportive and receptive to new policies and a new government. And as new ANC people entered the Department of Finance – people like Maria Ramos and Andrew Donaldson – they were put together on the 19th floor of the building on Proes Street in Pretoria. 'It was known as the ANC floor,' says Manuel.[9] But his analysis and recollections also reveal that, despite the initial tension and distrust that followed the change of government, he did not experience major incidents of subversion or overt hostility. It must, however, be added that Manuel is particularly strident and combative and has over the course of his career rarely entertained any form of resistance.

'I became minister of trade and industry, and the director general of trade and industry had left about a year before the elections because he didn't want to be part of this democracy. There was an acting DG, oom Gerrie Breyl, who ... was a mild-mannered chap. I got there and there was no computer in the minister's office. The only thing I remember was a pink chaise longue, a couch for the minister. So, I called the manager and said, "What is this?" They said, "No, ministers rest in the afternoons." I said, "Okay, but I haven't come here to rest, you know, I've come here to work and I need a computer," and so on. And they were very shocked, because none of the men who were seniors in the department were computer literate. There were secretaries to do that stuff. So, you were driving a cultural change. I'm not pretending that I was a computer whiz-kid, but psychologically there is a shift in what's happening, and I introduced a system of regular meetings.[10]

'I needed to bring in a transition team of people to the department. Included there were someone who became DG later – Alistair Ruiters, who came in as an adviser – Alan Hirsch, who's now a professor, and Mfundo Nkuhlu, who is now the chief operating officer at Nedbank. It was an all-male team; I apologise for that. And the guy who was head of human resources, a guy called Breytenbach. Breytenbach said, "Minister, you can't do this. You must put it out to tender," and so on ... I said, "No, there's a change of government, a fundamentally important change of government and I need to bring in some people." And he said, "No, I can't allow it." And I said, "Yes, you will allow it." And so eventually, you know, ministers get their way, and Breytenbach left and went across to the Department of Health.'[11]

Manuel's biggest run-in was with Estian Calitz, the director general at the Department of Finance. Calitz was appointed deputy director general in 1989 and elevated to director general in October

1993. 'He had taken over from a guy called Gerhard Croeser, and on 26 February 1996 Chris Liebenberg (who was Mandela's finance minister) told Estian that the president was announcing a change in the minister of finance that day. And Estian said, "Minister it's going to be very sad, but who's replacing you?" Liebenberg said, "Minister Manuel, because he was a minister in another department already." And Estian said, "Oh, but then I must redetermine my conditions of service. I must go, I can't work with him." That's where it starts.[12]

'So, when I get there ... in the building in Proes Street where the finance department sat, we were on the 25th floor and as you came into the reception there was a wall with bulletproof glass. And in that reception area there were photographs of past finance ministers. I think [Klasie] Havenga was the first finance minister in 1929, through to Barend du Plessis, their photos were there. And I said, "But Estian, those photos must come down." And he said, "No, that's our history." And I said, "Estian, that might be your history but I don't think it's our history." I said, "You didn't even have the decency to put up the photographs of Derek Keys and Chris Liebenberg. You stopped with Barend. There's a message. I'm asking you to take that down."[13]

'And he said, "No, I can't take it down, because the Auditor-General will come after me." So, I said, "Look, I will write to the Auditor-General and tell him that I asked you to take those photographs down. I don't know what will happen to them in the department. Why don't you take them with you because you're going? You can pack them into your *trommel*, you can hang them in your study. It's your personal history and you can have it."[14]

'But I'm saying in many cases, you couldn't build with the attitude of people who were very senior in the public service.'[15]

Tim du Plessis, who as a politics reporter in the 1980s and 1990s got to know the National Party establishment well, has a different perspective on the civil service and the transition, arguing that many senior bureaucrats were positive and welcoming of the new order: 'There were many people in those institutions of state who were well disposed to what was happening. Someone like Niël Barnard [head of the National Intelligence Service] became very friendly with Mandela and it turned out that they became relatively close, for example. He also worked closely with Mbeki, especially in the approach to the 1994 election.'[16]

He cites Fanie van der Merwe as the quintessential example of 'the good bureaucrat'. Van der Merwe was director general of the departments of justice and internal affairs before he was appointed constitutional adviser to FW de Klerk's government during the negotiations. He served on the secretariat at Codesa and the Multi-Party Negotiating Forum and helped establish the Transitional Executive Council ahead of the 1994 elections. After the elections he helped draft the country's electoral laws and was a commissioner of the Independent Electoral Commission until 2011.[17] 'Van der Merwe maintained his independence as a bureaucrat but made sure he understood what the [De Klerk] government wanted to do. He was very endearing but efficient. And in the ranks of bureaucrats he was considered an elder statesman with enormous stature. He never smothered dissent but worked to convince others not to get up to mischief. And that was important,' says Du Plessis.

'And then there was the symbolism of General Georg Meiring, the head of the apartheid South African Defence Force [SADF], saluting Mandela as the air force jets roared above at the inauguration in Pretoria. And that also sent a message to public servants. Obviously, there were many who were not so positive about what was happening and they eventually left or were shifted out. But unfortunately, the new government also got rid of a large cohort of civil servants who understood the system and could have made a big contribution in the early years. Remember, we inherited our civil service culture from the British. "We serve all governments with equal loyalty and equal contempt," was the saying. And it remained part of the culture. After 1948, with the victory of the Nationalists, they did get rid of English speakers, mainly in the defence force, but there weren't major purges in the civil service. As the English bureaucrats' periods of service ended, they were just replaced. I was never aware of mid-level resistance after 1994. But maybe there was ...'[18]

The GNU's priorities in rebuilding the public service rested on six pillars, including a belt-tightening exercise, reprioritisation of programmes, rationalisation and reorganisation, and restructuring of state assets, 'including privatisation'.[19] 'Where inherited policies and spending programmes are inconsistent with the policies of the GNU, they are undergoing revision and in some cases activities will be cut back or eliminated,' the finance department said.[20]

The biggest job was to get a handle on the vastness of the disparate arms of the civil service as the state functions of the four 'independent homelands' (Transkei, Bophuthatswana, Venda and Ciskei) and other 'self-governing' territories were integrated back into the central government. There were enormous implications: wage disparities had to be corrected, the duplication of functions had to be rationalised, fiscal transfers reversed and debt reallocated. And the various former state departments – including 'own affairs' for the different 'national groups' under apartheid – had to be welded together. For example, one national department of education had to be established where before 1994 there were several catering for the homelands and different race groups. Apartheid had created a byzantine organisational mess.

Pravin Gordhan says it is easily forgotten today that 13 administrations were consolidated in two years: 'That applied across the board. Education, health, housing, social security ... all of it. And revenue collection went through a similar exercise. You had to bring the tax authorities of the so-called independent states into the system and that affected the culture, because you brought the Bantustan culture of corruption and incompetence into what we planned was going to be a very modern administration.'[21]

Manuel says he was part of negotiations with Keys (the last apartheid finance minister) and Theo Alant (a National Party and government official), who were unable to say what the contingent liabilities of the self-governing territories were: 'There were major issues that arose consequently. In Bophuthatswana, that entire Mmabatho area was built with pension fund money without a revenue stream ... Then you had a situation where the pension funds of Venda and Ciskei were privatised and up to today many people have still not been able to recover money from them.'[22] By mid-1995, 'the functions and administrative structures of the former public services [had] been comprehensively reviewed and redeployed into new national departments and provincial administrations ... most of the functions and organisational components of the former national and regional authorities were transferred to new legal entities with effect from 1 July 1994',[23] the Department of Finance review read.

Within its first year in government, the ANC-led GNU launched broad and sweeping policy reform proposals. The minister of education, Sibusiso Bhengu, published a White Paper proposing significant reforms to basic and higher education and in 1996 started overhauling the school system and curricula.[24] The Department of Health was restructured and Nkosazana Dlamini-Zuma – the minister who would become a cabinet fixture for three decades – appointed nine committees to examine the government's priority areas. Joe Slovo, the housing minister, established housing programmes with the RDP office, planning to build 'millions' of 'RDP houses'. Funds and subsidies were redirected away from commercial farmers to small-scale subsistence farmers and land reform restitution projects were crafted. The security services – the defence force, police and intelligence – were also rapidly reconfigured.[25] 'The South African Police Service is in the process of changing its operational style to a community policing approach, which requires extensive and continuous community involvement. It is also involved in a transformation process involving amalgamation and rationalisation. The process will improve legitimacy by increasing transparency, accountability and sensitivity to human rights, thereby also contributing to reconstruction and reconciliation.'[26]

The GNU reforms were broad. Transport, water provision and sanitation, electrification, trade policy, industrial policy – every function and policy position inherited from the apartheid government went on the chopping block. The GNU launched the Masakhane campaign to improve the culture of payment for municipal services, immediately allocated millions of rand to improve local infrastructure and appointed the Katz commission to investigate the tax regime and make recommendations.[27] The government's activities in the first couple of years after 1994 represented nothing less than a complete reorganisation and fundamental reconceptualisation of the South African state and its government.

❖

Like all his colleagues in the executive, Manuel was under pressure from the start, first at the Department of Trade and Industry then at the National Treasury, formed by amalgamating the departments of finance and state expenditure. After the stoush with Breytenbach about the appointment of a new leadership team, Manuel says things settled down and started working reasonably well: 'For the rest, I thought we worked reasonably well together, because we introduced a new culture. We brought people together and we developed new approaches ... we needed officials who understood the situation a bit better and we got the show on the road. So, we built the system, working with the officials, and I didn't experience hostility [then]. Once we were over the first period we started involving people from the outside, for example pulling in academics and the unions to try and save the motor industry in South Africa. You had to harvest these things and we couldn't have done it without a reasonable amount of goodwill from public servants.'

Those examples of goodwill seem to have been prevalent at the Treasury. Manuel cites the instances of Hannes Smit, who was director general of the Department of State Expenditure, and Trevor van Heerden, commissioner of Inland Revenue, forerunner of SARS. The finance minister came to rely quite heavily on Smit, who was wont to whisper in Manuel's ear when provinces showed increased profligacy, after which the minister came down heavily on errant provincial deployees. But after some years in the new dispensation, Smit went to Manuel and said he and other deputy directors general believed it was time for them to transition out of the department to make space for new officials. And they agreed on a planned exit over a specific period, which meant not everyone left at once.

'It wasn't a hostile arrangement. They came to me. And there was an understanding of the fact that if you wanted to do new things, you sometimes needed new people and new approaches. So, the question about cadre deployment is a fundamentally important question. Because unless you can see eye to eye with these people, you'll see all these officials and say that you can't work with them.'[28] Van Heerden resigned as commissioner of SARS in August 1999 but stayed on as an adviser to Gordhan, who succeeded him, 'so that we could transition these things through because the establishment of SARS was a big issue.'[29]

Manuel admits that maybe he radiated 'sullenness' in the early years (moody, sour or glowering, according to the *Collins Thesaurus A–Z*, 2006) but that he tried to be 'present' when chairing meetings or rearranging and redesigning internal systems. 'It was about building a culture; it was about shifting a culture,' he says.[30]

❖

The GNU inherited a country racked by violence, bureaucratic inefficiency, a tepid and misfiring economy, enormous inequality, unemployment and poverty. Society had been arranged along racial lines for decades and it would take much more than an activist Parliament rewriting the statute books to correct matters. There is no doubt, therefore, that the ANC had an enormously complicated and delicate task ahead of it.

Forgotten today is that it wasn't merely a change of government and new ministers taking over existing departments of state: new legal entities had to be established, even though many of the apartheid government's structures were subsumed into the new government. The GNU inherited the bureaucracy and offices of state, yes, but it had to forge a new culture and align departments to the policy imperatives of the ANC. And it had to do so while the final constitution was being written between May 1994 and May 1996, the deadline for the finalisation of the supreme law.

Between 1990 and 1994, and despite not having any experience in economic matters, Mandela rather rapidly adjusted his view of how the modern South African economy should look and what was needed to ensure growth. He had rattled big capital on 23 May 1990 with his first major speech on the economy after his release from prison, reaffirming his commitment to the Freedom Charter to a constellation of business leaders at the Carlton Hotel in Johannesburg. The angry speech – written by Mbeki and quoting Shylock from Shakespeare's *The Merchant of Venice* – revealed the ANC's still deeply held antagonism towards capital.

Michael Spicer, an Anglo American executive at the time, later called the speech a disappointment: 'The ANC was still clearly wedded to nationalisation. After that we said to them, "Guys, get real. The

[Berlin] Wall has fallen, socialism has essentially been consigned to the rubbish bin and you're still talking the language of the old world." There were all these new ideas … We were telling them that whatever role they, the ANC, were going to play, they had to get up to speed with economic thinking and the way the world was changing.'[31]

After his visit to the World Economic Forum in Davos, where Chinese and Vietnamese leaders explained to him that the age of rigid socialist and communist economic theory was gone for ever, Mandela changed tack. 'At that stage, Madiba was going around talking about how we're going to nationalise mines because that's what the Freedom Charter said,' according to Manuel. But on his return to South Africa, things changed. 'He came back and in a quite undefiant way, said, "No, I've been convinced that you can't just nationalise, that we mustn't just nationalise."'[32] Spicer said it quickly crystallised in the minds of people such as Mbeki and Manuel – and Mandela – that left-wing economic positions were unsustainable if the ANC wanted to redevelop and reconstruct the country. They also started to understand former Conservative British Prime Minister Margaret Thatcher's catchphrase: 'There is no alternative.'

In the late 1980s and early 1990s, gross domestic product (GDP) saw its longest slide since the Second World War, with 51 months of negative economic activity. The promise of peace and democracy saw a recovery in 1993 and 1994, with growth – albeit tepid and insufficient – of 1.2 per cent and 3.2 per cent being recorded.[33] Ever since the foreign debt crisis of 1985, precipitated by PW Botha's infamous 'Rubicon' speech (a misnomer if ever there was one), foreign direct investment wasn't only halted but reversed. The rand had also depreciated badly, losing 11 per cent of its value between 1992 and 1993,[34] and government finances were in trouble. The budget deficit (when expenses exceed revenue) had reached 7.1 per cent of GDP in the year before the GNU was sworn in and in 1994 stood at 5.4 per cent.[35] And the government's debt – including foreign debt, which was negligible – stood at 43 per cent, rising to almost 50 per cent in 1996.[36]

The socioeconomic environment, shaped by apartheid and years of institutional discrimination and racism, was completely skewed. Unemployment was high, with a fifth (20 per cent) of all South Africans of working age unemployed; that number rose to 31.5 per cent on the expanded definition, which included those who'd given up looking for jobs. This disproportionately affected blacks: officially, 24.7 per cent of blacks were unemployed, compared to 3 per cent of whites, 17.6 per cent of coloureds and 10.2 per cent of Asians. And that number rose dramatically on the expanded definition, with 39.2 per cent of blacks jobless.[37]

The skewed pattern was replicated elsewhere, with more than 45 per cent of blacks living in informal or traditional housing in 1996, just more than 49 per cent of households not having electricity (the vast majority of them black) and only seven million households having access to piped water. These challenges were the product of deep-rooted patterns of economic activity, constructed not only on cheap black labour but also on expensive skilled labour.[38]

Some of these numbers do not look that disastrous compared to today. And this is surprising, if not deeply disconcerting, given the dire straits South Africa found itself in during the early 1990s, coming out of the strife-torn apartheid era in which the country was isolated, shunned and deeply divided. In 2023, after several election cycles during which legitimate governments had been repeatedly elected and with the country enjoying the benefits of an open economy and relative stability, a significant number of indicators were worse than in 1993 and 1994.

Ismail Momoniat, until 2023 the acting director general at the National Treasury, was exasperated in 2021 when he submitted a statement to the Judicial Commission of Inquiry into State Capture. Referring to the acute levels of corruption, mismanagement and misrule under the Zuma government, he told then Deputy Chief Justice Raymond Zondo: 'The erosion of the discipline of fiscal decision-making and value-for-money spending, combined with the misdirection of funds, not only reversed all these gains [referring to the fiscal and financial management progress under Mbeki and Manuel], moving us back into sub-investment grade, but took some key indicators to a level far lower than that which we inherited in 1994.'[39]

In the first quarter of 2024, unemployment stood at 32.9 per cent, a full 12.9 percentage points higher than when the GNU took office. The expanded definition in 2024 was approaching crisis levels and pointing to a structural and inherent unsustainability in society: 42.4 per cent.[40] In 2022, GDP remained stuck in a low-growth trap, recording expansion of 1.9 per cent, having grown by only 0.3 per cent from 2019 (before the Covid-19 pandemic hit).[41] Although the budget deficit in 2023 was better than in the first year of democracy, the country still recorded its 14th consecutive deficit, reaching 4.7 per cent of GDP (versus 5.4 per cent in 1994).[42] Government debt in relation to GDP in 2023 was clearing 70 per cent.[43] In 1994, a dollar was worth R3.55,[44] while in 2023 it fluctuated between R18 and R19 – although economists believed it was undervalued by half and should have been trading at about R8.94.[45]

And after being awarded investment grade status in 1994 by Moody's – and maintaining it with relative ease for many years – not a single ratings agency gave the country a high investment grade 30 years later. At least inflation – at 9 per cent in 1994 – retreated to below 6 per cent in the latter half of 2023,[46] thanks in no small part to the resilience of the Reserve Bank and its governor, Lesetja Kganyago, in resisting increased political pressure from a government bereft of ideas.

4
Bickering begins

THE ANC CAME INTO OFFICE ON THE BACK of an election campaign built on the Reconstruction and Development Programme, popularly and colloquially known as the RDP. It was the product of wide consultation within the broader liberation movement and focused on 'people-centred' and community upliftment programmes, encompassing social services, housing and infrastructure.

The ANC told its supporters that the RDP would provide millions of jobs and houses and ensure access to piped water and electricity. The idea originated among members of the National Union of Mineworkers (NUM) and was quickly taken up by the ANC department of economic planning, headed by Trevor Manuel.

The RDP policy document and Ready to Govern, a treatise setting out the incoming ANC government's policy priorities, became the GNU's new blueprint – and the symbol of most South Africans' hope for the future. But it became completely unworkable as the realities of a modern, industrialised economy functioning within an interconnected global economy and financial system collided head-on with a struggling local economy and a state with limited means. Jay Naidoo, the minister in charge of the RDP, later said it could have worked as an overarching government policy if the leadership (read: Mandela and Mbeki) had been fully committed to it. But Michael Spicer, from Anglo American, called it 'uncosted and typical of the left's flights of fancy'.[1]

Nevertheless, for the first two years of democratic government, the

GNU's priorities, policies and spending were arranged according to the tenets of the RDP. In tabling its first full budget at the beginning of 1995, the new government made clear that it did not want to compromise on its election campaign promises. In his first address to a joint sitting of Parliament, on 24 May 1994, Mandela announced a range of municipal, provincial and national projects, and by the following March 21 'presidential lead projects' had been activated, including a primary school nutrition programme, a rural water supply and sanitation project, limited free health services and a range of urban renewal initiatives.[2] These projects were more symbolic than anything else and demonstrated that the new government would redirect resources as it saw fit. Mandela had to announce something that would have a visible and lasting impact in communities and these projects gave him and the GNU a quick and easy win.

Despite the good intentions, many RDP promises were not kept. And in the two years of its existence, the RDP routinely missed its self-imposed targets.[3] Chris Liebenberg, the former banking chief whom Mandela called out of retirement to become finance minister, was frustrated with the lack of skills to be able to satisfy the promises so easily made during the election campaign: 'Housing has been a major challenge for us for a whole host of reasons. Can we build a million houses a year? Unlikely next year, very unlikely. Will we build more houses next year than we have done this year? Hopefully, because some of the blockages are being addressed.[4]

'Will the housing programme run as high as I would have liked it to run? Unlikely. Until you get this, what you call a culture of entitlement, and people making contributions [in the form of tax] to the full extent, until we remove all the blockages, the political interplay between the three levels of government where each one wants to do his own little turf issue … until you get all of that out of the way … we are not going to build houses at the rate that we want to. The building of houses is not a money problem. There is more than enough money for that. It's actually a capacity problem and I don't think we have enough builders and skills to transform the rands and cents into bricks and mortar at the rate that people have glibly thrown figures around from political platforms.'[5]

The capacity problem was to be the country's Achilles heel in later years: the ANC government would eventually chase away skilled workers almost as quickly as it produced unemployable matriculants.

❖

The Department of Finance, economists and distrusted institutions such as the World Bank and the International Monetary Fund all agreed that sustained and high GDP growth was non-negotiable if the government stood any chance of improving employment statistics, if it intended to lessen poverty and inequality and if it wanted revenue to finance the reconstruction of society. Liebenberg, who preceded Manuel as finance minister, said the country needed consistent GDP growth of 3.5 per cent to subdue unemployment[6] 'but we are targeting 6 per cent on a sustainable basis down the line'.[7]

Bureaucrats at finance told the new government it must adhere to crucial macroeconomic requirements for the economy to grow. And growth would not be possible without domestic investment, serious foreign direct investment and the deregulation and liberalisation of strictures placed on economic activities by apartheid governments. The minions at finance's high-rise building in Vermeulen Street, Pretoria, told the government it needed to maintain high levels of investment in infrastructure and manufacturing capacity; savings must be improved across the board; industrial and trade policies to ensure competitiveness must be implemented; foreign inflows of capital were crucial; and inflation must be kept in check.[8]

In the final days of apartheid and the first days of democracy, Mandela and his colleagues held out hope of a 'freedom dividend' to boost the economy and lift it out of the misery of low growth and high unemployment. The theory went that, given global enthusiasm about the transition to democracy and the importance of the South African story, foreign investors would rush to provide the capital that would allow the new government rebuild and redesign the country. But it didn't happen. The 'freedom dividend' never materialised. Jeremy Cronin, a leading light in the SACP at the time (and one of the architects of the RDP), says it was a great disappointment.[9] The expectation was for a so-called Marshall Plan for South Africa but the money all went to South East Asia and the rise of the 'Tiger' economies there.[10]

Liebenberg was wide-eyed about the problems the country faced and sober about how long the sins of the past would linger: 'Is the capital coming in faster than we would have anticipated before the 27th of April? The answer is yes. Are we getting enough fixed direct investment? No. Why not? There is still a concern. We've only been in the democracy for 18 months. People are still sitting back and saying, "Let's just see how it works out." People that I speak to overseas are still saying, "What's going to happen after Mandela? Are you sure you've still got a country that can survive after Mandela?" There are also investment cycles that people go through. They don't close their Budapest factory just because we have a democratic South Africa so they can open one in Cape Town. You've got to wait for the investment cycle for the Cape Town factory to be opened. Ultimately, if we are reasonably successful with our social stability and with our political stability, investors cannot ignore 40 million consumers.'[11]

The appointment of Derek Keys as finance minister, and having banker Liebenberg succeed him, was a signal to the markets and the international community that Mandela was committed to a gradual and orderly transfer of the command of the economy to the ANC. He was also open about the fact that the country 'wasn't yet ready for a black finance minister' even though it annoyed many in his inner circle. And for the first two years Keys and Liebenberg did a solid job of maintaining fiscal prudence as far as possible, even though there were serious and competing demands on the fiscus from within the fledgling government – and from a governing party that was starting to develop its theories and ideas about the 'developmental state'.

But the government had no macroeconomic package, or framework, that it could take to foreign investors and to the bond market (where the country raises most of its debt). The government's bedrock was the RDP, the vast package of promises and undertakings it sold to the electorate in 1994 and embodied in Naidoo's RDP office. But by 1996 it became clear the RDP was unworkable. The RDP office became a source of tension between various line-function ministries and Naidoo, and Mbeki had tired of what appeared to regard itself as a 'super-ministry'.

On 28 March 1996, Mandela stood up in the National Assembly to announce that Manuel would succeed Liebenberg and the RDP office would be shuttered. Naidoo was moved to the ministry of posts and telecommunications.

❖

During 1994 and 1995, senior officials and ministers went on several international roadshows, not only to sell South African bonds to overseas investors but to sell the South African story. Alec Erwin, Liebenberg's deputy, Manuel (then minister of trade and industry) and Maria Ramos (then a senior official at finance) were among the emissaries who came back frustrated. Erwin told his boss it was difficult when questions were asked about the country's macroeconomic framework and they couldn't provide coherent answers.[12]

In 1995, Liebenberg (with Mbeki's knowledge) tasked Erwin to commission economists and other experts to start working on a macroeconomic framework they could present to Mandela and the cabinet – and which they could sell as the country's economic roadmap. And when Manuel – after a period of unannounced apprenticeship (Mandela told Manuel before Liebenberg's departure that he should shadow the incumbent) – took over as finance minister, he found the process far advanced. A working group of economists from institutions such as the World Bank and the International Monetary Fund, as well as local economists and academics, held a series of meetings at the Development Bank of Southern Africa in Midrand, where they started to craft a new macroeconomic framework.

'Madiba asked me what keeps me awake and I said that by 1998 the debt service costs will be the greatest expenditure item in the budget,' says Manuel. 'Madiba said, "I'm not an economist, you know, just explain this to me." And somewhere in that discussion he said, "But that's money spent, this is interest on money that's already been spent, and so what you have already spent is costing us more than education, so we are not building for tomorrow. Education should be our number one priority. How can we do that?" And I said, "Well, it's about macroeconomics, we must tighten the fiscal envelope," and so on.[13]

'There was a team working on this issue. We then sat and eventually packaged this thing. We didn't just want a series of econometric equations and we looked at the elements, we revisited what we wanted out of the programme and we thought that we needed to grow the economy because we had a balance of payments constraint. We needed to create a lot more employment and we needed to focus on redistribution, and so that became Gear. We sat ... I don't know how many all-nighters we pulled in the week before Friday 14 June of 1996, but we just went round the clock, working through this thing. It must have been that Thursday that we thought that Growth, Employment and Redistribution is a very appropriate name for what we were trying to achieve.'[14]

Once the policy team finished the draft, it was kept in a tight circle around Mbeki and Manuel, eventually approved by Mandela, then shared with leaders of the broader alliance before being tabled in Parliament. There were fears that if the detail of the policy framework was disseminated too broadly, it could derail the whole process. Instead, Gear became perhaps one of the first, and one of the last major policy positions conceptualised, crafted and implemented (or imposed?) by the executive rather than through the protracted and paralysing broad consultation process in the governing alliance, where too often consensus was built around the lowest common denominator.

The purpose of Gear was to align the new government's flailing economic policies with the modern economic thinking necessary to stabilise the country and clear the decks for necessary investment, while pushing down unemployment, inequality and poverty. And the ANC government (by June 1996 the National Party had exited the GNU) did this by departing from the 'uncosted' wish list of the RDP and acknowledging that failed policies followed by other African states after liberation would not work in South Africa, a vastly different country and polity, and operating in a post-communist and post-socialist world.

Then Mandela called on Manuel to sell the policy to the ANC's partners. 'While the numbers were still softish, I briefed the president and deputy president and on the Sunday Madiba convened a meeting in that house in Houghton that he lived in, in 13th Avenue, that is now the hotel. At the back there was a kind of hut, a rondavel, and in that rondavel he called Cosatu, the SACP and the ANC. Gill [Marcus, Manuel's deputy] and I spoke about what we were trying to do and we didn't have a lot of detail, but Madiba asked them to back us as we walked that course,' says Manuel.[15]

Gear was presented to Parliament on 14 June 1996. It proposed a fundamental and significant move away from the ANC's initial guiding policy documents, including the Freedom Charter (1955), Ready to Govern (1992) and the RDP (1994). It proposed what was perceived at the time to be a classic neoliberal, Washington Consensus-inspired macroeconomic framework. And it precipitated a clash of ideologies, cultures and factions that led to Mbeki's ousting 11 years later and gave rise to Zuma, state capture and the aggressive dismantling of South Africa by a cabal of criminals and political opportunists. Although Gear became a source of bitter conflict later, Manuel is at pains to explain 'that there was broad support' for what the government was trying to achieve and how it wanted to do so. The SACP and Cosatu expressed their cautious backing.[16]

Propelled by Mbeki's desire to show that an African government can be a successful modern democracy, Gear was an attempt by the Mandela government to stabilise the country's finances. It sought to give certainty to the economy and to make South Africa attractive to foreign investors. It put economic growth at the centre, buttressed by stable fiscal and monetary policies, and sought to expand public and private investment and increase exports.[17] It tried to do all this by reining in public finances and spending, cutting the budget deficit and limiting tax increases. It completely enraged the ANC's leftist partners in the governing alliance, Cosatu and the SACP – despite their initial qualified support.

The government was accused of betraying the struggle and the Freedom Charter, of selling out to the West and pandering to the whims of Washington and the citadels of capitalism in Europe. Forgotten today, in the haze of ANC collapse and misgovernance, is how divisive Gear was and how it later became the single biggest driver of resentment against Mbeki. Cronin, deputy leader of the SACP, told me how angry they were, and Naidoo, Cosatu's first general secretary, how he felt betrayed and sidelined.[18] Many in the ANC and the broader movement were furious because they believed there hadn't been proper consultation before the policy was suddenly announced in Parliament.

Ben Turok, the veteran communist and one of the drafters of the economic clause in the Freedom Charter (about banks and mines being owned by the people), explained how the ANC parliamentary caucus was simply informed about Gear's tabling shortly before Manuel stood up in the chamber.[19] Manuel says he agrees there wasn't broad consultation but explains it by saying he, Mandela and Mbeki weren't going to treat the crafting of a far-reaching macroeconomic policy 'like it was wage negotiations … We were not going to do that.'[20] Mbeki defended Gear at a press conference after Manuel's announcement, goading his critics and declaring himself perfectly happy to be called a 'Thatcherite'.[21]

'We went off to meet the press but they were ignoring me and wanting to talk to Thabo, who was in the same room, and we talked about the degree of risk and how you take these things forward,' says Manuel. 'And that became quite important because there was cover for what we needed to do. And so, for a while Zwelinzima Vavi [Cosatu's general secretary] supported it and the party supported it, but it was clear that there were people who were losing influence, ideological influence, and it was biting at them. We worked over weekends to try and persuade people, but not everybody would come into that arrangement. Going into 1997, the issues were still unresolved. But the economic resolution at Mafikeng spells this thing out and says the basic policy of the ANC is the RDP and Gear is the macroeconomic means to achieve its implementation. So, you've married the two. It was approved with acclaim but the barking didn't stop. But it was a fundamentally important turning point.'[22]

Mbeki was clearly motivated by a desire to make South Africa, suffering from high unemployment and low growth, a more attractive destination for foreign investment, which the country desperately needed to lift it out of its post-apartheid malaise. And for those capital inflows to materialise, it had to adopt economic policies that would lure them in. The quintessential pragmatist, he had made the ideological conversion to a market economy stimulated by the private sector in the preceding decade, but most of his comrades in the ANC either did not make the same trek, sticking to the main tenets of the Freedom Charter and the broad aims of socialism, or exploited political dynamics and economic uncertainty to establish networks of patronage and extraction.

Manuel fundamentally rejects criticism of Gear as neoliberal or anti-poor, arguing that it was the opposite and saying the results confirm it: 'It was the first time that the ANC had to take decisions as government and not negotiate with trade union partners. The child maintenance grant that was extended to white, Indian, coloured with a differentiated matrix, including a very small percentage of African children, was replaced by the child support grant which was extended to all children where a means test was passed. That child support grant reached two-thirds of children in the country in a very short period of time. So, it's quite important to recognise that here this was being called out as an ultra-conservative and neoliberal approach that ignores the people, but one of the central issues which deals with poverty was able to be introduced within two years of passing that policy. So, these are fundamentally important questions that had not been given attention. The other issue is that we were spending less on funding the deficit and consequently less on debt service costs. We actually had more resources available to deal with social spending.[23]

'The other issue which I think you've got to compare then and now, the other issue which is quite important is state-owned enterprises [SOEs]. They were run as enterprises off the strength of their own balance sheet; there weren't annual grants from the budgets to parastatals to fund their debt. And you know, those debates weren't just there within Gear. When we drafted the Public Finance Management Act, which is Act 1 of 1999, there are schedules to the PFMA. And I think it's schedule 3 which deals with the larger state-owned enterprises, like Transnet, Eskom and SAA. And those enterprises could go to capital markets and borrow against the strength of their own balance sheet. The only thing that happened, and this was operational rather than statutory, was the asset liability division of the Treasury set up a queueing system so that it didn't get the government, Eskom and Transnet in the US market at the same time. You needed to just straddle this, and the other important point about that is for a long time during that period, Eskom's rates were much tighter than what the sovereign could borrow at.[24]

'*En kyk hoe lyk dit nou!* [And see how it looks now!] I mean, the scale of what happened at SOEs is quite phenomenal. But the point is: you set up something, you knew there was adequate air cover from the Presidency, you could take things into cabinet, deal with them …

sometimes there were debates that were quite intense but you could get things through. Gear laid the basis for better economic policy management and for the resolution of many of these issues.'[25]

5
Whiffs of corruption

DESPITE MANDELA'S EXHORTATIONS that South Africa would be governed under a different set of rules and a higher set of values than it had been during the previous years, it didn't take long for ANC cadres and comrades to identify and exploit the opportunities for self-enrichment that came with incumbency. The rise of the class of rent-seekers and javelin-throwers who eventually hollowed out party and state with their complex systems of patronage and extraction started almost immediately.

The first year of running the country was difficult for the party as it navigated the labyrinthine corridors of the state and sought to come to grips with leading the government. The best in class were deployed to Parliament, Mandela (and Mbeki) rewarded loyalty and seniority with cabinet posts and comrades gradually started to infiltrate the bureaucracy. Combined with the ANC's relentless march to stamp its ideology of party control and central deployment on the state and country, the ability of the unscrupulous and crooked to establish fiefdoms markedly increased.

When exactly did the ANC's fall from grace begin? For Stephen Ellis, the author of *External Mission*, it was probably sometime during the years of exile and deprivation that organised crime took root in the organisation. For many, if not most, it was the arms deal initiated during the first years of the Mandela presidency that set the party on the path to capture and a total abdication of ethics and morals.

But it might also have been the way in which Mandela dealt with the inquiry into the Shell House massacre, the ANC's refusal to censure Nkosazana Dlamini-Zuma for the *Sarafina 2* debacle or the cover-up of corruption claims against Stella Sigcau, a minister and Xhosa royal.

Tim du Plessis describes his newspaper, *Beeld*, as a 'vanguard' publication: 'We bought into the belief that the political transition wasn't just inevitable but that it was just. But it wasn't a case of us saying, "Okay guys, this is your honeymoon period, we'll give it to you to enjoy." We were critical of the government. The zeitgeist of the time, however, was one that said this is a new dispensation, let's work together. Today, looking at our news reports from then, I can see how carefully we chose our words. We were mindful of our audience ... that wasn't as taken with events and the spirit of the time. We did tell them that hey, this thing is working! I think it could have contributed to us probably not being critical enough at the start.'[1]

Nevertheless, corruption and a determination to avoid account-ability have been part of the ANC's culture and governing philosophy since Mandela was president. The ANC, from the start and despite statements to the contrary, believed itself to be above the law and beyond scrutiny. It shamelessly exploited the great national deference to its judgement and authority, burnished by its role during the tran-sition and aided by a general refusal to criticise the party, for fear of being branded apartheid apologists.

This ensured that the ANC was always given the benefit of the doubt, its leaders were forgiven quickly and matters of principle and law were too often ignored for the sake of expediency. To this day, even after the destruction caused by state capture and amid continued ANC mismanagement and misrule, many in the party – even the so-called good people – as well as commentators and analysts seek all manner of reasons to excuse the ANC from the glaringly obvious. The way in which the ANC was lauded, defended and coddled in those first years of democracy gave it a sense of godlike immunity and royal entitlement that continues to cloak it.

Some of the examples of corruption and crookery noted above might sound trifling compared to the depth and breadth of corruption and criminality in present-day South Africa. In fact, the *Sarafina 2* scandal, which caused a massive outcry at the time and almost permanently shaped Dlamini-Zuma's reputation, is piffling in hindsight. But the lack of accountability in every one of those instances, and Mandela's reluctance to act decisively, without doubt contributed to the latter-day malaise which makes the party and its cadres almost untouchable. Certainly Tony Leon, who sat across from Mandela in the National Assembly, believes him to have been 'careless at best, and, in some cases, even complicit, with public office seen by some as a shortcut to personal riches'.[2] Warning bells rang loudly during Mandela's term 'but he did not do much to answer the alarm'.

In April 1995, less than a year after taking office, Dlamini-Zuma's Department of Health agreed to pay R14.3 million to playwright Mbongeni Ngema to produce an HIV/Aids awareness play. The contract was awarded without a proper tendering process and the play was a disaster, containing false information about HIV and achieving the opposite of what was intended.[3] *The New York Times* reported: 'Aids experts called some of its dialogue dangerously inaccurate, its message unclear. And people wondered: why had it cost so much? How had the cash-strapped health department paid for it? Appalled Aids activists said the play sent vague and confusing signals about the disease. For instance, one victim limps and walks doubled over in the second act, symptoms not generally considered consequences of Aids.'[4] Dlamini-Zuma was caught lying to Parliament when asked to account for the play and the subsequent furore.[5] She told the portfolio committee on health that the play was financed by the European Union, which promptly denied it, then claimed it was backed by an anonymous donor.[6]

Dlamini-Zuma started her term of office at a gallop, tackling the health portfolio with gusto and launching into private health care, medical schools and 'diseases of the rich' (like heart conditions requiring heart transplants).[7] *Sarafina 2* was produced after an outcry about the government's lack of investment and sincerity in tackling the rising Aids pandemic, which saw infections double between 1994 and 1996.[8] She ignored the agreed Aids strategy, opting instead to spend time attacking 'big pharma' and the tobacco industry and redesigning post-qualification community service for medical students. Dlamini-Zuma, in those first years, became synonymous with ham-fisted and hard-handed government.

Sarafina 2 doesn't even register as a scandal by today's standards, but Leon says it was 'one of the defining moments of the new democratic dispensation'.[9] It was defining because it revealed a lot about how the ANC was to approach scandals involving senior leaders and how its ministers would later treat public resources. Although there was unease in the ANC Women's League[10] about the way Dlamini-Zuma handled the furore – bending procurement rules, lying about sources of funding and eschewing accountability – the leadership leapt to her defence. Mandela, revealing a trait that sometimes bubbled to the surface, used race to counterattack, accusing the 'white-owned media' of vilifying her.[11]

Sarafina 'was small fry', says Du Plessis. 'But it was the first scandal and signified a turning point. But the whole thing disappeared because Mandela said she was a good woman, she made a mistake but she acted in good faith. And if Mandela forgives someone, the president of the country and the party, who are you to disagree? But we should have made a louder noise, we should have called Mandela out and we didn't. We should have gone harder, looking back.'[12]

The New York Times quoted analyst Steven Friedman as saying: 'The ANC has established a very clear pattern and the pattern is simple. You can be whatever you like as long as you are loyal. The minister of health may be responsible for *Sarafina* but she is loyal, so she will be defended. The problem is you can't deal with corruption this way.' Nothing happened to Dlamini-Zuma, despite an investigation by the Heath Investigating Unit (later the Special Investigating Unit) calling her 'reckless' and 'negligent'.[13] She was 'royal game',[14] Leon believed, while political analyst RW Johnson ascribed her immunity from consequence to her being 'Mbeki's client and therefore unsackable'.[15]

Would it be disingenuous (or too easy and lazy) to argue that the ANC's latter-day tolerance, even acceptance, of senior leaders going astray and involving themselves in irregular activities at best and downright corruption at worst, stretched back to the early days of democracy? Because for all Mandela's traits as a unifier, he and his leadership were tolerant of many of the movement's indiscretions, often because they didn't want to show weakness in the face of a critical opposition and a press that Mandela sometimes branded as racist.

❖

In early 1995, Allan Boesak, a cleric, former UDF leader and prominent ANC figure, was accused by a Scandinavian non-governmental organisation of irregularities related to a church organisation he ran during apartheid. A forensic report claimed Boesak had 'misappropriated' funding to finance his lifestyle and the career of his television personality wife, Elna, and it seemed the money had been used to pay for ANC politicians' travel during the 1994 election. It emerged that the now-defunct state investigative unit, the Office for Serious Economic Offences (OSEO), was also investigating, but the ANC leadership, in the form of Mandela and Mbeki, leapt to Boesak's defence.

Mandela called the charges 'baseless' and praised Boesak – who had a sizeable following thanks to his activism in the church – as 'one of the most gifted young men in the country'. Mbeki's office went further, countering the forensic report with one by Mojanku Gumbi, later one of his most trusted advisers, exonerating Boesak. It was an extraordinary intervention by the deputy president. Leon called it 'farcical and [a] far-fetched ruse', the OSEO's head said he was 'taken aback' at Mbeki's move and the law firm that completed the forensic investigation said Gumbi's report was 'incorrect' and 'preposterous'. [16]

But the furore caused Boesak to withdraw from consideration as ambassador to the United Nations in Geneva, a role he had been promised. Four years later, he was found guilty of four charges of fraud related to R500 000 in Scandinavian donations to his church organisation, R240 000 given by music star Paul Simon and more than R300 000 from his organisation's 'discretionary funds'. The high court judge said that 'instead of making the 12 videos on voter education as he had promised, Boesak used the money to build a recording studio for his wife, Elna, a former television presenter'.[17] After taking the judgment and sentence on appeal, Boesak served two years of a six-year prison term and was later pardoned by Mbeki.[18]

Another harbinger of what was to come was the expulsion from the ANC of Bantu Holomisa, a former apartheid homeland leader, after he told the Truth and Reconciliation Commission that Stella Sigcau, Mandela's minister of public enterprises and an erstwhile 'prime minister' of the Transkei, was bribed by gaming king Sol Kerzner.[19] Holomisa, a Transkei general, took power from Sigcau in a coup in the 1980s but the ANC welcomed both into the party before the 1994 election. Holomisa said Kerzner not only paid R2 million to another Transkei government head, George Matanzima (Mandela's nephew), he gave Sigcau a R50 000 cut for gaming licences. He also bankrolled the ANC to the tune of R2 million before the election. This incensed Mandela and the ANC, who accused Holomisa of 'treachery' and proceeded to suspend and expel him from the party. Meanwhile, nothing happened to Sigcau, and Mandela later admitted that the ANC took Kerzner's money.

At a press conference after his dismissal as deputy minister for environmental affairs due to 'political indiscretions', Holomisa said it appeared that the ANC took the money in return for a promise not to prosecute Kerzner.[20] He said the casino and hotel mogul helped pay for Mbeki's 50th birthday party and helped Steve Tshwete, the minister of safety and security, with free hotel accommodation. 'Again, as a loyal member of the ANC, I would hate to draw an inference that these sponsorships by Mr Kerzner were in return for him escaping the due process of criminal justice,' he said. Kerzner, indeed, was never prosecuted. The incident showed how conflicted Mandela was. 'There was his sincere respect for the Constitution and the rule of law, on one hand, and his deep organisational loyalties and ties, on the other. He found it hard to stamp out these practices when they were manifest,' Leon said later.[21]

Mandela saw things differently, and despite the damage the *Sarafina 2* and Holomisa affairs did to his image and that of the ANC, he reverted to blaming the media for waging a campaign. He quickly became wont to accuse white journalists of resisting change and black journalists of either not understanding what was happening in the country or being 'co-opted', presumably by 'backward-looking interests'.[22]

Mandela railed against journalists for raising the *Sarafina 2* and

47

Holomisa issues as matters of principle and tests for the ANC on corruption. 'Both black and white journalists are waging a biased and venomous campaign against the ANC,' he said.[23] He continued to make the extraordinary claim that 'some black journalists have been co-opted' by 'traditionally white parties and their surrogates' and that they were being used 'to destroy the ANC'.[24] This tactic – of targeting black journalists who were doing their job of identifying corruption and malfeasance, then pointing it out – was to become pervasive in later years and the tone was set by Mandela. During the era of state capture, in which corruption and criminality were embedded in the DNA of state and party, black journalists regularly faced the wrath of the party and its acolytes, with entreaties of ethnic loyalty over the rule of law a regular line of attack.

The *Sarafina 2*, Boesak and Holomisa affairs shocked the country as they played out in full view of the nation – and revealed the ANC's true colours when confronted by wrongdoing in its ranks. But they were nothing compared with what was to follow. Du Plessis says many did not understand the fault lines in the ANC, believing them to be between returning exiles and the so-called 'inziles', the Lusaka ANC versus the UDF and the Robben Islanders. 'But those weren't the real fault lines. The real lines were between those in the party who were honest and those who were dishonest. And those lines did not follow ideological divides. You had free market adherents who were exposed as dishonest and staunch communists who were honest, the good guys. And Mandela's sharply critical speech about redistribution and the white face of business at the ANC conference in Mafikeng in 1997 was music to the ears of the dishonest faction in the party. It gave them a shield behind which they could hide while doing their deeds. And when "transformation" became established policy, it was the fig leaf they used to cover up their activities.'

6
The poisoning of the well

TOWARDS THE END OF 1994, the newly constituted South African National Defence Force (SANDF), which brought together statutory and non-statutory forces, including the old SADF and MK, proposed to the cabinet a deal that would see the country acquiring warships from a Spanish manufacturer. It would transform a navy that had never been much more than a coastal patrol service, three old French Daphne-class submarines representing the height of its strike power.

But when Mandela received the proposal via his defence minister, Joe Modise, he rejected it, apparently 'furious' after being presented with a done deal and feeling as if the military was 'behaving as if it was not accountable to the new government'.[1] A thorough review of the SANDF's capabilities was launched, leading to the adoption of the White Paper on National Defence in 1996 by Parliament and the Defence Review in 1998. These processes sought to position the armed forces within the framework of post-apartheid South Africa, with its urgent and competing social justice needs, such as health, education and welfare.

Mbeki subsequently chaired a cabinet subcommittee including Modise and finance minister Trevor Manuel which recommended moving forward with what was called the Strategic Defence Procurement Package (SDPP). The R29.9-billion SDPP contracted manufacturers and suppliers to provide the SANDF with four frigates, three submarines, fighter and trainer jets and helicopters. The cabinet decided on

18 November 1998 to endorse the SDPP and the recommendations by Mbeki's subcommittee on the main contractors. The cost of the deal eventually ballooned to R143 billion and many of the promised industrial offsets and reinvestments into the local economy by contractors failed to materialise. Mandela's government wasn't only pulled into the international arms trade's vortex of corruption and skullduggery, it plunged headlong into it.

What unfolded was, by common cause, the ANC's loss of innocence. Many in the party's upper echelons weren't only receptive to bribes and largesse, they encouraged and solicited them. And when law enforcement agencies in South Africa and Europe started to pick apart the deal, following the money and logging the receipts, the ANC shamelessly used its position in government to cover it all up. In doing so, it prevented a proper investigation that, had it been conducted without interference, might well have set the standard for post-apartheid South Africa and the continent.

Instead, the arms deal became the first mega-scandal in democratic South Africa and further set the tone for how the ANC would handle corruption in future. As was to become the norm later – most notably during the era of state capture – it refused to investigate senior party men before allowing a limited inquiry conducted by compromised institutions, then quashed any hope of accountability and reform in Parliament.

During the Mandela era, and despite having the hallmarks of an executive based on the agreed liberal constitution, the ANC-in-government always retained its centralist, statist and, as it later became clear, anti-democratic impulse. Boesak, *Sarafina 2* and Holomisa were the first warnings, but the arms deal was the real thing. It showed South Africa what the ANC was and provided a clear indicator of what it would become.

The arms deal was conceived halfway through Mandela's term and the cabinet's final decision was taken at the end of 1998 while he was still head of state. Contracts with the main suppliers were signed a year later, after Mbeki had succeeded Mandela as president. But by then

Mbeki had effectively been in charge for five years. He was the main driver of government policy and execution as deputy president and took over as party leader in December 1997.

Despite Mandela delegating much of his work to Mbeki, he was president when the deal was conceptualised and finalised. He cannot escape blame for what it became and for how the ANC smothered any hope of accountability. During negotiations with contractors, the secretary of defence (Pierre Steyn) and the chief of the SANDF (Georg Meiring) wrote to Mandela, warning him about aspects of the deal. Willem Hechter, the air force chief, also rejected the government's choice of fighter and training jets.[2]

On 9 September 1999, Patricia de Lille, then an MP for the Pan Africanist Congress, stood up in the National Assembly and made startling claims of corruption related to the arms deal. She claimed that millions of rand in bribes were paid to a host of ANC figures and their families through networks of companies and shady interests to influence the outcome of negotiations. Her claims, met with howls of derision and boos, were based on a memorandum signed by 'concerned ANC MPs'.[3] It provided clear insight into unfolding events in the ANC as the arms deal was negotiated and accused Tony Yengeni, the ANC chief whip, of buying a Mercedes-Benz SUV with money he received from British Aerospace, now BAE Systems.

On 15 September 1999, the government announced that it was committing to an arms acquisition package costing R29.9 billion. The deals – with contractors committing to subcontracts and industrial participation programmes – would generate business to the tune of R110 billion and create 65 000 job opportunities, the government claimed. The arms deal, it was argued, would pay for itself. When the contracts were signed, the amount came to R30.3 billion, with expected offsets of R104 billion.[4] It was a coup for Mbeki's government. It had negotiated with the devil and won.

De Lille handed all the information she had to Judge Willem Heath, who headed the Heath Investigating Unit. His bloodhounds had the statutory powers to declare state contracts null and void if it could be proven that irregularities had occurred – but he had to get a presidential proclamation first. And that was never forthcoming. Then, a year later, in September 2000, the Auditor-General tabled a report in Parliament. It was a review of the selection process of contractors, and even though it was a mere six pages, it was explosive.[5] There were deviations from procurement policies; the independence of different role players was questioned; there appeared to be irregularities between primary and secondary contractors; the consideration of cost was removed in the air force's fighter programme; and no formal budget was compiled beforehand – it was approved by the cabinet only during negotiations.

'Many allegations regarding possible irregularities in contracts awarded to subcontractors exist ... I recommend that a forensic audit or special investigation into these areas be initiated,' Auditor-General Shauket Fakie concluded. What unfolded was to become the ANC strategy during every subsequent crisis or conflagration in which the party and its deployed cadres were at the centre of corruption claims. It shamelessly used its position as the governing party to intimidate, manipulate and dominate the investigation and oversight process, eventually neutering it.

This is where the tale of the ANC-in-government segues into the Mbeki era, when the party undermined the separation of powers and the crucial parliamentary function of oversight and accountability. Mandela, his biographers and critics agree, held Parliament in reverence and believed the legislature should be respected and allowed to fulfil its constitutional role.

Andrew Feinstein, in his remarkable memoir *After the Party*, details the events he experienced as an idealistic and faithful ANC MP and party caucus leader on Parliament's powerful and important standing committee on public accounts (Scopa). After informing Jacob Zuma, who was then deputy president, of the course of action decided on by Scopa, Feinstein and another ANC MP on the committee, Laloo Chiba, were called into Yengeni's office and told the arms deal matter should be 'dealt with internally'.[6] They refused and the Scopa hearing that followed made party bosses apoplectic with rage.

Chippy Shaik was the defence department's head of procurement and part of a triumvirate of ANC brothers who were prominent during the early days of democracy. One brother, Mo, became the country's spy chief, while the other, Schabir, oversaw a host of private businesses, including one that looked set to make enormous amounts of money as a secondary defence contractor. The conflict of interest was glaring, but to the ANC at the time there was nothing wrong. Feinstein and his colleagues grilled Shaik and others about the contracts, the steep escalation in costs and why cost had been removed as a deciding factor during the contracting process. Shaik flailed about, trying to explain why South Africa was paying so much more than other countries for the same armaments. MPs did their best but even then, Feinstein wrote, 'I feared Yengeni's response and wondered whether the ANC was going to allow us to continue this search for the truth.'[7] The answer was to become patently clear.

After the dramatic and much-publicised Scopa hearing, a series of whistleblowers came forward with information about Chippy and Schabir's involvement in soliciting bribes and obtaining advantages for Schabir's businesses. Contractors were asked to appoint complete strangers as 'consultants' on monthly, dollar-denominated retainers – without knowing that those individuals were linked to Modise, the minister of defence.[8] It was later claimed that Modise received between R10 million and R35 million in bribes from a range of contractors. One of the contractors, Conlog, allegedly bought Modise shares in the company shortly before it won a secondary contract bid. British Aerospace donated R5 million to the ANC Veterans League, chaired by Modise.

'In addition, speculation has refused to go away that the ANC received millions of rands from successful bidders, money that was probably used in the 1999 election campaign,' Feinstein wrote.[9] Some of the winning bidders gave the ANC money, an NEC member told Feinstein, asking, 'How do you think we funded the 1999 election?'[10] Then there was Yengeni's Merc.

The ANC quickly developed the ability to lie to South Africa. As was to become apparent later, during the Nkandla scandal and state capture and in recent times with its strategy to blame apartheid for the country's multiple crises, the party and its leaders inhabit an alternate universe where sound governance, honesty and ethical dealings do not feature.

The arms deal was deeply flawed and highly problematic from the start. Chippy Shaik was head of acquisitions and his brother Schabir's company stood ready to secure lucrative contracts flowing from the deal. Yengeni, the ANC chief whip, took a bribe, seemingly to frustrate any parliamentary oversight process. Zuma was earmarked for a bribe while serving as deputy president. After he retired, Modise – known for his elastic commitment to honesty and his liking for the good things in life – became the chairperson of a company that benefited from the arms deal. Various fixers, 'consultants' and go-betweens with demonstrable links to the ANC allegedly scooped millions of dollars in 'facilitation fees'.

Then there was the role of Mbeki, who was implicated based on two serious claims. The first was that he held a secret meeting in Paris with Thomson, the French partner in the German consortium that won the bid to build four frigates for the navy. 'The implications were far-reaching. Firstly, it would have been in flagrant violation of the tender procedures governing the deal since the company was bidding to supply a combat system contracted to the South African Navy. The second trapdoor was that the company, in the form of its South African subsidiary, Thint, was the same entity that ended up in the dock with Jacob Zuma [whom they were accused of bribing] on charges of corruption,' wrote Tony Leon.[11]

The second claim is based on a raid by German authorities on the offices of ThyssenKrupp in Hamburg. The company was responsible for the frigate and submarine contracts. The Germans found evidence of R130 million in bribes paid to 'a senior South African politician', with Chippy Shaik being named.[12] Mbeki was at the forefront of pushing South Africa towards the German consortium and in 1997 Mo Shaik was sent to Hamburg as consul-general to 'midwife the deal'.[13] Between the involvement of the Shaik brothers, ANC MPs, fixers, senior cabinet members and the deputy president, there was a whole latticework of impropriety, conflict of interest, corruption and bribery. The ship and submarine contract was tainted and the contracts for the fighter and trainer jets were enormously problematic (the air force did not want the fighters that were bought).

Feinstein recalls a meeting between ANC members of Scopa and the ANC governance committee (later the political committee) that steers the party in Parliament. It was an angry and ill-tempered encounter because Feinstein and his colleagues had shepherded a resolution through the National Assembly calling for a multiagency forensic investigation into the arms deal. They soon received reports of Mbeki's 'apoplexy' over events,[14] and the role of some of the attendees in browbeating Feinstein and his colleagues remains flabbergasting. Zuma, as leader of government business, attended the meeting and said the SIU needed to be excluded. Johnny de Lange accused the ANC MPs of conducting an 'unjustified fishing expedition'.[15] But it was Essop Pahad, one of Mbeki's closest confidants and his undisputed attack dog, who tore into Feinstein and his colleagues. In a 'ferocious diatribe' he spluttered: 'Who the fuck do you think you are, questioning the integrity of the government, ministers and the president?'[16] Yengeni was there, as was Vincent Smith, an ANC MP who in later years would be accused of corruption related to another ANC scandal, Bosasa.

The intimidation of Parliament continued with more meetings between Feinstein, his fellow ANC MPs on Scopa and the party leadership. Alec Erwin told them 'they won't find anything there' if there had been corruption. Charles Nqakula, who occupied a series of senior cabinet posts and served in advisory roles for every successive president, accused Feinstein and company of 'betrayal'.[17] Then the speaker, Frene Ginwala, intervened. Feted after her death in 2023 as a steadfast and principled presiding officer in Parliament, she helped to stymie Scopa's investigation and prevent the SIU from being included in the multiagency investigation. Ginwala 'was a key player in neutering the investigation'.[18]

After meeting Mbeki, Public Protector Selby Baqwa and prosecutions head Bulelani Ngcuka changed their minds about the SIU and agreed it should not be part of any investigation. Everyone seemed to work in concert to prevent the SIU from being included in the investigating team: key ANC people, the president's office, the speaker, the chief whip, the deputy president. In early 2001, the die was cast: the SIU was excluded and Judge Willem Heath was removed as its head. Feinstein was fired as the ANC's Scopa head and Ginwala declared that Parliament never intended the SIU to be part of the investigation. Mbeki appeared on television claiming that Heath was targeting him and Mandela as culprits, and used it as an excuse for getting rid of the judge. Parliament was now an 'ethics-free zone', Leon said, accusing Ginwala of joining 'the other side' instead of defending the legislature against executive-minded 'bullying and cajoling' of MPs.

The joint investigative team delivered its report in November that year and declared 'no evidence was found of any improper or unlawful conduct by the government'. The investigation was led by Ngcuka, an ANC loyalist, Baqwa, who revealed his 'shyness' in holding ministers to account during the *Sarafina 2* scandal, according to Leon, and Fakie. 'None had either the hunger or the inclination to unpack the scandal and trace its perpetrators, no matter their office or status,' he said.[19]

The report was severely criticised as a whitewash that pandered to the executive. Then it emerged that there was significant interference in its compilation, with an original version containing notes in Pahad's handwriting instructing the author of the final document, Fakie, to make findings exonerating the government, even when no such finding was made.[20] The report ignored a 'detailed and damning' critique by secretary of defence Steyn and the 'large-scale irregularities' that he said 'riddled' and 'flawed' the process. His statement that the investigation was designed to give legitimacy to the 'political manipulation of the process' was left out of the report.[21]

Chippy Shaik resigned from the defence department and later emigrated to Australia. Schabir was jailed in 2005 after being found guilty of fraud and corruption related to the arms deal, and Mbeki, in a cynical move given his involvement with the SDPP, fired Zuma because of his proximity to Schabir and his imminent and expected prosecution on the same charges. And when Yengeni, having been found guilty of corruption, arrived at Pollsmoor Prison in Cape Town's southern suburbs to start serving his sentence in August 2006, he was carried shoulder high and loudly cheered by no less than the speaker, Baleka Mbete. The Western Cape premier, Ebrahim Rasool, the minister of housing, Lindiwe Sisulu, and a host of ANC luminaries went to support Yengeni, who told the crowd he had been 'hard done by'.[22]

In angry missives, Mbeki accused opposition parties, journalists and non-government organisations that pursued the arms deal of 'a fishing expedition' with a strong hint of racism. A letter he wrote to Gavin Woods, the IFP Scopa chairperson, was later cited in Schabir Shaik's corruption trial. In the letter, which was signed by Zuma, he ominously declared that 'special steps' would be taken to ensure Scopa respects the rule of law and the government would 'act vigorously to defend itself' against misinformation and attempts at destabilisation. Judge Hilary Squires, who presided over Shaik's trial, opined that it was 'almost as if the writer took special delight in rubbing the collective nose of Scopa – and Woods in particular – in the rejection of the recommendations of Scopa'.

Mbeki, in an interview with his biographer Mark Gevisser, was 'breezily dismissive' of subsequent British and French investigations into the arms deal. They were 'based on … nothing,' he said, sticking to the findings of the joint investigative team. And he rejected any responsibility for corruption related to secondary or subcontracts. Mbeki's response to the allegations of corruption was to claim a conspiracy driven by the media and 'fishers of corrupt men, determined to prove everything in the anti-African stereotype'.[23]

There were no more significant investigations or prosecutions of major arms deal figures. In 2011, Zuma – having neutered the criminal justice system by installing pliant functionaries at the National Prosecuting Authority, South African Police Service and Public Protector, appointed judges Willie Seriti and Hendrick Musi to conduct a judicial commission of inquiry. It was another whitewash, with the judges finding no evidence of corruption, exonerating everyone involved and claiming evidence presented to the commission amounted to 'hearsay'.

The high court, however, set aside the report, slamming the inquiry's 'inexplicable' decision to exclude a raft of evidence of corruption implicating Chippy Shaik, fixer Fana Hlongwane and many others. The court said there was 'a complete failure to rigorously test the versions of these witnesses by putting questions to them with the required open and enquiring mind. The questions posed to these individuals, in particular, were hardly the questions of an evidence leader seeking to test the extremely serious allegations that went to the heart of the reason for the establishment of the commission. This is hardly an investigation whose objective is to get to the bottom of the allegations.'[24]

❖

The arms deal was a significant moment in post-apartheid history, but Tim du Plessis did not think so at the time: 'That was because the White Paper on defence made a plausible argument about the urgency of re-equipping the defence force. We had tanks with bodies that dated from the Second World War, our Mirage fighter jets were old, other aeroplanes also served in the world war and we didn't have much of a navy to speak of. So, they had a strong case. We didn't realise it was just one big corrupt scheme. And it was only when a whistleblower, Richard Young, raised the alarm that we realised something was amiss. But again, Mandela was president and the government had this enormous legitimacy. It was difficult to ask hard questions. And black journalists were not critical enough.

'I was at *City Press* at the time and every Sunday Khulu Sibiya, the editor, went to Pretoria for a meeting of Mbeki's so-called consultative group. Black editors, black businessmen, black public servants, black ANC politicians. That was where Mbeki blew them away. The white guys … if you asked questions, you were against transformation and obviously longed for the olden days.

'But even when black editors and journalists, such as Barney Mthombothi and Moeletsi Mbeki, started pushing back against what was happening, the ANC's legitimacy was so great they were ignored. The ANC was a colossus and it was so powerful that revelations about something like the arms deal were just swept aside. Yes, Anton Harber and the *Weekly Mail* and later the *Mail & Guardian* soldiered on, but the ANC didn't care. And Parliament was captured … it started under Mbeki. He had other people do the dirty work. But he was behind the deal, even though he didn't want his fingerprints on it.'[25]

With the arms deal, the ANC set its course for the future. Corrupt networks of patronage and rent-seeking started to emerge, then embedded themselves in the party and the state. Crucially, these networks were not only focused on self-enrichment and resource extraction but seemingly channelled money back to the perpetually cash-strapped party – a pattern that continues to this day. There is never any incentive to clamp down on them, or to reform and modernise the criminal justice system, because they fund the party and the lifestyle of many of its members.

The arms deal also saw the ANC government asserting its dominance over Parliament, with strict directives from Luthuli House setting a line of march for everyone from the speaker to the chief whip, committee whips and chairpersons and ordinary MPs. The first years of democracy might have been different – Mandela showed real deference to the legislature – but once scandals and corruption started in and around the ANC, the party never wanted an independent Parliament. And the way it manipulated and intimidated the system of oversight and accountability meant that once other scandals emerged, bending rules and convention – and expanding the 'ethics-free zone', as Leon called it – they were never questioned.

In fact, much of the ANC's later modus operandi in Parliament – naked partisanship by the speaker, blatant manipulation by committee chairpersons, suppression of questions and motions by the opposition – became part of normal parliamentary culture.

PART TWO
CONSOLIDATION

7

The house never wins

WHEN I ARRIVED IN PARLIAMENT AT THE END OF 2006 as a correspondent for *Beeld*, the Johannesburg daily newspaper, it had been through the wars in the years since the end of apartheid. It was clear that parliamentary norms and culture to shield the executive from scrutiny had become entrenched, despite the best efforts of the opposition and parliamentary staff to maintain tradition and convention.

The smothering of any proper parliamentary oversight into the arms deal – and speaker Frene Ginwala's complicity – removed any veneer of the legislature's independence under an ANC government. And after Mbeki was elected president, his prickly nature, indomitable central control of the party and a weakening of the government benches led to a further dilution of Parliament's role in oversight and accountability, and certainly in the quality of its lawmaking. Committees were mostly run on a strict partisan basis, the ANC often bludgeoning through the majority decision without input from the opposition (although the portfolio committee on justice has over the years been the exception). Chairpersons, appointed by the ANC political committee on instruction from Luthuli House, executed their duties wholly in favour of the interests of the party and the executive.

According to the Constitution, alongside the state and the judiciary Parliament is one of the centres of public life and vital to maintaining democracy. But apart from a 'Prague Spring' between 1994 and 1996, the ANC effectively subjugated Parliament to serve its needs.

I remember how astounded I was when figures such as Manto Tshabalala-Msimang, then minister of health, were treated like demigods in committees, with the chairperson and ANC MPs openly fawning over the party deity descending to room E249. Most of the time there was a visceral refusal from party members to ensure accountability from senior officials like ministers or directors general, with most of the heavy lifting left to the opposition. In later years, as we shall see, Parliament abdicated its role as an independent arm of the state and went from being a lapdog of the executive to becoming an enabler of state capture and grand corruption.

The ANC sent its best people to Parliament in 1994, Tim du Plessis, a former parliamentary correspondent, told me when I arrived in the parliamentary press gallery. They were smart, formidable, occupied the moral high ground and ushered in an era of transparency and accountability. Committees were chaired by high intellects such as Pravin Gordhan, Gill Marcus and Blade Nzimande. 'The ANC had its A team there, but only for a short while and to their detriment,' says Pieter Mulder, whose career as a Conservative Party and Freedom Front Plus parliamentarian straddled apartheid and democracy.[1]

He calls the A team 'impressive and relentless' and names Cyril Ramaphosa, Mac Maharaj, Valli Moosa, Gordhan, Joe Slovo, Mathews Phosa, Penuell Maduna and Mbeki as some of the formidable opponents he came across in those first years: 'Of them, only Mbeki was in Parliament for longer than 10 years. Apart from Slovo, who died in 1995, all of them left Parliament early. Of the 274 ANC MPs that went to Parliament in 1994, only 49 remained after the 1999 elections – 82 per cent of them left the legislature. Most of them left for better-remunerated positions in the civil service or the private sector. And as the ANC's A team gradually left for the business world, the ANC in parliament became staffed by the B team. That probably explains why the C team serves at municipal level.'[2]

Tony Leon remembers the ANC benches being chock-full of heavyweights: three Sisulus (Albertina, Max and Lindiwe), Saki Macozoma, Raymond Suttner, Barbara Hogan and prominent unionists Johnny Copelyn and Marcel Golding.[3] The strongest went to the cabinet but the ANC caucus remained talented, says Leon. 'Its strength was its intellectual depth and community credibility its members represented. This, alas, was not to last. With the completion of the Constitution in 1996 a steady trickle of the best and brightest, led by Ramaphosa, left legislative politics for the lure – and rewards – of the private sector, parastatals and the upper echelons of the public service.'[4]

The impact of the ANC brain drain was severe. The loss of so many capable MPs, who seemingly understood the importance of oversight and proper democratic accountability, was calamitous. A decade and more onwards, Leon later said, 'much of Parliament and its proceedings had become a pale shadow of the imperatives designed for it by the framers of the Constitution.'[5]

For the first two years after 1994, Parliament sat as the Constitutional Assembly, and the final draft of the Constitution it negotiated was adopted on 8 May 1996. Leon, who was elected to Parliament in 1989, said it was everything the apartheid Parliament was not. It was racially integrated, constrained by checks and balances and representative of all people.[6] 'The early years [1994 and 1995] were filled with hope and promise; a spirit of innovation washed through the stodgy halls, replacing old conventions with new perspectives and new aspirations. The legislators set about energetically dismantling what remained of apartheid's legal edifice; but it also introduced exciting new political and ideological debates whose depth was matched by their vigour. One example was the abortion debate of 1995, in which the full range of religious, medical and socioeconomic issues was probed from a variety of perspectives in passionate but respectful exchanges.'[7]

Many of the old Parliament's best features were transferred to the new one: ministers were summoned to question time in the National Assembly where MPs could grill them. The president and deputy president had similar dates with MPs. The committee system was expanded and Scopa was established to keep a check on public spending.

The interim constitution, agreed in 1993, contained 34 principles that the final constitution should adhere to, and the Constitutional Assembly set about its work through various themed committees. 'My ANC colleagues were completely convinced that one could and should legislate for every contingency and the betterment of the human condition,' Leon recalls.[8] The crunch came in the final three months, when a raft of significant issues could not be agreed upon, including aspects of labour rights, such as the right to strike and employers' right to lock striking workers out of the workplace; the property clause, and the ANC's insistence that the state should be able to expropriate land with zero compensation; and language rights. In total, 60 matters of concern remained outstanding.

The ANC majority in 1994 fell a little more than four percentage points short of the magical two-thirds majority it needed to finalise and later change the Constitution on its own. But it seems its impulse to squash dissent and bulldoze through its own positions, without regard for opposition or minority rights, started there.

There was significant unhappiness that in the approach to the final deadline for the Constitution-making process, smaller opposition parties were excluded from backchannelling between Ramaphosa and the senior National Party negotiator, Roelf Meyer, and attempts to put further checks on the powers of the executive were met with derision. Gordhan gave glimpses of what was to come when he told the negotiating council that 'minority parties are often concerned not with creating a democratic state but rather with checking the power of the majority party in the interests of minority groups, which are often racially biased. The debate is often masked in democratic terms but it is frequently used to protect the rights of the privileged.'[9]

This approach to lawmaking and governance – referencing white or minority rights – was to become de rigueur for the ANC over the next three decades. In the early years, Gordhan's argument had some cachet and many were reluctant to push back when the country had just emerged from a racially divided and racist past. But it quickly became the catch-all for the ANC when it was confronted with its own failings or restraints on its powers with which it did not agree. Mandela finally signed the Constitution into law on 10 December 1996 after the Constitutional Court certified it as having complied with the 34 principles in the interim constitution. Parliament's work could begin.

Leon, who was leader of the tiny DP before it took on the mantle of official opposition in 1999, argues that Mandela had high regard 'for the rigours and niceties' of a legislature designed to provide oversight of the executive. But, he explains, the party quickly started to flex its centralist muscle, something that did not bode well for the institution in later years.

Mbeki was the executive-minded deputy president, Mandela more removed from the daily cut and thrust of nascent democratic politics. The former, Leon contends, 'had an impoverishing, indeed withering, effect on the politics of democratic accountability.'[10] It was clear that in the contest between the interests of the party and oversight and accountability, any dispute would be settled 'in favour of the former'.

And in 1994, according to Leon, Ramaphosa – then the ANC secretary general and in charge of Luthuli House – compelled ANC MPs to sign a code of conduct that forbade any 'attempt to make use of parliamentary structures to undermine organisational decisions and policies'.[11] This effectively put paid to ANC MPs relying on their own judgement and conscience in the execution of their parliamentary duties, which nominally were supposed to be discharged in accordance with the Constitution, not ANC diktats. But it was also a function of the electoral system, which gave party bosses power over MPs because they were dispatched to Parliament based on a list and a proportional representation system. If MPs refused to toe the party line, they were easily replaced by the next candidate on the list. Even if there had once been a semblance of independent thought and action among ANC MPs, this neutered it.

Despite Ginwala's strong hand as speaker in the first democratic Parliament – upon her death she was praised as 'exemplary' and ruling with 'a firm yet fair hand'[12] – her role in Parliament's first big test was disappointing but in keeping with the ANC's authoritarian bent. During the arms deal investigation, as Andrew Feinstein noted, she believed the party had to be protected and played a starring role in directing parliamentary affairs in favour of the ANC. 'Provided no vital ANC interest was threatened, Ginwala defended Parliament as an institution and provided some protection to House minorities,' was Leon's assessment.

Ginwala, although nowhere near the toadying and pathetic servility of Baleka Mbete, her successor, set the tone for how Parliament's presiding officers would arrange the legislature's affairs in future.

Parliament was merely another terrain of struggle where ANC strategy and tactics were to enforce the movement's hegemony over society. Parliament, in the beginning, might have been seen as an independent arm of the state with a specific constitutional mandate, but once the ANC saw how a real legislature could and should function, it set out to bring it to heel. It became apparent under Mbeki's presidency, and more so during the destruction of the Zuma years, that the ANC would not countenance a robust Parliament with presiding officers who acted in the legislature's interests, MPs who held the executive to account and an opposition left to fulfil its role.

Leon, regularly accused by the ANC and its alliance partners of only looking after white and elite interests, was one of the few who saw danger lurking in the way the ANC set about governing. He identified the Shell House massacre, which occurred as the April 1994 elections loomed, as the first big red flag. On 28 March 1994, a 20 000-strong Zulu impi marched on ANC headquarters in central Johannesburg. It was a period of heightened rhetoric and tension and those inside the building feared the Inkatha supporters were going to kill them. As the impi approached, ANC security staff in Shell House opened fire. When the smoke cleared, 53 people lay dead on the tarmac. Mandela's response to the events was instructive to Martin Meredith, one of his biographers. It 'tarnished Mandela's reputation', he wrote.[13]

When the police arrived the following day to search the building for weapons and compile forensic evidence, Mandela personally refused them access. For Leon it was a harbinger of what was to come, and he was particularly worried about 'what the event suggested for the rule of law in the country' once the ANC took over. The Shell House massacre was also one of the first issues Leon took up in the new Parliament. At the first available question time, a month after new MPs were sworn in, he questioned the new minister of safety and security, Sydney Mufamadi, about the matter. The minister mumbled and scraped his way through the session, which was followed by a debate on the massacre. Leon would not let it go, believing it was important to hold the new government accountable and to gauge its commitment to the rule of law.

A parliamentary committee was appointed to deal with the issue, but with 'its inbuilt ANC majority' it exonerated Mufamadi. Mandela was furious with Leon's approach and summoned the whole DP caucus to his office, where he confirmed that he gave the 'shoot to kill order'. Mandela dismissed the criticism of Leon and his colleagues, saying their party 'is essentially all white'. A few weeks later Mandela took another dig at Leon, telling the Senate (today the National Council of Provinces) that 'the DP proved itself to be more right-wing than the National Party'. If the arms deal was Parliament's first big test, then Shell House was the primer. And it failed both. An 'opening up' of Parliament was short-lived. 'The ask-no-questions, brook-no-dissent exile liberationists began to find the scrutiny to which they were now subjected a little too uncomfortable,' says Leon.

Leon details how the new Parliament, initially dynamic and brimming with fresh ideas and enthusiasm, eventually succumbed to a lack of focus and weak management – something that would worsen significantly in later years, culminating in the devastating 2022 fire. But in those early years, Leon and his colleagues were confronted by problems that now seem almost quaint. Opposition parties complained about delays in meetings and absenteeism by ANC MPs affecting quora. Parliament, Leon thought, was being treated by ANC MPs as not much more than 'a tiresome inconvenience' and efforts to convince the speaker to act against errant and truant MPs came to nought.[14] When Leon led his caucus to meet the president about the increasingly malfunctioning Parliament, Mandela was at pains to explain that his party and its parliamentary caucus had not had the benefit of serving an apprenticeship in the opposition benches. They had no experience of formal politics and parliamentary cut and thrust.

Mandela told the assembled DP MPs that the transition from the National Party to the ANC was the biggest in South African politics since 1948, when the National Party became the majority party. 'The ANC went straight from the bush into power,' he said.[15] It was clear to Leon that Mandela meant to say that the ANC could not be expected to immediately have an effective parliamentary operation. This would prove to be true not only in the 1990s but deep into the 21st century. The ANC would continue to treat Parliament as an inconvenient check on its untrammelled power. And it would eventually destroy the institution.

8
Total control

BEN TUROK OCCUPIED A SPACIOUS OFFICE in the Old Assembly wing of Parliament, almost directly above Poorthuis, the security gate that gives access to the legislature's precinct. Two large bay windows let in sunlight that illuminated a giant framed poster of the 156 accused in the Treason Trial of 1956 mounted on the opposite wall. Somewhere in the giant picture sat a young Turok, a fiery communist. Around the corner from his quarters was the office of Jeremy Cronin, who was deployed to the National Assembly and later the cabinet as the SACP deputy general secretary. I frequently visited the two senior communists while I was a member of the parliamentary Press Gallery Association.

A leading member of the SACP before it was banned, Turok helped craft the economic clauses of the Freedom Charter in 1955 ('The national wealth of our country, the heritage of South Africans, shall be restored to the people; the mineral wealth beneath the soil, the Banks and monopoly industry shall be transferred to the ownership of the people as a whole …') and was an ANC MP between 1994 and 2014. His guidance was indispensable to me as a young parliamentary reporter trying to understand the arcane ways of the governing party – or, as many called it, the ruling party. 'What is it you want now?' he used to say in a gruff voice as one of his two secretaries ushered me into his office when I visited him on a random weekday. 'What don't you understand?'

Turok, a leading figure in the struggle intelligentsia, cut an intimidating figure, especially since he made it clear that speaking to an upstart Afrikaner journalist from *Beeld* was at the very bottom of his list of priorities. His lectures and monologues directed at me were often difficult to understand and follow, especially as they were brimful with explanations of the role of the 'vanguard party in the class struggle', the different phases of the revolution and the Marxist-Leninist character of policy. Almost all of it was beyond me and I told him so.

It was during one of these visits, in the months before the ANC's national conference in Polokwane in 2007, that Turok took me to task for asking questions that he believed any proper journalist should have the answers to. 'You must read more. Everything that we [the ANC] plan to do is in our policy documents. Everything is there. But the problem is people don't read. And then they act all surprised. Have you read Strategy and Tactics? Have you read Through the Eye of the Needle? No? Then don't come back to me unless you've read through all of it. We can talk once you've read them.' And with that, Turok sent me packing. I went to look for Strategy and Tactics and just as he said, found answers to most of my questions.

By 2007, the ANC had been in power for 13 years. It had seized control at every level of government – municipal, provincial and national – and across the breadth and depth of the public service. By then, it had also taken charge of state entities and agencies, independent state institutions and SOEs. The party was asserting increasing control in broader society, where its ideology and doctrines – democratic centralism, transformation – were becoming embedded. In fact, by the time delegates gathered for the showdown between Thabo Mbeki and Jacob Zuma that December, ANC dogma had become part of the state's institutional and organisational DNA. Society had begun to arrange itself according to ANC dictates and anything to the contrary, any challenge to ANC policy and beliefs, was considered racist and anti-democratic heresy.

The ANC is guided by a latticework of ideological foundational documents. These include the Freedom Charter, antiquated as it might be; the party constitution; Through the Eye of a Needle; policy and

71

discussion documents that are produced between national conferences; and resolutions taken at these conferences. But marching orders to carry out the National Democratic Revolution, the ANC's foundational theology, are contained in Strategy and Tactics. It is the ANC's sacred ideological treatise and guiding doctrine, updated at every national conference, and sets out the domestic and international framework and conditions under which the NDR, as it is referred to, continues to be executed by 'the movement'. It contains the long-term vision for the organisation and analyses prevailing and future conditions in the context of the party's worldview, using mostly Marxist and socialist themes as points of departure.

Strategy and Tactics is replete with Marxist and Leninist phraseology, which is to be expected since the organisation was marinated in these ideas while in exile. The posture of the ANC, according to the document, is that of an organisation which remains deeply engaged in ongoing revolutionary conflict with the goal of eradicating any opposition, whether ideological or political. The tone is antagonistic and couched in military terms – it tells the story of an organisation still at the height of conflict. It tells its readers – ANC members – that just because it emerged as the party of government after 1994 does not mean the struggle for supremacy and control is over. The 1994 political solution is cast as a beachhead, with ANC control of the state merely an enabling development that will in time help it to transform society into its image.

The document analyses the 'balance of forces' as it seeks to identify the 'terrain of struggle' where 'the motive forces of the revolution' can 'attack the enemy on all fronts'. The 'liberation movement' is the 'vanguard of the NDR', is 'always in political motion' and seeks to 'capture the primary centres of power'. The 'neoliberal agenda' will be defeated by 'militant and brave cadres' who exert a 'hegemony of ideas' in the 'current epoch and this stage of the revolution'. And so on.

Strategy and Tactics is the basis from which the NDR is launched and waged, with the NDR being the ongoing struggle to create, in the ANC's ideology, a non-racial and non-sexist society. But the NDR also details the continuous assault on all vestiges of power that do not fall under the ANC's control. The state and its institutions cannot remain independent; they must become a constituent part of the movement in its efforts to attain the goals of the NDR. The NDR seeks to disrupt and transform every aspect of life, public or private, in line with the organisation's aim of uniting the country under the ANC flag and in accordance with its ideology and purpose.

Not many South Africans – including ANC supporters and voters – know and understand the ideological scaffolding that supports party and government policy. In 2007, at the insistence of Turok, I tried to unpick whether the ANC meant what it said and why it did what it did. At that time, it was still standard practice to refrain from assigning overtly malign intent to ANC and government policy decisions as they related to the broad transformation of state and society. Mandela, although having retreated from public life, was still close to the forefront of the national consciousness and the reconstruction and reconciliation project he once led.

But a decade earlier, in 1997, it was Mandela who initiated the departure from a national reconstruction and reconciliation project to an ideological enforcement project when he laid the groundwork for an acceleration of the NDR. By 1996, he had handed over much power to his chosen successor, Mbeki, and at the ANC's 50th national conference the following year he stepped down as party leader and Mbeki was elected unopposed. But it was Mandela, after a year in which the party started to question and query its progress in government, who set the tone for what was to come when he delivered an ill-tempered and angry speech at the party gathering in dusty Mahikeng, then still called Mafikeng, in North West. By then it was clear the ANC had begun to grow in confidence and wanted to assert its control over state and society more forcefully.

Tim du Plessis attended the conference as a reporter and says, for him, it signalled the end of the honeymoon phase: 'The Mandela speech set off alarm bells, even though it was the voice of Jacob but the hand of Esau. In that period – 1996 and 1997 – you had major changes in education, minister Sibusiso Bhengu's outcomes-based education began to be implemented, the White Paper on defence, *Sarafina* ... and then the Mandela speech. I think we should have realised back then that these guys had bigger plans than just happy and jolly and hail to the chief Mandela. When they spoke about transformation, they meant it.'[1]

❖

By the time Mandela took to the podium in Mahikeng on Tuesday, 16 December 1997, the ANC was completely in charge of the government after the National Party's withdrawal from the GNU earlier in the year. It had bedded down its macroeconomic policy, Gear, which sent a strong message to the international investment community. And the first ANC minister of finance, Trevor Manuel, had been appointed in 1996.

Early in 1997, the ANC leadership gave a sign of things to come when it lamented in the annual January 8th statement that party members in government should not think they were individuals, or that they could steer their careers in accordance with their own belief systems and mores. 'You aren't only cadres after hours,' was the admonishment. The message was clear: public servants remained under the whip of the party's leadership and they should seek to advance the cause of the organisation wherever they found themselves. It didn't matter whether they were lowly municipal employees or the directors general of national departments – matters of the movement remained their primary endeavour. If the ANC wanted to mould South Africa into its image, the state would be its most important tool. And to control the state it had to embed itself in the marrow of departments, entities and agencies. The ANC had to become the state and for that to happen it had to formulate official policy to enable nothing short of a complete takeover of the public service.

Mandela spoke for more than six hours, even taking a break for lunch. Anthony Sampson, his biographer, called the speech 'bewildering' and argued it 'destroyed much sympathy he had built up while in office'.[2] Author Mandla Langa, who worked on Mandela's incomplete presidential memoirs after his death, wrote that the president voiced his 'concerns about media ownership and governance' in the speech.[3] Tony Leon said it was 'unprecedented and revealing' because Mandela 'gave clear notice that the heights the ANC commanded across politics and much of civil society were insufficient for the party's appetite'.[4] And the 'sharp tone caused a stir inside and outside of the ANC', wrote political reporters Tim du Plessis and Peet Kruger on the front page of *Beeld*.[5]

The ANC needed cover for its assault on the state and its intention to assume complete command and control – and it needed justification for what would become its cadre deployment policy. This was amply provided by Mandela, who identified enemies of the ANC and threats to the movement almost everywhere, but specifically in the civil service, the media and opposition parties. And this provided justification for the acceleration of the NDR and transformation policies. The ANC, he told delegates, was facing significant resistance from those aligned to the previous dispensation in its efforts to transform the country and to uplift those who had suffered under racism and apartheid.

'The counter-revolution has also sought to regroup to create the possibility for itself to act decisively to compromise the democratic system at whatever moment it considered opportune,' Mandela said. 'This counter-revolutionary network, which is already active and bases itself on those in the public administration and others in other sectors of our society who have not accepted the reality of majority rule, is capable of carrying out very disruptive actions. It measures its own success by the extent to which it manages to weaken the democratic order.[6]

'Consistent with the objectives we have just mentioned, it has engaged in practical activities since our last conference which include: the encouragement and commission of crime; the weakening and incapacitation of the state machinery, including the theft of public assets, arms and ammunition being among these; the hiding of sensitive and important information from legal organs of state; and the building of alternative structures, including intelligence machineries as well as armed formations. Evidence also exists that elements of this counter-revolutionary conspiracy have established or are maintaining a variety of international contacts.'[7]

Mandela repeatedly identified the public service as an impediment to the ANC's transformation policies but also accused the media and opposition parties of defending the old order. 'Further, even a cursory study of the positions adopted by the mainly white parties in the national legislature during the last three years, the National Party, the Democratic Party and the Freedom Front, will show that they and the media, which represents the same social base, have been most vigorous in their opposition, whenever legislative and executive measures have been introduced seeking to end the racial disparities which continue to characterise our society.

'Equally, we have experienced serious resistance to the transformation of the public service, with representatives of the old order using all means in their power to ensure that they remain in dominant positions. Some among these owe no loyalty to the new constitutional and political order nor to the government of the day and have no intention to implement our government's programmes aimed at reconstruction and development.'[8]

The media was reserved for special criticism, having positioned itself as 'as a force opposed to the ANC'. It exploited its ill-gotten gains to campaign against change and the ANC and resisted its own transformation, labelling it an attack on press freedom, Mandela charged. 'Thus, the media uses the democratic order, brought about by the enormous sacrifices of our own people, as an instrument to protect the legacy of racism, graphically described by its own patterns of ownership, editorial control, value system and advertiser influence. Consistent with the political posture it has assumed, it has been most vigorous in disseminating such information as it believes serves to discredit and weaken our movement.

'By this means, despite its professions of support for democracy, it limits the possibility to expand the frontiers of democracy, which would derive from the empowerment of the citizen to participate meaningfully in the process of governance through timeous access to reliable information.'[9]

The opposition parties – the National Party (then still the biggest), the DP (the antecedent of the DA), the fledgling United Democratic Movement (UDM) and the Freedom Front (then without the 'Plus', which was added when remnants of the Conservative Party joined later) – sought nothing but the destruction of the ANC. The 'white parties' had nothing to offer but defending white interests and discrediting the 'ruling party', Mandela said, while cadres had to guard against infiltration from UDM spies. The opposition, including non-governmental organisations funded by foreign powers, wanted to destroy the ANC and the revolution.

Mandela said there was an urgent need 'for the fundamental transformation of all sectors of our society'. He told delegates that the easiest part of the job – holding elections and changing the legislative environment – was done. But the hard work, that of fundamental transformation, was yet to begin. And the ANC, in the process of 'abolishing the apartheid state and replacing it with a democratic state', had to 'speed up' the theoretical work related to the nature and the role of the new state.

Kruger, writing in *Beeld* the following day, said it might have been Mandela delivering the speech, 'but the report was unmistakably the voice of Mbeki' and an indication of what the country could expect from Mandela's successor. He told his readers – the newspaper remained influential in government circles until well into the democratic era – that there was much to be upbeat about but a lot to be concerned about, too. Mandela spoke of creating dialogue with whites, of convincing them to vote ANC and urging the private sector to move more quickly in changing the business environment. But the attack on the media and Mandela's warnings about 'counter-revolution' sounded paranoid and reminiscent of hardline apartheid president PW Botha.[10]

Du Plessis, Kruger's colleague, took a different line and said it would be daft to fixate only on the 'paranoia'. The Mandela speech and Mbeki's media engagements afterwards explaining the rationale behind the political report convinced him that 'a door opened' to the ANC. Mbeki, Du Plessis said, made it clear that he was willing to seek consensus on pressing issues with social actors but that there must be agreement on the source of the country's ills, and that was the immorality of apartheid. There was a new drumbeat in the country, that of Mbeki, Du Plessis added. 'The days of *die groot oubaas* walking out in front, hoping to let the country feel better about itself by saying nice things, are over.'[11]

On 22 December, before Mbeki closed the conference, delegates adopted the party's resolution on 'the deployment and redeployment of our cadres'. It would lead to the ANC's rapid takeover of the entire state and its institutions and agencies and eventually to the creation of a sprawling, metastasising network of patronage and extraction. 'State machinery must be transformed as quickly as possible so that it can be used as an instrument to serve the needs of the people, President Thabo Mbeki said in his closing address at the ANC national conference,' reported *Beeld*.[12]

A *Beeld* editorial warned of the disappearing line between party and state. There was an increased tendency to appoint senior state functionaries into party positions, it said. Frank Chikane, director general in Mbeki's office, Joel Netshitenzhe, chief director in the president's office, Saki Macozoma, Transnet managing director, and Thenjiwe Mtintso, a commissioner at the Commission for Gender Equality, had all been elected to senior party positions. There was no reason to maintain the previous dispensation's traditions and customs but the separation between party and state wasn't always clear, the newspaper said.

'The ANC must motivate and explain this new practice … it will be better if guidelines can be laid down within which office bearers that also occupy important positions in political parties can function. The dividing line between the state and the governing party isn't always easily visible. But that doesn't mean that the line doesn't exist, or that it mustn't be respected.'[13]

Du Plessis, who thinks he wrote this editorial, says the ANC was not transparent about its plans or the real purpose of cadre deployment. 'They were not open about it. And it was the end of innocence for the country. The ANC and Mbeki sold it to us by saying this is what all democratic governments the world over do. That was how they cloaked it. But it was more sinister than that. It was, indeed, a power grab.'[14]

Shortly after the ANC conference, *Sowetan* published a cartoon by Zapiro illustrating the outcome. Mandela is at the wheel of an enormous truck named 'transformation', a pipe-smoking Mbeki beside him. Mandela, calm and collected, hoots at a small car right in front of the truck, urging it to get out of the way. The words 'white privilege' are emblazoned on the car and the horn scares the bejesus out of the grimacing white driver and his passenger, a woman.[15]

Mandela, Leon observed, 'had to conjure up some ghosts and phantasms to make it clear that the organisation, far from being secure, was in fact facing some kind of threat'.[16] The outgoing ANC president paved the way. The ANC was now Mbeki's party. And he would put the country on a path that would lead to the ascension of Jacob Zuma, the institutionalisation of corruption and broad state collapse. The ANC was obsessive about central control and from 1998 onwards it pursued this goal relentlessly.

❖

Mandela's speech that prepared the ground for the ANC's grand project of state and social engineering was not well received outside the party. Many discounted it 'as simply addressing an internal audience' and as an attempt to placate 'some of the wilder ANC elements', Leon said. 'This immediately led ANC-inclined sympathisers to play down the rhetoric as being of less importance than the economic substance.'[17]

Sampson said the speech was 'was far from radical', arguing that Mandela even quoted 'American arch-capitalists George Soros and David Rockefeller'. But it was 'quickly presented by the white media as an attack on white enemies and a clean break with Mandela's earlier conciliation'.[18] He conceded that the speech was not in line with the tone Mandela had struck over the years but added that 'it was not a policy statement', simply an analysis of the problems facing his government and a 'rallying call' for the 1999 election. *Beeld* called it 'ominous'.[19] *Business Day* rejected the speech, as did the *Citizen*. Foreign observers were equally negative, with Britain's *Daily Telegraph*, *Independent* and *Observer* slating it.[20]

In briefings with journalists at Mafikeng, Mbeki tried to contextualise Mandela's remarks and his tone was 'conciliatory and accommodating'[21] but Leon was not convinced. 'Those who assumed the surrender of socialism meant the abandonment of the party's national revolutionary agenda were mistaken,' he said.[22] Resolutions taken at the conference accelerated the party's transformation agenda, including decisions on regulations that would see more rapid affirmative action, primarily but not exclusively focused on the state.

The national mood changed after the Mafikeng conference, says Du Plessis. 'Especially after we were able to digest what happened, and after everything could be analysed, and bills to give effect to it started coming before Parliament. The whole climate changed. More critical voices started to emerge from business too and the consensus reached, for example, at the Brenthurst meetings (between the ANC and business leaders at the Oppenheimer estate) was becoming increasingly weak.

'The 1999 election, when the ANC increased its majority, also wasn't a shock to anyone, nor was it necessarily a bad thing. And it was because we did not fully comprehend what was happening behind the scenes. We believed Mbeki was keeping things together with his force of personality, his stature as an intellectual and his management style. He didn't only convince the white minority of this but also the business community and the international community. We accepted his bona fides. As long as Mbeki was there, we thought things were going to be okay.'[23]

Years later, in the cold and dark of the winter of 2022, while Eskom was collapsing under the weight of ANC interference and the resultant waves of power cuts were destroying the economy, Chief Justice Raymond Zondo found 'cadre deployment' to be 'unlawful and unconstitutional'.[24] The ANC's obsession with democratic centralism and the party leadership's insistence on ANC hegemony and total control would eventually destroy almost all institutions afflicted by the deployment of party cadres. Ministers would be summoned to the deployment committee to explain their choices for senior civil servants – and be sent away to compile a new shortlist if the committee was dissatisfied.[25] The committee would issue commands to cabinet ministers, who would be 'taken to task' for presenting some appointments as their own personal choices.[26] It would insist that it be told before positions were advertised.

It would be with 'the party that power resides', Ramaphosa told Zondo. The ANC would not countenance members of the executive acting outside party prescripts. 'Decisions of the organisation are final and a breach of policy shall constitute a serious offence … deployees of the ANC should always be loyal to the organisation,' the deployment policy stated.[27] Appointing authorities in the state – including ministers – were bound by decisions of the committee. 'Its "recommendations" are in fact instructions,' Zondo later found.[28] The ANC's 'self-identification as leader of society' meant the party was unable to distinguish between the interests of the party and the constitutionally enshrined public duty of those in government.[29]

But Zondo's denunciation of democratic centralism and cadre deployment still lay in the future, and in December 1997 ANC delegates to the national conference instructed their leaders to 'put in place a deployment strategy which focuses on the short-, medium- and long-term challenges, identifying the key centres of power, our strategy to transform these centres and the attributes and skills we require from our cadres to do so effectively'.[30] The resolution was short and lacked details, bar adding that 'deployment committees' must be established at every level of the organisation to oversee and decide on where party members should serve in the government and the state.[31]

As furiously explained to me by Turok, the ANC has a strong ideological basis which is codified every five years at its national conference and provides the framework and arc for what the party seeks to achieve. And the ANC's 1997 conference set the country on course for the era of state capture. According to Frederik van Zyl Slabbert, the charismatic politician who was well disposed towards the ANC before it assumed power in 1994, the ANC's ideology was so deeply influenced by communism because it was the 'dominant secular liberation ideology of the 20th century'.[32] He explained this 'liberation theory' as one that guaranteed the 'unavoidable victory of the working class over capitalist exploitation through a national democratic revolution'.

This ideology, Slabbert held, collapsed in the early 1990s with the crumbling of the Soviet empire and the socialist world. The ANC, Slabbert argued, not only agreed to but argued for a liberal democracy and market economy. But Mbeki, working in close partnership with Netshitenzhe, one of the foremost intellectuals and ideologues of the Mbeki era, tried his best to maintain the liberation movement's ideological flourish and focus.

9

Here come the cadres

THE REVIEWED STRATEGY AND TACTICS that emerged from
Mafikeng in 1997 codified cadre deployment in ANC policy, detailed
the goals of the NDR and placed the state at the centre of the party's
transformation plan. It also declared that ANC members deployed in
government and the state must be loyal to the party – with little if any
mention of fealty to the Constitution, signed into law the year before.

The ANC 'should exercise maximum discipline among its members,
and ensure that, after ideas have been exchanged and decisions taken,
all its structures and members pursue the same goal'. The inference is
clear: the ANC and its policies take precedence over anything else.
ANC cadres should use Parliament as a 'forum' – therefore, not as
the only legislative authority – 'to lay the detailed legal framework
for transformation, creative employment of public representatives in
organisational work, a cadre policy ensuring that the ANC plays a
leading role in all centres of power, and a proper balance in its day-to-day
activities between narrow governmental work and organisational tasks.
In all centres of power, particularly in Parliament and the executive,
ANC representatives must fulfil the mandate of the organisation. They
should account to the ANC and seek its broad guidance.'[1]

Just as Ben Turok said, everything the ANC intends to do is in
its policy documents. Deployed cadres, regardless of their station in
government or the state, were to toe the party line. And every centre

of power – the executive, Parliament, the state, institutions – would be primed to fall in line behind the ANC. For example, Strategy and Tactics demanded that MPs would henceforth have no space to vote differently from the party's line of march and ANC members deployed to the state would have to execute party policy regardless of whether it was contrary to the national interest. This was to play itself out repeatedly in later years, feckless ANC MPs keeling over when instructed to by Luthuli House and ministers and directors general mindlessly parroting whatever a miscreant like Jacob Zuma required.

Strategy and Tactics is remarkable in the way it demands all-consuming loyalty to the party, the NDR and the broad movement. There are some references to the ANC following the prescripts of the law and adhering to the tenets of democracy, but the reader is left in no doubt about the party's purpose and mission. The party 'is the vanguard of all the motive forces of the NDR, the leader of the broad movement for transformation'.[2] After getting its hands on the state machinery, the 'revolution' must use it to drive social transformation. Its success depends critically on the role of the state. 'For this reason, we reject insinuations that our country needs "less government", which is in essence a ploy aimed at weakening the democratic state,' the document declares.[3]

The ANC was, and remains, incredibly paranoid. Strategy and Tactics repeatedly warns about 'counter-revolution' and about those who want to 'destroy the ANC, the vanguard of the NDR, both from within and outside its ranks'.[4] And among those who seek to weaken and destroy are the civil service, the security sector, the economic sector and the media.[5] 'In this phase of transformation, we seek to expand and deepen the power of democratic forces in all centres critical to the NDR, at the same time as we improve the people's quality of life.' One of the key pillars was the state. 'Strengthen the hold of the democratic movement on state power and transform the state machinery to serve the cause of social change.'[6]

❖

When the ANC was elected to form the first democratic government, it took over a state constructed over more than eight decades, ever since the South Africa Act in 1910 gave independence to the Union of South Africa. This state, built by legislation in a Parliament that represented the white minority, was used to oppress the majority. The administration of government, the institutions that executed policy, the arms of state – including the judiciary – and particularly those who staffed it, were all engaged in supporting apartheid.

When ANC ministers and senior officials moved into national departments in June 1994, they understandably did so with suspicion and trepidation. After all, they were inheriting systems designed to fight the liberation movement. But the transition would not have happened as it did without the cooperation of apartheid civil servants, many of whom were careerists who chose to maintain the systems of governance rather than sabotage and destroy them.

Of course, there were many elements, like those in the security establishment, who opposed and resisted the passage to democracy and used violent means to do so. But there was little evidence of a civil service in revolt and engaging in a silent war of resistance against the democratic state. In fact, most if not all civil servants continued with their jobs as normal, serving the government of the day. Senior ministers from that era have told me how they relied on the 'old guard' to keep things afloat while the new executive was settling in.

One man, widely regarded as one of the most efficient ministers in the democratic era – and certainly one who did not suffer fools or apartheid apologists – explained to me in detail how easily many mid-level Afrikaner civil servants in his (strategic and crucial) department went on doing their jobs, sticking to routine and executing the work of government. You could say what you wanted about Afrikaner nationalism but its inherent Calvinist ethos caused many civil servants to transfer their professional loyalties very quickly to the incoming government.

The minister tells a colourful and rich tale of how his posse of senior Afrikaner bureaucrats helped orientate him in his department and steer the democratic ship. When one of them retired, he personally delivered a bottle of whisky to the minister's house as a farewell gift. Of course, anecdotal evidence cannot pass for scientific proof. Niël Barnard, the former head of the apartheid National Intelligence Service, was asked to leave his senior position in the Department of Constitutional Affairs by Valli Moosa, an ANC deputy minister, because he simply 'could not' work with the former apartheid spymaster.[7] And Trevor Manuel, upon entering the Department of Finance, similarly forced out Estian Calitz, the director general. But in general, and in the absence of major conflagrations, the ANC government took charge of a largely stable and acquiescent civil service.

It was natural that the ANC wanted to ensure its policies were adhered to by the large and disparate bureaucracy and that it wanted to staff the state with a new breed of public servant. Yes, it did 'inherit' the state and its constituent parts from the apartheid government, but it was also building a new state machinery – including new legal entities. The new government had to combine as many as ten different bureaucracies – including those of the former homelands and TBVC states – into one national body. In forging the post-apartheid state, the ANC agreed to a set of sunset clauses which guaranteed job security and pensions of all civil servants until 1999.[8] This was to ensure continuity and stability – and went some way to pacifying latent animosity towards the new government from the incumbents.

But in 1995, amid a cash crunch and after a comment by Mbeki that the civil service had to be streamlined, the government offered voluntary severance packages, hoping to reduce the headcount by 300 000 over three years.[9] Historian Thula Simpson calls this a 'miscalculation' after it led to an exodus of the most highly skilled and the deterioration of financial management and administration. Education was an area where the loss of skills was felt most acutely, and in February 1997 the government admitted it had approved more than twice as many voluntary severance packages than the education system could afford.[10] It was to have disastrous long-term consequences.

❖

The year after the adoption of cadre deployment as a central feature of the NDR – 1998 – was, in hindsight, a watershed. Mbeki, now in charge of the party and shadowed by Joel Netshitenzhe and the brothers Pahad (Essop and Aziz), moved assiduously to extend the party's influence and control over the state and its entities. Netshitenzhe was installed as the head of the government's central communications unit, the GCIS, in January.[11] Former MK soldiers Siphiwe Nyanda and Gilbert Ramano were installed as head of the SANDF and army in quick succession in April and May,[12] in accordance with revolutionary theory which dictates control over power structures (army, police, intelligence) as non-negotiable. Tito Mboweni, who had been an ANC MP and labour minister, went to the Reserve Bank in July.[13] In the same month, Bulelani Ngcuka, another ANC MP, became the first 'super attorney-general' in the new position of national director of public prosecutions (NDPP), which meant that he oversaw the NPA.[14] The prosecuting authority went on to become arguably the most politically contested state institution.

In October, the party distributed another seminal discussion paper that codified the rationale for cadre deployment and, more importantly, what it sought to achieve and how it was going to do it. As a Marxist extension of Strategy and Tactics, the document titled The State, Property Relations and Social Transformation made the case for the ANC's complete annexing of the state. 'The state is not a neutral, non-partisan entity, but it is an instrument that is used to pursue the interests of a class or group of classes,' the document states.[15] This is of course contrary to a state that, although headed by political appointees executing a party-political mandate obtained through a majority vote, should be apolitical when executing the functions of government.

According to the document – authored by Netshitenzhe – the state the ANC inherited remained hostile to the party's goals of complete societal transformation, therefore 'the balance of forces' in the state and the broader country must be 'continually shifted in favour of the movement of transformation'.[16] The ANC could never just take over the state as it was, the document argued, and hope to realise its aims. 'The apartheid state has to be destroyed in a process of fundamental transformation,' was how Netshitenzhe, Mbeki's policy guru, summed up the party's goals.[17]

Recall Manuel's case for cadre deployment: 'In many cases you couldn't build with the attitude of people who were very senior in the public service … if you wanted to do new things, you sometimes needed new people, new approaches … so the question about cadre deployment is a fundamentally important one.'[18]

From the outside, says Tim du Plessis, it was difficult to gauge what exactly was happening in the ANC and what precisely its plans were. 'It was like a new building being constructed, with the building site shielded from view by screens all around it. You can't see what's going on; all you know is they're erecting a new building and that Thabo Mbeki is the architect and engineer. And you think, well, it's going to be fine. Yes, we were worried and of course there were critical voices, but the feeling was still, Mbeki is in charge. And maybe they haven't completely gotten rid of their old communist ways, but Mbeki is a good president, he runs foreign policy too, the economy is being run well and Gear is starting to produce dividends with Trevor Manuel in charge ... And when the screens were taken down from around the building and we could see what they built, around the time of Mbeki's HIV/Aids disaster and the Zimbabwe issues, we saw it wasn't exactly a thing of beauty.'[19]

The ANC, a governing party that was supposedly guided by a higher set of values and ostensibly believed in democracy, wanted total control. And the way to achieve it was to inject the party's DNA into the body politic. It wanted everything. 'Transformation of the state entails, first and foremost, extending the power of the NLM [National Liberation Movement] over all levers of power: the army, the police, the bureaucracy, intelligence structures, the judiciary, parastatals, agencies, regulatory bodies, the public broadcaster, the central bank and so on.'[20]

By 30 November 1998, the party had formalised cadre deployment. The deployment committee was formed after a meeting of the ANC NWC, with the party's deputy president, Jacob Zuma, as chairperson. The first deployment committee also included Nkosazana Dlamini-Zuma, Mbhazima Shilowa and Blade Nzimande. Two days later, on 2 December, the cabinet adopted the Public Service Amendment Bill, which made cadre deployment much easier. It allowed for the appointment of national directors general and provincial heads of department by the president and respective premiers 'in order to allow for redeployment and utilisation of these public servants on a government-wide basis'.[21]

The following day, the ANC told the media at a press conference that 'every deployment will now go through the committee, be it in national, provincial or local government'.[22] And less than a week later, the ANC national executive formally adopted the party's cadre policy and deployment strategy. It would henceforth seek to ensure 'hegemony in broader society around our agenda' while 'strengthening the hold of democratic forces on state power'.[23]

During 1999, the ANC-in-government implemented the new doctrine at lightning speed, promulgating the Public Service Amendment Act to speed up cadre deployment and moving apparatchiks into every leadership position across the state. The dividing line between party and state was overrun by cadres as ideologically pliant deployees took charge of all levers of power.

Between June, when Mbeki took over as head of state, and December an enormous change of guard at national departments occurred. Only nine of 31 departmental heads were retained by the new Mbeki government, with 12 new appointments, five moved to other positions in the state and five vacancies opening up.[24] James Myburgh, a respected researcher for the then DP, said that all security and intelligence portfolios were led by 'former ANC exiles close to Mbeki'.[25] They included former diplomat and exile dogsbody Jackie Selebi as the new national police commissioner.

Cadre deployment was the death knell for the independence of institutions such as the NPA and Parliament. Du Plessis says: 'The ANC for so long got away by maintaining the fiction that these institutions are independent. But all of them were deployed cadres following the resolutions at Mafikeng. But the party remained Mandela's party at the time, so there wasn't a lot of criticism. Because Thabo was still there and we knew him. As long as he and Trevor were there, we'd be okay ...'[26]

'Hence, at a time when government was lamenting the haemorrhaging of skills and experience from the state sector, it was simultaneously committed to a mass purge of existing personnel that would leave no part of the civil service untouched,' was University of Pretoria historian Thula Simpson's verdict.[27] And he cites fears by then Auditor-General Henri Kluever that Mbeki's South Africa faced major challenges if it wanted to avoid a rapid decline in the 'quality of financial management and administration' in the public sector.[28] Tony Leon feared that the country could be 'succumbing to something darker'.[29]

But criticism of the ANC's nascent transformation and deployment policies was often met with accusations of racism or being anti-democracy. The ANC had now set the country firmly on the path to entrenched politics of patronage and rent-seeking. And under the ANC, it would never recover.

10
Mbeki takes charge

I NEVER DUCKED AN OPPORTUNITY to attend a press event at either the Union Buildings, the presidential residence Mahlamba Ndlopfu in Pretoria, or Tuynhuys, the president's office next to the National Assembly in Cape Town.

The south-facing Union Buildings on Meintjeskop in Pretoria are stately and magnificent, looking out across the capital. The clocks in the two towers chime every 15 minutes and the serenity and silence is only (just) broken by pigeons cooing and the distant hum of the city's traffic, way down beyond the terraced gardens. Mahlamba Ndlopfu sits to the east of the Union Buildings on the crest of the same hill in the Bryntirion ministerial estate, with its lush, manicured gardens and large traffic circles. Mahlamba Ndlopfu was first occupied by Jan Smuts, who named the mansion Libertas. And Tuynhuys was originally a garden shed used by the Dutch East India Company.

I always found it fascinating to see the ANC-in-government occupying the same buildings and offices where British governors and National Party prime ministers once worked. Much of the antique Dutch or British furniture remained in place after 1994, yellowwood tables where hardline premiers ate now being used by democratic leaders. Just outside the president's office in the west wing of the Union Buildings there are still large oil paintings bearing inscriptions testifying that they were gifts from European countries 'on the attainment of the republic, 1961'.

The president's office in Tuynhuys is at the back of the whitewashed two-storey building, looking across the parliamentary gardens and towards the Company's Garden. During my first year as a parliamentary correspondent, I decamped to Tuynhuys to attend a press conference by Mbeki. I forget what it was about but when Mbeki had finished delivering his statement and answering questions, I walked up to query him further. He was already leaving the room to cross the hallway to his office. Mbeki put his hand on my shoulder and asked, 'What did you not understand? Walk with me.'

We sat down in the president's outer office and he took time to answer whatever questions I had before his aides and assistants extricated him and he disappeared into the main office. He was engaging, friendly and had a clear grasp of the details. The bookshelves behind him were filled with green and brown bound copies of Hansard, green being pre-1994 and brown post-1994. There were other books on the desk in front of the shelves and Hansards – including green ones – lying open. When I returned to the office some years later to interview Zuma, the shelves were empty.

The interaction at Tuynhuys happened towards the end of Mbeki's presidency; his enemies abounded and he wasn't the confident and assured leader who had taken office in June 1999. But he remained determined and committed to the task as he saw it. Mbeki desperately wanted to prove to the world, especially the West, that Africans could govern a complex, dynamic and developing state like South Africa efficiently and effectively. Mandela's 'sanctity' was assured because of the entrenchment of a Bill of Rights during his presidency and the fact that a racial and ethnic conflict did not materialise, Mbeki's biographer Mark Gevisser argued. 'But he was a far better liberator and nation-builder than he was a governor. In contrast, Mbeki marketed himself as the technocratic, truth-telling antidote to the madness and magic – the scattershot celebrity – of the Mandela era.'[1]

Although Oliver Tambo was leader of the ANC-in-exile, Mbeki was the movement's most important statesman. He travelled the world stating the ANC's case, working ceaselessly to isolate apartheid South

Africa and helping to arrange contact with Afrikaner and apartheid government functionaries. Mbeki prepared the ANC for its return to South Africa and negotiated with Afrikaner emissaries and the National Intelligence Service. And he started to modernise the ANC as it prepared to enter government, establishing his influence through the organisation's economic desk and a handpicked group of leaders who went on to shape the country's fortunes for more than a decade. He was the natural successor to Mandela, despite attempts to anoint Ramaphosa.

Allister Sparks, the veteran journalist and former *Rand Daily Mail* editor who wrote a trilogy about South Africa's transition from apartheid to democracy and was a big Mbeki admirer (he called the second democratic president 'brilliant'), says Mbeki was 'the key player' in many of the pivotal strategic moves that led to the negotiated settlement. 'It was he who was instrumental in persuading the ANC, first, to abandon its armed struggle, then to agree to the dropping of international sanctions against South Africa. Both were highly emotional issues that encountered fierce resistance within the liberation movement, but Mbeki won his colleagues over with his cool, reasoned arguments that they were weapons of the past that would have to go and that it was therefore better for the ANC to manage their removal and win moral high ground for doing so,' he wrote.[2]

Mbeki was chiefly responsible for neutralising the threat of the militant white right and convincing a recalcitrant Mangosuthu Buthelezi and the IFP to take part in the 1994 election. 'This is a formidable record of achievements. Mbeki must go down in history as one of the key players in bringing about South Africa's miracle of transition,' Sparks wrote in 2002, five years before Mbeki's dramatic ousting at Polokwane and six years before he was 'recalled' from government by the Zuma ANC.

Tim du Plessis first met Mbeki at a 1987 conference in Arusha, Tanzania, organised by the Institute for Democratic Alternatives in South Africa, the think-tank run by Frederik van Zyl Slabbert and Alex Boraine. 'There were many journalists and Mbeki was the prettiest girl on the political dancing floor. Everyone wanted a dance. I tried talking to him about the release of his father, Govan, but he didn't have a clue who I was.'[3]

Shortly after the Arusha visit, Du Plessis was contacted by Artem Grigorian, a representative of Komsomol, the Soviet Communist Party's youth section. 'Artem had all these ANC connections and completed his doctorate at the Moscow State University on the development of trade unions in South Africa. He had enormous knowledge about the country and was a very pleasant Russian. He invited me and Johan Vosloo, a reporter at *Rapport*, to Moscow. We just laughed but it turned out he was serious. One evening in early 1988 I received a phone call at home and someone from the Soviet embassy in Maseru tells me in broken English to go to the Soviet embassy in Maputo and that a visa for the Soviet Union would be waiting for me there. So, we went to Maputo and were quickly issued with our travel papers.'

The trip to Moscow for the two Nasionale Pers Afrikaans journalists was arranged by the Afro-Asia Solidarity Committee, a Soviet state entity that channelled support to the ANC. 'And there on one afternoon in Moscow, Vossie and I were sitting in the Kremlin office of Vasily Solodovnikov, a major Soviet figure who was ambassador to a range of African countries and who also worked for the KGB, chatting away with Thabo Mbeki. Remarkable.'[4]

Du Plessis was deeply impressed by Mbeki's intellect. He would build argument upon argument when discussing a particular subject, then step away from it before tackling the same issue from a different perspective. 'And he spoke, and he spoke, and sometimes I got lost in his explanations and arguments, but it was clear that our fates were intertwined. He told us, two Afrikaans newspapermen, that Afrikaners have a special role to play in South Africa and that they shouldn't leave the country; that the ANC did not view them as foreigners. When I told this to people afterwards many said, *Aag, hulle het jou lekker gebreinspoel!* [Ag, they just brainwashed you!] But what else could I have thought as a journalist after sitting and talking to the man and everything he says is contrary to the horror image that we were served by PW Botha and Magnus Malan and Adriaan Vlok? Mbeki was easygoing, he was incredibly polished and well-travelled. It made a massive impression on me.'[5]

When the two journalists took their leave, Mbeki asked where else they had been and Du Plessis told him about their visit to Zagorsk, the seat of the Russian Orthodox Church. 'He said that when he returns to

South Africa, he will give me Russian church music, which he loved. And when I saw him when he was president, he always told me that he still owed me those tapes.'[6]

❖

Educated at the University of Sussex (he earned a master's degree in economics) and given military training in Moscow, Mbeki was erudite, ambitious, intellectual and an Africanist. Post-apartheid South Africa is arguably the creation of Mbeki more than any other leader, including Mandela. It was under Mbeki that government processes, systems and culture were established. He was the architect of the ANC's insertion into the state, the driving force behind economic reconstructive policies and the broad project of transformation. And the ANC's descent into misrule and corruption – possibly inevitable – was triggered by Mbeki's iron grip on the party and the subsequent vehement response to his autocracy.

After establishing himself as Mandela's heir and moving into the Union Buildings, he moulded government and governance and set the policy agenda for the ANC and the cabinet. And after succeeding Mandela as party leader, he established Pretoria, not Luthuli House, as the 'motive force' in politics, vastly expanding the operations of the office of the president into a formalised Presidency which eventually occupied the whole of the Union Buildings, originally designed by Sir Herbert Baker to house the entire government.

Van Zyl Slabbert, the one-time Mbeki acolyte and former leader of the opposition in the white Parliament, told Sparks that Mbeki used 'authoritarian and undemocratic' methods to entrench his dominance and control of party and government. 'So, he makes the ANC undemocratic in order to preserve a democratic system,' he said.[7]

Mbeki's vision of South Africa was in line with the prescripts of the NDR: ANC hegemony in the state and society, electoral dominance, accelerated transformation – including aggressive policies of racial redress and rebalancing – and black economic empowerment (BEE). Mandela was the conciliator, the founding democratic president who sought to keep a fractious and anxious country together by any means possible. For Mbeki, however, the task was complete transformation, economic reconstruction and a national and continental project of African nationalism in opposition to the West. Devoid of Mandela's charm and human touch, Mbeki had a clear resolve to reorganise and rearrange society and to upset the prevailing status quo. Mandela moved easily among people, his regal manner earning their allegiance. Mbeki could never do that – he wanted to be respected, even feared.[8]

Tony Leon, who as leader of the opposition in the National Assembly sought to build a relationship with him, was taken aback at Mbeki's transition from 'the clubbable smoothie of the mid-1990s to a distant, aloof figure' by the turn of the century.[9] He wanted to build the black middle class and saw the job of the second democratic government as actively and tangibly restoring the dignity of black Africans. This he sought to do by methodically implementing ANC policies using the full powers of the state. 'Mbeki saw his mission as effecting real transformation – the flip side of the coin of reconciliation, as he said repeatedly – even if this meant disrupting the comfort of the white South African population,' argues Gevisser.[10]

To do so, he had to 'capture full control of the ANC as a party', wrote William Gumede, an associate professor in the School of Governance at Wits University, who argues that Mbeki was bent on enacting an 'ambitious conservative economic and social reform agenda'.[11] (The word 'capture' would take on a different and more sinister meaning in later years.) Gumede and others argue that Mbeki had by then adopted the ideas of British prime minister Tony Blair and his Labour Party's 'Third Way' that he defines as 'less government, using the market to deliver, distancing themselves from the unions and moving closer to business. They ['Third Way' leaders] keep a tight rein on their parties.'[12]

After his election as ANC leader in 1997 and his ascension to the presidency two years later, Mbeki was in complete control of party and state. He taunted his opponents and detractors on the left from the stage at the Mafikeng conference, saying nothing had come of warnings that the ANC would 'tear itself apart' over economic policy and Gear.[13] He managed to install his loyalists and supplicants in all senior party positions bar one – Mosiuoa 'Terror' Lekota wasn't his first choice for the party chairmanship – and started a process of governmental reconfiguration which would culminate in an almost entirely redesigned state.

It seemed as if Mbeki, unshackled from the Mandela era of bridge-building and attempts at national unity, wanted to shape the country to his vision. The ANC had to bend to his will, the state had to march to his orders and meddlesome alliance partners that disagreed with his policies and macroeconomic vision were to be put on terms. It was Mbeki's suite of policies – agreed to by the party but designed and ushered through the system by his functionaries – that were to be implemented by the state, despite stiff opposition from Cosatu and the SACP. And it was Mbeki's intransigence and bloody-mindedness as president that would eventually lead to his downfall.

Mbeki's control of the ANC was almost absolute until 2007. In the previous decade his supporters and confidants took control of the whole ANC leadership structure. The party's NEC and NWC, the youth and women's leagues, internal committees and commissions, as well as the cabinet, parliamentary leadership and caucuses at all three levels of government were packed with loyalists. Mbeki, under whose patronage the ANC formalised its cadre deployment project, was ruthless in implementing the policy in the state, where key positions like national police commissioner, NDPP and head of the National Intelligence Agency (NIA) were quickly filled by party loyalists.

The president and his strategists – Joel Netshitenzhe, Aziz and Essop Pahad, and later Mbhazima Shilowa and Lekota – sought to 'modernise' the ANC and depowered the secretary general's office, locating influence and power in the party president's office. The secretary general's office, returned to the days pre-Ramaphosa, was now a little more than an 'administrative hub'.[14]

Mbeki appointed Smuts Ngonyama as head of the Presidency and developed a reputation for cracking the whip on errant party leaders.[15] The ANC president, according to Gumede, wanted to push the ANC to a more centrist path, inspired by social democratic movements in Europe and Blair's 'New Labour' – and he was not going to be challenged. 'Some changes in the ANC happened so quickly that many members were not even aware that they had taken place or grasped their significance. Mbeki was determined to remake the ANC into a modern political party with a social democratic orientation, something of a mix between the Swedish Social Democratic Party, the German Social Democratic Party and Britain's Labour Party, adapted to the demands of Africa and run efficiently along business lines. The oldest liberation movement in Africa was to become a hybrid that appealed to both business and the poor, while holding on to its mass base.'[16]

It proved to be an impossible task, partly because of the range of irreconcilable ideologies and beliefs within the organisation but also because of the rise of criminality and sanctioned corruption. Mbeki set about changing the structure into a 'lean and mean election machine', which included an overhaul of election strategy and the appointment of a permanent head of elections.[17] Peter Mokaba, the firebrand former leader of the ANC Youth League (ANCYL), was the first holder of that position, with Manne Dipico, the first premier of the Northern Cape, succeeding him in 2004. The party also adopted modern polling and research techniques, roping in election consultants such as Stan Greenberg from the United States and Labour Party expert Philip Gould from Britain. They had rebranded the Democratic Party in the US and Labour in the UK before helping to recast the ANC.

The party moved from its Shell House pile near Joubert Park in the Johannesburg CBD to a new office block named Luthuli House, across the road from *The Star* office in Sauer Street. Kgalema Motlanthe, the staid former trade unionist from the NUM who served as the ANC secretary general under Mbeki, proposed issuing new electronic membership cards. And the party's donor base expanded, with corporate benefactors in 2005 accounting for more than half of inflows.[18] Under Mbeki, Gumede argues, the ANC became increasingly removed from its members, with the 'top echelon of the party adopting the cold formalism of a business operation'.[19]

Mbeki's ANC switched the party's focus from the nine provinces to the metropolitan areas, which saw branch numbers reduced significantly. Leaders became 'too busy with "national concerns" to spend time with members. The identity of the old ANC was changing fast and its soul became harder to locate.'[20] The Mafikeng policy positions became Mbeki's lodestar, and for those policies to succeed he and his movement had to have untrammelled power over the government. After transforming the ANC, he set about redesigning the state. There were disastrous consequences for both.

11
Re-engineering the state

MBEKI'S ENEMIES HATED HIM FOR IT – many in the governing alliance even detested him – but for the ANC leader between 1997 and 2007, absolute control over the party machinery and the state was non-negotiable. His overriding commitment to a fundamental South African reset – true to Strategy and Tactics and party ideology – demanded ruthless command, and Mbeki brooked no dissent.

ANC policymaking ostensibly revolved around the parliamentary caucus and its study groups attached to portfolio committees, NEC subcommittees and the permanent staff at Luthuli House. In reality, however, it became the redoubt of Mbeki and his cabinet, their directors general and certain committee chairpersons in Parliament, a far cry from the bottom-up, democratic process of policy formulation that marked the era of the UDF and, to a large extent, the preparations for democracy. But in truth, the UDF tradition was impractical and unwieldy, and Mbeki wanted a strong, centralised government with clear overarching policy and a civil service that could execute. After the anger from the left over Mbeki and Manuel's implementation of Gear, there was immediate friction with Cosatu and the SACP, which feared they would be marginalised – which is exactly what happened.

For Tony Leon, the markers that would define Mbeki's presidency were quickly set, and in a speech in the National Assembly during the early days of his tenure the new president lashed out at the DA-led opposition, calling them peddlers of a 'soulless theology' who defined some races as 'sub-human and believed in the survival of the fittest'. To Leon, this was an indication of Mbeki's leadership style: mischaracterise opponents, malign their motives and stick to his decisions and appointments 'no matter how rotten, drunken or maladroit they might be'.[1]

But the trajectory of Mbeki's presidency and insight into how his core beliefs might have developed since 1994 were revealed in a speech to the National Assembly on 29 May 1998, months after being elected ANC president. Gone was the charming, warm and affable Mbeki of the transition years and the first steps into democracy. In his place was a dispassionate ideologue who, despite the validity of much of what he said about the legacy of apartheid, became unyielding in the face of rapidly diminishing returns from ANC government policy.

Addressing the issue of reconciliation, Mbeki delivered his thesis on South Africa being 'two nations', one prosperous and largely white, the other impoverished and largely black. And he proceeded to lambast 'those sections of society' that he believed were not committed to nation-building, reconciliation and upliftment. Even though the message was one that should have been heard by some in society who, at that point, weren't enamoured with how democracy was unfolding, Mbeki came across as antagonistic, bitter and pining to take charge and force change.

Nation-building, he said, was not being achieved. Neither was national reconciliation. And the longer the situation persisted, 'the more entrenched will be the conviction that the concept of nation-building is a mere mirage and that no basis exists, or will ever exist, to enable national reconciliation to take place'.[2] There was resistance to transformation and increased racial representation, he said, while many were unwilling to commit the kind of material support needed to lift the poor masses out of their squalor.[3] Additionally, there were elements in the security establishment – on both sides of the historical divide – that wanted to see democracy fail.[4] Rage, Mbeki said, was starting to build in society. And he quoted a favourite poet, the African-American Langston Hughes, who asked, 'What happens to a dream deferred?' 'His conclusion,' Mbeki said, 'was that it explodes.'[5]

The speech jolted Du Plessis, who believes the president should have taken greater care with the language he employed that day.

He could have transmitted the same message without the division. 'Professor Willie Esterhuyse from Stellenbosch, an Mbeki confidant, responded to criticism asking where Mbeki was wrong. And he used the metaphor of a double-decker bus, with white people on top and black people at the bottom and no staircase for blacks to ascend to the top. He was right about the top and the bottom, of course, but he was wrong about the staircase. There was enough realisation among everyone that we had to build that staircase; business knew it, we knew it. But the speech "othered" white people. Two nations. As crass as that. Mbeki was of course good at spin and would invite select journalists and thought leaders and explain that he didn't mean it this way or that. But for many white South Africans a disillusionment started setting in.'[6]

One of Mbeki's first projects as president was to oversee a sweeping review of the operations and functions of the Presidency. Mandela's executive office, although adapted to his needs and those of a new government, was largely the same one vacated by FW de Klerk, who had stripped it down from the 'imperial presidency' of PW Botha. Mbeki wanted a powerful centre to implement and execute the policies agreed at the ANC's Mafikeng conference in 1997. And for that to happen, he had to overhaul the national executive to serve his needs.

Shortly after the 1994 elections, the government published a White Paper on the transformation of the public service which found that it was inefficient, ineffective and racially skewed.[7] In early 1996, in a process driven by Mbeki, Vincent Maphai was appointed to lead a presidential review of the public service, while Mbeki's office investigated the structure of the offices of heads of state in other countries. In early 1999, Mbeki accepted Maphai's recommendation 'for an enhanced Presidency and for an expansion of the inherited cabinet secretariat into a strengthened cabinet office'.[8] The result was a dramatic restructuring, 'a functional redesign', of the executive office of the president within days of Mbeki's inauguration.[9]

Four months after taking office, the reorganisation and restructuring was concluded and an integrated Presidency with a new corporate identity, sitting atop a superstructure primed to execute the new president's mandate, came into being. It was under Mbeki that the functions of the deputy president were formulated. Jacob Zuma was made head of the government in the National Assembly, given leadership of various binational commissions, appointed to chair the South African National Aids Council (Sanac) and placed in charge of the moral regeneration movement.[10] This was to prove bitterly ironic, as Zuma was completely ill-suited to lead Sanac or any form of moral campaign. He later had sex with the daughter of a friend and took a shower to prevent the transfer of HIV, for which he was roundly criticised and mocked. And his presidency became synonymous with corruption, thievery and a complete abdication of public duty.

Mbeki did not consider Zuma a political threat and regarded him as pliant, unremarkable and unambitious. He could not have made a worse appointment as deputy president but, given ANC dynamics and the fact that he was elected deputy ANC leader in 1997, there wasn't much Mbeki could do. Zuma, however, eventually became the insidious enemy in the Union Buildings and Luthuli House.

Essop Pahad, a close confidant of Mbeki since their days at the University of Sussex, was appointed to the new position of minister in the Presidency; he was to be Mbeki's enforcer in the ANC, the government, the Presidency and Parliament. He was repeatedly dispatched to Parliament to club the caucus into line, as he did during the arms deal saga, and often tried to quash any accountability – as he did when dealing with questions from journalists. But Pahad was also the president's hatchet man, his consigliere, as he showed when he marched into FNB's Bank City in Johannesburg to confront chief executive Paul Harris about the bank's new anti-crime campaign. (Mbeki refused to acknowledge the severity of the crime crisis at the time.) After a barrage of invective from Pahad, Harris and FNB cancelled the campaign. His bloodlust quenched, Pahad returned to the Union Buildings to report back to his principal. Pahad was the ultimate ANC operative and a nasty piece of work.

The Rev Frank Chikane, a former anti-apartheid cleric and chairperson of the South African Council of Churches, was appointed director general of the Presidency, but his role was also completely redesigned when compared to his predecessor, Professor Jakes Gerwel.

The DG in the Presidency now oversaw the new cabinet office (modelled on 10 Downing Street in London), where the cabinet secretariat and an operations team ran cabinet committees and units.

Mbeki also changed the line functions of directors general in government departments, with all of them now appointed by him and reporting into a directors general forum chaired by Chikane. This meant that Mbeki, directly and indirectly, had sight of every director general in every department – and that, for ministers, there was nowhere to hide. There wasn't a single aspect of the government that did not give Mbeki greater control than Mandela ever had.[11]

In addition to directors general – and importantly, in the context of ANC politics – the right to appoint provincial premiers and even mayors of ANC-run metropolitan municipalities was relocated to Mbeki.[12] The president had direct power to ensure that heads of provincial executives toed the line, which in turn gave him significant influence at party provincial level. Mbeki was known for choosing acolytes for senior positions across government and party to ensure uniformity of policy. Those who didn't fall into line were sidelined or removed.[13]

One of the biggest additions to the Union Buildings was the establishment of the Policy Coordination and Advisory Services unit, or PCAS, headed by Joel Netshitenzhe, perhaps Mbeki's closest adviser and the president's policy tsar.[14] Netshitenzhe was Mbeki's principal ideological foil during his years as head of state. During exile he had overseen Radio Freedom, the ANC radio station that broadcast messages of liberation to the subcontinent, and later emerged as Mbeki's alter ego. They echoed each other's mannerisms and spoke in the same deliberate, measured tone (and often in the third person). Mbeki and Netshitenzhe were kindred spirits: it was all about the NDR, seizing control and accelerating transformation. Netshitenzhe was responsible for all the ANC's seminal policy documents during the Mbeki era – including updated versions of Strategy and Tactics – and helped draft the policy papers that laid the groundwork for interventions such as cadre deployment.

PCAS was arguably the most important addition to the new Presidency and central to Mbeki's centralisation of policy development and implementation. It was based in his office and run by his functionaries but, crucially, it was removed from Luthuli House and away from the ANC. Netshitenzhe and PCAS enabled Mbeki to drive his government's main policy positions as he saw fit – and allowed him to refine ANC policy without interference from the rabble in Sauer Street. The unit became the Presidency's nerve centre, where ministers had to submit all policy proposals and where Netshitenzhe decided whether they passed muster before they could go forward into cabinet processes. If they did not, they were sent back.

PCAS consisted of five chief directorates that mirrored the reconfigured cabinet structure and clusters (and which wouldn't really change for the next 25 years). 'The unit coordinates and monitors the progress of all departments in compliance with government's own core policies of transformation in these areas,' Chikane stated. 'The branch is the engine room of the new Presidency's drive for coherent policy and implementation.' Netshitenzhe, schooled in the art of mass communication, also took charge of GCIS, the government communications arm, which meant that not only were senior appointments done from the Union Buildings, but all policy development as well as messaging and communication were now located in the new-fangled Presidency.

Mbeki constructed the executive edifice, the structures and systems that enabled Zuma to launch his project of subversion and capture so efficiently and that later prevented Cyril Ramaphosa from enacting the necessary reforms. For Zuma, the powerful, centralised and well-resourced Presidency was the perfect tool with which to dispense patronage and manipulate systems of government and state. In contrast, when faced with the urgent need for reform and intervention, Ramaphosa was reluctant (perhaps afraid) to use the Presidency's enormous inherited superstructure to do what was necessary.

The functions, norms and rhythms of the executive and state as we now know them (cabinet functions, the planning cycle, imbizos, advisory councils, and so on) were also established under the direction of Mbeki and his associates. Although there were structural changes in subsequent presidencies – Zuma, for example, killed off PCAS within a year of coming into office and appointed more ministers at the Union Buildings – the Presidency became the most powerful entity wielded by ANC leaders in executive office. It enabled the party, through its ideology of cadre deployment and unquestioning fealty to ANC ideology and policy, to completely erase the dividing line between party and state, between factional interests and the national interest – and between corruption and good governance.

And it was Mbeki and the ANC cadre deployment policy which ensured that corrupt networks of extraction were able to latch onto the state and penetrate its institutions; it was deployment that enabled ANC rent-seekers to flood the body politic and, like parasites on a host, extract and steal public resources on an astonishing scale.

Mbeki's control of the party, achieved in 1997, was strengthened in 2002 at the ANC's next national conference, in Stellenbosch, where his allies dominated the election of the NEC. Manuel, the bête noire of the left, rocketed to the number-one position, followed by Ramaphosa in second place. With the exception of Winnie Madikizela-Mandela at number six, the rest of the top ten were also made up of Mbeki loyalists: Nkosazana Dlamini-Zuma, Thoko Didiza, Penuell Maduna, Sydney Mufamadi, Kader Asmal, Zola Skweyiya and Pallo Jordan.

Strategy and Tactics, the ideological treatise that guides the ANC, enjoined the party's cadreship to take control of the state and government at every level. Once it did so, it could rapidly execute its broad transformation policies and ensure that the state was firmly under the control of the party. Mbeki's redesign and re-engineering gave him and the party leadership 'unprecedented control of both the party and government, concentrating enormous powers of patronage in the hands of party bosses. The changes have been wrought in the name of more efficient governance and delivery, but they have worrying implications for internal debate and democracy,' William Gumede wrote in 2005, a year into Mbeki's second term as president.[15] Some years later, during the hearings of the Zondo commission, the corrosive effect of ANC policy and cadre deployment became clear.

Tony Leon, leader of the opposition between 1999 and 2007, when he retired from politics, was under no illusion what the ANC wanted: accountability of deployed cadres 'lay to the party high command and not to the institutions they were serving'.[16] Mbeki and the ANC engaged in 'stripping South Africa's constitutional instruments of real authority and locating effective power in the hands of the party, particularly its NEC', Leon argued in 2008.[17] Or, as Tito Mboweni, labour minister under Mandela, governor of the Reserve Bank under Mbeki and later finance minister under Ramaphosa, said: '[Those] of us in government are answerable to the ANC. I can't just proceed because I'm minister of labour and do whatever I want because I'm governing. I became minister of labour because I went into government on an ANC platform, was deployed by the president to that position, [and] so I'm answerable to the president, yes, of the Republic, but fundamentally in terms of policy and politics I'm answerable to the NEC of the ANC.'[18]

Van Zyl Slabbert understood Mbeki's power moves as trying to manage inherent contradictions between what he sought to achieve as president of the country and what his party's ideology allowed him to do. If he wanted to achieve higher investment and economic growth, he would have to go against party dogma: stricter fiscal and monetary policy, privatisation and a flexible labour regime. Those choices would have political consequences. 'And he's doing it [managing the consequences] by taking control of the ANC. He is determining the public representatives right through from the national to the local level, which is authoritarian and undemocratic,' Van Zyl Slabbert said.[19] The ANC, Mbeki and Mboweni had started to exhibit the fatal flaw in their view of democracy: that they were the state.

12

Failing the big tests

DURING THE YEARS OF MISRULE AND DYSFUNCTION that accelerated after Jacob Zuma's election as head of state in 2009, there has been an often-repeated nostalgia for the Mbeki years. Many critics of Zuma and his successor, Cyril Ramaphosa, have voiced a longing for the halcyon days of Mbeki, effectively between 1994 and 2007, when the government seemingly functioned properly, budgets balanced and the machinery of state worked. But that would be a misjudgement of an era that laid the foundation for the years of deep capture, endemic corruption and poor governance.

'A big factor that we should not forget when analysing the period was the country's good economic performance,' says Tim du Plessis. 'Unemployment started to decrease and employment started to increase, interest rates were low, foreign debt was paid off, the commodities cycle was booming and money was coming in. It started going better with the man on the street ... media companies were making lots of money. All this acted as a counterweight to what was starting to go wrong. Yes, people were seeing what was happening in Zimbabwe and were uncomfortable with Mbeki calling Robert Mugabe his brother and holding hands in public. But then again, Trevor Manuel and Tito Mboweni were managing the economy, we saw good GDP growth, low deficits and eventually a budget surplus. Yes, there was the commodities boom, but you must admit they did a damn good job with the economy. It elevated Mbeki's stature and it was difficult to take him on.'[1]

As we have seen, Mbeki set about transforming party and state into the tools needed for the ANC to implement its broad and deep reorganisation and redesign of society and state. Government and state subservience to Mbeki and ANC structures had a profound long-term impact on constitutional democracy, parliamentary oversight and accountability and good governance. And what Mbeki nostalgists often omit from their analyses was the second democratic president's descent into the netherworld of internet conspiracy theories, race-fuelled diatribes and intransigence during the HIV/Aids crisis of the 1990s and 2000s.

While Zuma was undoubtedly the most corrupted and destructive post-apartheid leader, and Ramaphosa suffered from an astonishing lack of conviction and bravery, Mbeki distinguished himself as an Aids dissident, fiercely swimming against the tide of peer-reviewed science. His approach to HIV/Aids and the concurrent crisis in Zimbabwe probably reveals the most about the type of leader he was: suspicious of established science and wisdom, inherently distrustful of and antagonistic towards those who differ from him and unable to admit to mistakes.

For years Mbeki resisted the introduction of antiretrovirals (ARVs) to combat the transmission of HIV, first due to their expense, then because he questioned their efficacy and finally on ideological grounds. His government sent confused messages about the severity of the HIV/Aids pandemic, he supported the clueless rants of a quack – Manto Tsahabalala-Msimang as minister of health – and single-handedly did some of the worst damage to the country's credibility in years. He also racialised the national debate about HIV/Aids, preferring to see analysis of the issue and criticism of his government through the prism of colonialism, Western oppression of Africa, capitalist thievery and white racism. And through all of it, people were dying, unborn babies contracted HIV and the virus spread.

Much of Mbeki's dissidence and revisionism was motivated by his desire to eschew American and European approaches to HIV/Aids, including treatment and prevention. His unfounded conviction that there must be a non-Western alternative was one of the prime factors that motivated him. Professor Malegapuru Makgoba, a medical scientist who later headed the South African Medical Research Council

(SAMRC), told Allister Sparks he believed the pandemic 'could have been curbed during the early period of its incursion'. When it was not, and when it became clear that the government did not have a clear strategy, it 'retreated behind revisionist theories'.[2]

Tony Leon calls the pandemic 'the greatest tragedy of post-apartheid South Africa', explaining in 2007 that 'millions are dying early deaths, life expectancy has dropped precipitously in the past decade ... [and] an estimated 320 000 people died of Aids in 2005, roughly 900 per day.'[3] It was a political tragedy, Leon believes, that could have been avoided had different decisions been taken.[4]

Mbeki's foray into the politics and misgovernance of HIV/Aids started in the second half of the Mandela presidency. Seemingly obsessed with finding an original, African solution to the pandemic, he took up the cause of Virodene. A group of scientists attached to the University of Pretoria, sidestepping the institution's regulations governing ethics and Medicines Control Council (MCC) prescripts on testing, pitched the drug to Mbeki and Nkosazana Dlamini-Zuma, then health minister, as a homegrown, cheaper alternative to the ARVs offered by the world's big pharmaceutical companies. Mbeki threw his weight behind it, even inviting the developers to address the cabinet, and dismissed criticism of it as 'motivated by racism'.[5] He led a purge of the MCC and had the chairperson and senior executives removed after they refused to license the product. But he was left high and dry after an independent study commissioned by the SAMRC found that Virodene, far from being effective, was highly toxic.[6]

By 1999, the new president was on a mission. His biographer, Mark Gevisser, says that this was the year in which Mbeki became a dissident and during which a confluence of factors combined to launch him in that direction. Mbeki was at the height of his sensitivity about Afro-pessimism, there were clashes about pharmaceutical patents with the US government and 'rapacious' drug manufacturers, and the government was tightening its belt.[7] In July, Aids dissident Anthony Brink sent him a booklet he had written questioning the efficacy of the ARV azidothymidine, or AZT (ARVs were then unavailable in public health facilities, despite pleas from civil society).

Mbeki started sleuthing on the internet and stumbled across virusmyth.net, a favourite site for dissidents. Seduced,[8] he started corresponding with them about the science of HIV and Aids, the causes of both and the efficacy of ARVs.[9] In October, he questioned the efficacy of AZT in a speech in the National Council of Provinces and said MPs should 'access the huge volume of literature on this matter available on the internet ...'[10]

It was mystifying. Mbeki, the head of state, was being influenced by quacks and Aids dissidents and was set on his course by an advocate from KwaZulu-Natal (Brink) who had self-published a pamphlet. 'In questioning AZT – one of the most widely used antiretroviral drugs – and citing the internet as his basic source, Mbeki opened a bizarre debate that confused and detracted from South Africa's efforts to fight HIV/Aids. He took the campaign further, openly questioning the link between HIV and Aids. Encouraged by a small and largely discredited group of international Aids dissenters, he portrayed HIV/Aids as a form of conspiracy by pharmaceutical companies bent on testing and selling their products in Africa, where its inhabitants could be more easily exploited,' Leon wrote.[11]

In April 2000, Mbeki wrote a strange letter to UN Secretary General Kofi Annan and US President Bill Clinton, 'passionately defending' his appointment of several dissidents to his presidential HIV/Aids advisory council. He also suggested that something other than HIV could be responsible for Aids (Mbeki and Tshabalala-Msimang later argued that poor socioeconomic conditions could also be to blame) and called for 'a uniquely African solution'.[12]

Amid all of this, Mbeki's government was engaged in a fight with the big pharmaceutical companies, which opposed a legislative amendment that would enable it to manufacture generic products at much cheaper rates than they were charging. After protracted legal battles, which stopped just short of the Constitutional Court, the companies relented and the makers of AZT offered it at much reduced rates.[13] South Africa was now able to afford these lifesaving ARVs but Mbeki and Tshabalala-Msimang refused to relent and introduce a mass rollout, including the use of another ARV, nevirapine, to prevent mother-to-child transmission. Frustration among activists and civil society began to escalate.

Mbeki's denialism was elevated to government policy, with his spokesperson Parks Mankahlana (who died of Aids) lashing out at critics,[14] ANC heavyweight Peter Mokaba (who also died of Aids) declaring that HIV 'doesn't exist'[15] and even Cheryl Carolus, now a respected ANC veteran and former high commissioner in London, questioning the link between HIV and Aids in a letter to the *Financial Times*.[16]

Another factor that prevented the introduction of a universal ARV programme was the 'underlying belief in Mbeki's inner circle' that spending money on ARVs would be futile, because those with Aids are economically ineffective anyway and orphans would have to be cared for by the state.[17] Manuel, the finance minister, said: 'It does not make financial sense to spend money on people dying anyway, who are not even economically productive in the first place.'[18]

In January 2001, after months of wrangling about the cause of Aids, the role of HIV, the efficacy of ARVs and their affordability – and after consistent negative international press – Mbeki acknowledged during a cabinet meeting that there wasn't consensus in government on what its message must be. But it wasn't until April 2002 that the cabinet agreed to make ARVs available to pregnant women and rape victims at public hospitals.[19] And that July, the Constitutional Court sounded the death knell for Mbeki's obstinance when it ordered the government to make nevirapine available. The state 'had not met its constitutional obligations', the court said.[20]

Mbeki's government, however, continued to drag its feet and missed every deadline in 2003, 2004 and 2005 to launch the necessary massive rollout.[21] Tshabalala-Msimang, meanwhile, continued on her heretical path, promoting garlic, beetroot and the African potato at the International Aids Conference in Toronto, Canada, in August 2006. Stephen Lewis, the UN Aids envoy, declared that South Africa 'is the only country in Africa … whose government is still obtuse, dilatory and negligent about rolling out treatment. It is the only country in Africa whose government continues to propound theories more worthy of the lunatic fringe than of a concerned or compassionate state.'[22]

Mbeki's destructive response to HIV/Aids was rooted in his abhorrence of what he perceived as the West's racism in reference to African stereotypes, male sexuality and how the virus spread. He repeatedly hit out at critics he believed to be racist, from rape victims calling for the introduction of ARVs to scientists who mapped out the link between HIV and Aids. Mbeki refused to bend to Western scientists and their views on Africa. By 2007, he remained an Aids dissident.[23]

❖

Mbeki's approach to Zimbabwe resembled his position on HIV/Aids. Around the same time Mbeki was drafting his letter to Annan and Clinton, mass land invasions and widespread violence and intimidation erupted in Zimbabwe after the defeat of a constitutional referendum that would have given its octogenarian ruler, Robert Mugabe, increased powers.[24] The electorate, already starting to favour a new opposition party, the Movement for Democratic Change (MDC), balked and rejected Mugabe's obvious power grab. The country was experiencing steep economic decline directly related to mismanagement and corruption, with rural citizens suffering from hunger.

Mugabe turned to a ragtag militia under the leadership of Chenjerai Hunzvi, who revelled in his moniker of 'Hitler' Hunzvi. 'In a wildly destructive populist campaign of seizure,' the group started to occupy white-owned commercial farms that until then had formed the bedrock of Zimbabwe's agrarian economy, while also attacking the political opposition, civil society and the courts.[25] Violent mobs of Hunzvi's 'war veterans' stormed thousands of privately owned properties, beating and sometimes killing owners and workers, while the police and authorities did nothing. Mugabe and his party openly supported the use of brute force to drive white owners and workers off the land.[26]

Mbeki, increasingly agitated by what he saw as Western paternalism and racism, refused to admonish or criticise Mugabe in public, opting instead for 'quiet diplomacy'. It entailed using backchannels and private meetings with Mugabe in attempts to persuade him 'over a cup of tea' to change course.[27] It never worked and Mbeki was time and again lied to, deceived and humiliated by Mugabe, who believed himself to be an elder African statesman and the South African president his clear junior.

Initially, the ANC parliamentary caucus wanted to condemn the violence as strongly as possible, while the Africanist grouping in the party expressed its support. Mbeki argued that any public condemnation would inflame the Zimbabwean leader and sent his foreign affairs minister, Dlamini-Zuma, to Harare with orders 'not to be too harsh on Mugabe'. But she was an Africanist and consistently expressed support for the tyrant.[28]

The impotence of South Africa and Mbeki in the face of the complete breakdown of the rule of law north of the Limpopo River was put on global display when, during a meeting with Mugabe and leaders of the Southern African Development Community (SADC) to discuss the crisis, Mbeki and Mugabe held hands and smiled for the cameras. The following day the men appeared together at a trade fair. Mugabe warmly embraced Mbeki, who didn't utter a word about the collapse of the rule of law and the increasing violence.[29] It sent out a potent message of fraternal solidarity.[30] It was clear where Mbeki's sympathies (nominally) lay and that South Africa was not about to take a tough stance on Mugabe's violence.

Mbeki argued that his quiet diplomacy would bear fruit and believed he had secured an agreement from Mugabe to start withdrawing his 'war veterans' from the farms. But Mugabe, who looked at Mbeki with disdain and detested South Africa's position as a regional superpower, repeatedly reneged on any informal undertaking or agreement about settling the matter peacefully. In April 2000, shortly after the SADC meeting, Mugabe publicly encouraged the 'war veterans' to continue occupying white farms. And in August, after assuring Mbeki he would order the violent mobs to stop their rampaging, he again did a volte-face and announced that another 3 000 farms would be taken.[31] 'This is just the start. We will be going on from here,' he declared.

Du Plessis says Mbeki's support for Mugabe's blatant subversion of democracy helped prop up the Zimbabwean authoritarian. 'Trevor Manuel explained the reasons behind Mbeki's support for Mugabe to me, and even though I understood it there was no way you could condone it. It was clear that there was a solidarity that transcended everything else, that transcended nation-building and a coming together and we're all South African, and so on. There was a type of a race-bound loyalty and dynamics at play that was more important, that transcended the message of reconciliation, cooperation and a new beginning. Mbeki's uncooked plan for a national unity government later enabled Mugabe to sideline [MDC leader] Morgan Tsvangirai.

And this was done with the knowledge and approval of the ANC. As far as I know, no one in the ANC challenged Mbeki on this.'[32]

Mbeki kept trying to cajole Mugabe into changing course, making regular trips to Harare, the Zimbabwean capital. Mugabe used every visit to his country by Mbeki or senior officials to legitimise his actions. And it was left to Dlamini-Zuma to publicly say what everyone knew – that South Africa would not condemn Mugabe's land grabs and brutalisation of the opposition: 'It is not going to happen as long as this government is in power.'[33]

Mbeki opposed international sanctions implemented by the West and was bitterly disappointed when the Commonwealth suspended Zimbabwe. Mugabe continued to win a succession of fraudulent elections (South Africa was often alone in declaring these victories 'free and fair') and his crackdown on the rule of law and civil society went unpunished. All international aid dried up, the economy cratered, hyperinflation made the currency worthless and millions plunged into poverty and hunger. The collapse of Zimbabwe also had dire effects on South Africa as refugees streamed south in search of survival. By 2004, more than two million Zimbabweans had entered South Africa, most illegally.[34]

Mbeki's position on Zimbabwe changed Du Plessis's estimation of the president. For him, the 'two nations' speech was a red light because it revealed how Mbeki thought about reconstruction and nation-building. But Zimbabwe set off warning bells because Mbeki offered tacit approval of Mugabe's power grab and mutilation of the rule of law: 'So Zimbabwe was the moment for me. But besides the economy, another factor why there wasn't this strong push against Mbeki was because at the time there was never talk about changing the Constitution. They obtained 69.69 per cent in the 2004 election but there was no breath, no inkling from the ANC, that they wanted to change the Constitution to make things easier for them. Of course, what we later learned was even though the Constitution stood, thanks to cadre deployment they had everyone in place anyway.'[35]

The year 2000 was, in Sparks's estimation, an 'annus horribilis' for

Mbeki. He was able to control the state and his party but was exposed when the HIV/Aids and Zimbabwe crises erupted. In both instances his feelings and convictions about the West, race and the desire for African solutions trumped science and principle. If Mbeki hadn't been so fixated on refusing Western drugs because of politics and ideology, hundreds of thousands of lives might have been saved. A 2008 study by the Harvard School of Public Health determined that 'more than 330 000 people died prematurely from HIV and Aids between 2000 and 2005 [because of] the Mbeki government's obstruction of lifesaving treatment, and at least 35 000 babies were born with HIV infections that could have been prevented'.[36]

And if he hadn't been so enormously sensitive to Western criticism of Mugabe's abandoning the rule of law, perhaps Zimbabwe could have survived. Du Plessis says: 'Yes, it made me concerned about what could happen here. We had assurances, yes, and people said our Constitution won't allow for something like that to happen here. But a constitution is also just a piece of paper. Mbeki then blocked the release of the Khampepe report into the Zimbabwean election that found Mugabe lost, fair and square. And then we saw him removing Vusi Pikoli as NDPP; he removed the country's chief prosecutor after interfering in the pending arrest of Jackie Selebi, the police chief. It's easy today to criticise Zuma for that sort of thing. But Mbeki set the precedent for it.'[37]

In the final analysis, though, when confronted with two of his presidency's biggest crises, Mbeki, his government and the ANC failed to act on principle. In both cases, many innocent people died. And South Africa suffered for it.

In South Africa's post-1994 constitutional democracy, the national legislature was perhaps the most important institution on which the future health of the country depended – but a semblance of an effective and efficient Parliament probably only existed between 1994 and 1999.

The first democratic Parliament, during Mandela's tenure, was characterised by the yeoman work it did in crafting the outlines of a new society. Parliament's business for the first two years was dominated by the final phase of the negotiations by various committees that comprised the Constitutional Assembly, the forerunner of the National Assembly. It culminated in the vote on the Constitution in May 1996, the subsequent certification by the Constitutional Court and the signing into law of the country's foundational statute by Mandela in December of that year.

Parliament was also tasked with repealing apartheid legislation still on the statute books and completing the process started in 1990 by the last white Parliament when it began to remove the legislated vestiges of the apartheid edifice. The Group Areas Act and the Population Registration Act, two of the laws that formed the basis of apartheid, were repealed in 1991, for example, followed by a slew of land laws. (Other apartheid laws, including the Immorality Act and the Prohibition of Mixed Marriages Act, had been repealed in 1985.)

MPs of the first Parliament crafted a range of groundbreaking laws that set a precedent not only in Africa but also in the rest of the world. The Choice on Termination of Pregnancy Act of 1996, for example, gave women autonomy over their bodies and legalised abortion within a medico-legal framework.

But it was also during this period that the ANC was confronted with the realities of a constitutional democracy where the legislature ensures oversight and accountability of the executive – and it didn't like it. Parliament, Mark Gevisser argues, 'was perhaps the biggest sacrifice' made during the Mbeki years, when compared to those of his predecessor. 'Mbeki used the party to rein it in: within the ANC caucus loyalists were promoted, often without the necessary skills, while free-thinkers were iced out and began haemorrhaging from the institution.'[38]

Political analyst and former parliamentary correspondent Christi van der Westhuizen cites the arms deal as a demonstration of 'heavy-handed intervention by the executive'. And ANC MPs' response to Mbeki's Aids denialism and his government's disastrous handling of the HIV epidemic 'is a more insidious example of the stultifying effects of a forceful executive'.[39] Governing-party MPs were simply too afraid to speak out publicly and challenge the president and his health minister, Tshabalala-Msimang.

The tightening of political control over Parliament 'effectively neutralised it' and a line was crossed in 2002 when the ANC took control of Scopa, which according to convention was chaired by an opposition MP.[40] But not only was Parliament unable to check the executive, it also became a site of extraction for ANC cadres. In 2004, it was revealed that 40 MPs were being investigated by the Scorpions for fraud after they defrauded the legislature of millions of rands. The scheme involved MPs claiming travel vouchers to which they were entitled and then, with the help of travel agents, using them for a range of other purposes, including holidays, cars and entertainment. Of the 31 MPs who eventually pleaded guilty in a plea-bargain arrangement with the state, 29 came from the ANC (the other two were from the DA). They included Bathabile Dlamini, who defrauded the exchequer of R254 000 but who went on to enjoy a long career in the cabinet under Zuma despite her criminal record.[41]

The ANC has always had money problems. After the fall of the Soviet Union, assistance from Moscow dried up, and following its unbanning and the 1994 elections, donations from Nordic supporters also evaporated. Mandela was initially used as the organisation's chief fundraiser and he had no qualms about securing cash to contest elections from a variety of dubious sources, including Libya's Muammar Gaddafi. The party also discovered how easy and lucrative it was to use its incumbency in government to gather funds.

In 2000 and 2001, businessman Sandi Majali repeatedly travelled to Baghdad, Iraq, where he was introduced as an ANC representative. Majali's company was granted allocations of oil to sell under the UN's oil-for-food programme. It allowed Iraq, which was under sanctions, to sell crude oil and the proceeds to be placed in trust and used only for humanitarian purposes. Majali was either accompanied or assisted by a range of ANC luminaries, including Kgalema Motlanthe, the secretary general, who penned a letter introducing him as the party's agent. Majali was also assisted by Mendi Msimang, the party treasurer, and senior officials from the Department of Minerals and Energy, including its director general. Phumzile Mlambo-Ngcuka, who succeeded

Zuma as deputy president in 2005, was the department's minister.

The message, in the face of global condemnation of the dictatorship of Saddam Hussein, was that the ANC and the South African government remained committed to advancing the cause of Iraq. Veteran investigative reporters Sam Sole and Stefaans Brümmer described it as South Africa 'trading its principles for profits'. The scheme saw Majali's company, Imvume Management, scoring lucrative contracts from PetroSA to supply the Strategic Fuel Fund with Iraqi crude – and, in turn, Majali channelled millions to the ANC to help fund its 2004 election campaign.

The crookery was revealed by Sole and Brümmer in the *Mail & Guardian* and later confirmed in a report by the UN. The ANC's response, as was to become standard, was flippant and dismissive. Motlanthe simply rejected allegations of gross impropriety and said the money was a donation from a private company. The Public Protector later rejected a complaint from the DA that public money found its way into ANC coffers, while a commission of inquiry led by advocate Michael Donen was hamstrung in its ability to properly investigate the matter.[42] 'Oilgate' died a slow death but the ANC performed brilliantly at the polls in 2004, obtaining 69.69 per cent of the total vote.

Oil-for-food was scrappy but the governing party soon improved its ability to gerrymander the state and the private sector for its financial benefit. In 1998, the Department of Minerals and Energy released a White Paper warning that, despite having the fourth-largest installed electricity capacity in the world, the country would run out of energy in a decade's time without significant investment in generation.[43] The cabinet approved the first Eskom build programme since the 1980s in June 2004.[44]

So, in 2005, in anticipation of what was to come, the ANC's investment arm, Chancellor House, paid R1.2 million for a stake in Hitachi Power Africa.[45] It was a masterstroke. For a pittance, Chancellor House became Hitachi's BEE partner before Eskom issued contracts for the construction of the multibillion-rand Medupi and Kusile power stations. They were to be among the largest coal-fired power stations on the planet and there was a lot of money in the offing.

Thanks to the ANC's policy of cadre deployment, the governing party was well informed of unfolding events on the Eskom board and the committee adjudicating bids before the final contracts for boilers and other builds were issued. A Hitachi executive, Klaus Dieter Rennert, even met Taole Mokoena, the chairperson of the Chancellor House board, imploring him to apply pressure on Eskom on Hitachi's behalf.[46]

Eskom's board was chaired by Valli Moosa, an ANC luminary who had served in the Mandela and Mbeki cabinets and who was then a member of the party fundraising committee.[47] Moosa's attachment to Eskom and the ANC seemed to be enormously fortuitous for the party. Hitachi won the R38.5-billion contract to supply Eskom with boilers for the two power stations – and from that, Chancellor House scored a handsome R97 million, including a 'success fee', dividends and a share buyback.[48]

Hitachi understood Chancellor House was the ANC's funding vehicle and the ANC shamelessly offered its political influence to serve private interests. Both entities were richly rewarded, but flaws in the tendering process, design and construction subsequently cost South Africa dearly. 'For the ANC's 97 pieces of silver, the taxpayer is paying billions. Because of Kusile's design flaws, we've lost around 2 100 MW of generation in 2023, enough to eliminate two stages of load-shedding. To fix some of the boiler mistakes will cost R4.2 billion and we've already burnt R30 billion of diesel due to lost capacity,' André de Ruyter, who was Eskom's chief executive between 2020 and 2023, said later.[49]

Medupi and Kusile have been abject disasters. As of 2024, neither power station has ever run at full capacity and their generating units are continually in states of disrepair, with some not even finished or synchronised to the electricity grid. Cost overruns have been gigantic, ballooning to more than 100 per cent to bleed the taxpayer to the tune of more than R120 billion each.

When the White Paper on energy was forwarded to the cabinet and Parliament for comment in December 1998, warning of a crisis within a decade, the governments of Mandela and Mbeki decided to ignore it. Between 1998 and 2004, Eskom sent at least ten memorandums to the Department of Public Enterprises warning that new generating capacity was urgently required. No response was received.[50] The focus was on rearming the air force and the navy – the arms deal.

And in June 2008, two months before construction of Kusile commenced, the country was subjected to its first bout of rolling blackouts, or load-shedding. Demand was too high and supply too low. The government had waited too long to address the impending energy disaster. There was some contrition from Mbeki, at least. 'When Eskom said to the government, "We think we must invest more in terms of electricity generation," we said, "No, but all you will be doing is just to build excess capacity." We said not now, later. We were wrong. Eskom was right. We were wrong,' he said.[51]

PART THREEE
EXPANSION

13
Before the fall

THE ANC'S NATIONAL CONFERENCE held outside Polokwane in Limpopo in December 2007 was the most important inflection point in post-apartheid history. Zuma's victory over Mbeki signalled the start of an era in which corruption became rampant and pervasive, facilitated by an extensive network of patronage and politically connected cadres who would, over the next decade and more, extract vast resources from the state. And thanks to the ANC's policy of cadre deployment implemented since the 1997 conference, these patronage networks were already in place by the time Zuma took control of party.

The Polokwane putsch also led to a dramatic weakening of the state, with every department and institution, at all levels of government, afflicted by the ineptitude of legions of civil servants deployed as part of the ANC's transformation of the state into a party employment agency. The state also became the victim of Zuma and his network's cynical attempts to entrench their power and influence by neutralising key institutions and destroying their capacity. The Zuma victory at Polokwane amounted to an almost complete political revolution and it upended Mbeki's attempts to modernise the state and hold firm to the prescripts of responsible government. One of the first priorities in the Zuma era was loosening the National Treasury purse strings, for example – but more on that later.

The genesis of Mbeki's humiliation at Polokwane lies in widespread unhappiness about his iron grip on the ANC, his paranoia about plots and conspiracies and Zuma's deeply corrupt relationship with his 'financial adviser', Durban businessman Schabir Shaik. Out of this emerged a powerful bloc in the ANC, Cosatu and the SACP strongly opposed to Mbeki and intent on replacing the party leadership with a cohort of cadres committed to new government policies and a renewed deference to party structures. It is not an exaggeration to argue that, even though the ANC has been in charge since 1994, events at Polokwane amounted to a change in government.

On the afternoon of Tuesday, 14 June 2005, Mbeki took to the podium in the National Assembly and announced that he was firing Zuma as deputy president. It followed a judgment two weeks before by Judge Hilary Squires in the KwaZulu-Natal High Court in Durban that found Shaik guilty on three charges of corruption and fraud. Shaik had been Zuma's moneyman. The hapless former freedom fighter, once a favourite of Mandela and in charge of ANC intelligence structures before 1994, had no idea how to manage his personal finances, almost no moral or ethical compass, and was easily taken in by Shaik's corrupt network.

Shaik used his proximity to the deputy president to help his company – Nkobi Investments, named after a former ANC treasurer – solicit business related to the arms deal. In return for Zuma's political blessing, Shaik maintained his lifestyle, giving him cash, taking care of school fees, hotel bills, travel expenses, car payments, legal fees, a Cuban holiday, and making payments to the ANC.[1] It was all there in the exhaustive forensic investigation by the Scorpions, a specialist corruption-busting unit established in 1999. And the expectation was that, after Shaik, Zuma was next.

In his address to the joint sitting, Mbeki reminded MPs that no adverse finding had been made about the government's handling of the arms deal and that the joint investigative team (see Chapter 6) said 'no evidence was found of any improper or unlawful conduct by government'.[2] The government's integrity in negotiating the arms deal, Mbeki declared, was beyond reproach. But he acknowledged that more investigations were sure to follow Squires's judgment: 'As president of the republic I have come to the conclusion that the circumstances dictate that in the interests of the Honourable Deputy President, the government, our young democratic system and our country, it would be best to release the Honourable Jacob Zuma from his responsibilities as deputy president of the republic and as a member of cabinet.'[3]

Mbeki had had enough of Zuma. He had manoeuvred him into position as deputy party leader in 1997 and deputy president two years later on the premise that the Zulu chief from Nkandla would not pose a political threat. But Zuma fell out of favour and became the fulcrum around which the disgruntled started to coalesce. Shaik's conviction was the perfect opportunity for Mbeki to reassert control.

By then, Mbeki was aware of increased chafing in the governing alliance as more and more cadres in the ANC, Cosatu and SACP started voicing their disillusionment with his leadership. He had enough reason to rid himself of Zuma but knew he had to mitigate the inevitable fallout. So he gave Zuma a grand send-off. 'Personally, I continue to hold the Honourable Jacob Zuma in high regard,' Mbeki concluded. 'And I am convinced that this applies to most members of Parliament. We have worked together under difficult and challenging conditions for 30 years. In this regard, I wish to thank him for the service that he has rendered as part of the executive, at national and provincial levels, sparing neither strength nor effort to ensure that, with each passing day, we build a better life for all South Africans.'[4] It is unlikely that Mbeki believed what he was saying because he knew full well what the repercussions for the country would be under someone like Zuma.

Squires, in his damning judgment of Shaik, made no finding against Zuma, but thousands of hours of testimony and forensic evidence made it clear the deputy president had a case to answer. His name appears 474 times in the judgment – 14 times with the words 'corrupt' or 'corruption' in the same sentence. Shaik knew exactly what he was doing by courting Zuma and how he could benefit from his relationship with the deputy president, Squires argued. The two men enjoyed 'a mutually beneficial symbiosis' and Shaik's payments to Zuma 'generated a sense of obligation in the recipient'.[5]

During the Shaik trial, the Scorpions identified payments from him to Zuma totalling R1.3 million between 1995 and 2002. It emerged later that between 2002 and 2006 – a year after Shaik was found guilty and after Zuma was fired – Shaik made hundreds more payments to Zuma, bringing the total to more than R4 million.[6]

Here was a deputy president completely beholden to private interests. In return for Shaik overseeing his personal finances, using his company to assist Zuma with everything from his tax affairs to preparing his annual statement of personal interests to Parliament,[7] Zuma assisted Shaik in a series of business transactions – including a deal with French arms manufacturer Thomson-CSF (later Thales). Letters of endorsement from Zuma were even sent from Nkobi Investment offices.[8] The NPA was preparing to indict Zuma on the same charges as Shaik, and investigators and prosecutors were convinced that by using the same body of evidence they would be able to secure a conviction.

The civil war in the ANC exploded into the open after Mbeki's dismissal of Zuma. The fired deputy president had grown close to Cosatu, the trade union federation led by Zwelinzima Vavi, and the SACP, led by general secretary Blade Nzimande, who carried significant personal animus against Mbeki. Both organisations were avowed and vocal opponents of the Mbeki government's conservative economic policies, deriding them as the '1996 class project', a reference to the implementation of Gear.

'There is anger on this matter, lots of anger. The deep sense is that this is just a plot, a political gimmick to get rid of Zuma,' Vavi said. 'I am very worried about that. I am hearing it everywhere, that this is an ethnic thing.'[9] The narrative was that Mbeki was settling scores and trying to prevent Zuma from succeeding him as head of state, that he was abusing his position and that in reaching his decision he had sidelined not only the ANC but the whole alliance. And there was increased talk of the Scorpions being used to wage factional battles, specifically targeting Zuma.

Open rebellion ensued and mass support for Zuma erupted in the immediate aftermath – Mbeki had to dispatch party leaders and allies to all corners to try to quell anger.[10] The ANCYL, led by Fikile Mbalula, made clear its support for Zuma as Mbeki's successor weeks before he was fired, then invited him to address a rally in Mpumalanga two days after the announcement. There was 'nothing' that forced the youth league to reconsider its support of Zuma, Mbalula said.[11]

On Wednesday, 20 June 2005, the NPA announced that it was charging Zuma with, among other things, two counts of corruption. Vusi Pikoli, the NDPP, had already informed Mbeki and Brigitte Mabandla, the justice minister. He also went to Luthuli House to tell Zuma, who launched into a monologue about plots and conspiracies.[12] The announcement was followed by Scorpions raids in Cape Town, Johannesburg and Pretoria, including at Zuma's home and the Union Buildings, to seize documents. The NPA was gearing up for the Zuma trial.

It led to an outcry. Vavi labelled it a 'full-frontal attack on our revolution itself' and said it constituted the 'brutal persecution of Zuma'. He added: 'The political prosecution of Jacob Zuma risks plunging our new democracy into turmoil. It has already begun to divide our movement.'[13]

Days later, the ANC held its National General Council (NGC) at the University of Pretoria. This is a mid-term gathering that the party uses to gauge progress since the last national conference. It was billed as a show of strength for Zuma – and it was. The fired deputy president was mobbed by ordinary delegates wherever he went and it was abundantly clear that there was great anger among the rank and file about Mbeki's decision. Delegates cheered when Zuma declared that he had been treated unfairly in a trial by media. In fact, he said, the high court had tried him in absentia. 'The confidence which members of the ANC have in his leadership remains undiminished,' Kgalema Motlanthe declared.[14] No fewer than seven provinces, in addition to Cosatu and the SACP, demanded that Zuma be reinstated as deputy president.[15]

Zuma's first court appearance on charges of fraud, racketeering and corruption happened on the same day the NGC met, 29 June 2005. He wasn't asked to plead and the matter was postponed and transferred to the high court. The criminal trial was set to commence in June 2006, more than a year before the ANC's next conference, at Polokwane.[16]

A 'garish and motley carnival' of supporters followed Zuma to every court appearance and every postponement that pockmarked the next two years.[17] They held night vigils outside the courts in Durban and Pietermaritzburg; they sang songs venerating him and deriding Mbeki; and they lived and breathed the outrage fuelled by Vavi, Nzimande, Mbalula and others that Zuma was the victim of a political show trial.

'We will ensure that whenever comrade Zuma appears in court our people will demonstrate en masse,' Vavi thundered. Nzimande attacked the state, saying it was being abused to target Zuma. And Mbalula, a loudmouthed and vacuous bulldozer, held firm that Zuma would become president: 'Jacob Zuma has been subjected to a campaign of disinformation and a campaign of ill-administration and justice. This is just political malice of desperate people who are misusing the justice system ...'[18]

Then came the next hammer blow: in December 2005, Zuma was charged with the rape of the young adult daughter of a family friend. He had unprotected sex with the HIV positive woman and later testified that he quickly showered after the encounter to reduce risk of infection. But it simply added to Zuma's victimhood complex and assisted with the weaving of a narrative of unfair persecution and political meddling to scupper his chances of becoming president.

Zuma was acquitted of the rape charge on 8 May 2006, and four months later Judge Herbert Msimang threw out the corruption charges against him, saying the NPA's case 'limped from one disaster to another'.[19] Zuma, it seemed, was marching inexorably towards becoming the next ANC president.

By then, however, the intelligence services – the National Intelligence Agency, the South African Secret Service and the SAPS crime intelligence division – had been thrust into the middle of the power struggle. Zuma had deep connections in the shadowy world of intelligence and a lot of support at the NIA. Mbeki, by contrast, had to rely on crime intelligence, led by a former apartheid policeman, Richard Mdluli.

Under Mbeki, the size of the intelligence services increased significantly, especially during the ministry of Lindiwe Sisulu, and the various agencies became enormously well resourced. In 2003, the Presidency expanded the NIA's mandate to include political and economic intelligence and gave it wide new powers. It led to a host of new spies and agents being appointed.[20] From then on, the intelligence services became enmeshed in ANC internal politics, with spies, money and equipment being used in the service of different factions. It would become one of the most visceral examples of how the state became the ANC and how the ANC abused state resources.

But Mbeki was unperturbed. He planned to win a third term as ANC leader and would then repair to Luthuli House and continue to direct the affairs of state. He surrounded himself with trusted lieutenants, people who told him what he wanted to hear. The Pahad brothers, Mosiuoa Lekota and Mbhazima Shilowa were all aboard with 'the chief's' plans. But hubris led to catastrophe.

14

The Polokwane putsch

THE WHOLE COUNTRY BECAME EMBROILED in the governing party's civil war as both sides started mobilising support and resources for a ferocious leadership battle. Mbeki was clear that he was going to contest the leadership election at Polokwane. It was highly unusual. His term of office as head of state was set to conclude in 2009 and constitutional limits prohibited a third term as president. If he were to win a third term as party leader, it would mean the new head of state would be subject to someone outside the executive. Debate centred on the difficulties of 'two centres of power': one in Pretoria, the other in downtown Johannesburg. Who would hold sway? But Mbeki believed he still had work to do, that he couldn't walk away from the African nationalist and transformation project he had directed since 1994. And his kitchen cabinet – most notably the Pahad brothers – encouraged him to run.

There was growing hubris in the Mbeki camp, with acolytes and hangers-on telling the president exactly what he wanted to hear. Mbeki was clearly being poorly advised,[1] while the 'yes men' around him isolated him from what was happening at grassroots level[2] – and that was the beginnings of a 'Zuma tsunami'. Zuma emerged as the classic populist, embracing conspiracy theories and making up stories and lies to help cultivate the image of victimhood. He also encouraged being cast as the embodiment of the new struggle against political interference, against a system dominated by white monopoly capital and against the abuse of state institutions.

All of this, real or imagined, appealed to Zuma's ever-increasing support base. His hand was strengthened by the organisational efforts of Zwelinzima Vavi's Cosatu, Blade Nzimande's SACP and Fikile Mbalula's ANCYL. Their supporters booed Mbeki at party or national gatherings, they burned T-shirts bearing his face, and Zuma became the fulcrum around which rallied the so-called 'coalition of the wounded' – those who had been sidelined or slighted by Mbeki, or who reviled his policies.

Trevor Manuel says that, thanks to the implementation of Gear and improved economic performance in the decade before the Polokwane conference, a decision was made to accelerate the economic reconstruction project. 'We wanted to go faster and be more inclusive. So, in the approach to the conference, I went to Harvard and brought in Professor Ricardo Hausmann, the famed economist, and we held workshops involving local and international academics and the unions and business. The initiative was convened by Deputy President Phumzile Mlambo-Ngcuka and … produced 24 research papers with recommendations about what we needed to do to accelerate economic growth. These included recommendations about rail, ports and the electricity system that were not fit for purpose. And after Polokwane the entire initiative was thrown out; I don't think anybody looked at the proposals. I can't even begin to recall how many hours we spent on it. It was thrown out because they didn't like it, because it carried an ideological tag.'[3]

Whereas policy and governance had been the focus of the state and legislature, everything was now seen through the lens of what became known in newspapers as 'the succession battle'. Luthuli House, the party headquarters, was starting to drift away from Mbeki, who became ensconced at the Union Buildings, using his position as head of state to direct affairs before the Polokwane conference. The party machinery, led by secretary general Kgalema Motlanthe, was divided between the Mbeki and Zuma camps. The ANC parliamentary caucus was also split. And the state and its institutions became party to the ANC's mortal conflict, with the NIA, crime intelligence and even the NPA drawn into the collision – and often abused to obtain a strategic advantage. It was to set a precedent for later years, when the reach and resources of the state were regularly brought to bear in factional conflicts. The dividing line between party and state was well and truly breached.

The destruction wrought by the Mbeki-Zuma conflict did lasting damage to the body politic. It inflicted wounds from which the ANC would never recover (because it rooted a culture of factionalism in the organisation) and it established the state and its institutions as another front in the battle for supremacy. South Africa, its citizens and its system of government became beholden to the ANC and its catastrophic internal machinations.

Tim du Plessis says all bets were off in the approach to the Polokwane conference. Suddenly the roof was blown off the ANC house and everyone could see that the organisation was more divided than ever before: 'Mandela and Mbeki couldn't shift the culture from an organisation in exile, living in squalor in Lusaka, to that of a modern political party. And the transparency was simply too much for them. Everyone saw what was going on inside. And add to that cadre deployment and the effect it was starting to have on the public service. The public sector started to decay and many cadres were shown up: they couldn't do the job.'[4]

In May 2007, on a Sunday, I was in the Media24 offices at Parliament when the fax machine spluttered into life and a long statement by Cosatu came through. Attached to it was a document titled 'Special Browse Mole Report', which detailed support given to Zuma's campaign against Mbeki by several African countries, including Libya and Angola. Cosatu claimed the document had been leaked to it and was part of an Mbeki-inspired disinformation campaign. Firing Zuma hadn't worked, charging him with corruption had failed and the rape accusation had been thrown out of court. Now this, Zuma's defenders argued.

Browse Mole was a bombshell – only it was a lie. Mbeki ordered an investigation led by former freedom fighter Arthur Fraser, then head of NIA operations. As part of his 'flimsy and one-sided' inquiry,[5] he tapped the phones of a range of law enforcement figures – including Leonard McCarthy, the head of the Scorpions, the crime-fighting unit so hated by Zuma, Vavi, Nzimande and others. The recordings became known as 'the spy tapes' and occupied a central position in South African politics for the next decade, becoming a crucial weapon for Zuma in his quest to stay out of prison. And Fraser would become known as Zuma's personal spy, the man who helped get him off the hook for corruption and would later run a spy ring in the personal service of the president – Zuma.

❖

By the end of 2007, my first year as a parliamentary reporter, I was dead tired. As a junior reporter in Media24's parliamentary team, I covered the portfolio committees on health, social development, communications and sometimes sport. Of those committees, health was the most exciting (it saw the passage of a new bill championed by Manto Tshabalala-Msimang that drastically reduced the public space where smokers could enjoy a cigarette), followed by communications, which had to deliberate on new members of the SABC board. I forced myself to try to understand the social welfare system and only rarely ventured to the sports committee, whose existence I saw no need for.

To break the tedium, I attended as many meetings of the justice committee as I could. It was clearly to justice that political parties sent their best minds and it was instructive to see heavyweights such as John Jeffery (ANC) and Dene Smuts (DA) approach matters from different perspectives, only to compromise somewhere in the middle. I also saw the valuable role smaller parties could play in brokering understanding and helping to reach common ground. Steve Swart (ACDP) was an effective legislator in that regard. Another committee I covered was Scopa. No reporter on our team seemed to be permanently assigned to it, and once I understood the vital role it played in the system of oversight, it became clear it could provide me with a steady supply of lead stories.

I intensely enjoyed debates in the National Assembly. The government benches seemed to be stacked with heavy artillery, while the opposition benches held their own and returned fire in kind. Mbeki always seemed to be above the fray, rarely entering combat. It was left to his adjutants – Manuel, Nzimande, Essop Pahad and Pallo Jordan – to defend the government's position and respond to barbs and insults.

From my position in the press gallery – right above the leader of the opposition and his chief whip, looking towards the government –

I could see notes being delivered by parliamentary messengers and the reactions of recipients. Often, during heated exchanges, Mike Ellis, DA leader Tony Leon's right-hand man and chief whip, would scribble a note and I'd watch the messenger as he wound his way to the government benches to deliver the missive to Nzimande, who'd burst out laughing while Ellis pointed a finger at him, also grinning. The same happened with Leon and Manuel, who would go hammer and tongs at each other during a debate or question and answer session, but for most of the time maintained good humour and grace once tempers cooled.

MPs of all stripes and varying degrees of ability were accessible. One only had to knock on an MP's door to gain access and a hearing. Even ministers were within reach. More than once, I made the daunting trek to the floor at 90 Plein Street that housed ministerial offices and sheepishly knocked on Manuel's door, hoping to get a knockout quote from the finance minister. 'What do you want now?' he once threateningly asked. 'If you're going to ask me another stupid question, I'm going to knock your block off.' He was only half joking.

But the whole year was dominated by the succession battle. MPs in different camps were often seen huddled in corridors around the old House of Assembly or smoking in the courtyard next to the National Assembly. In the marbled hallway behind the ANC benches, Mbeki's closest supporters would sit on brown leather benches, planning and strategising as the Polokwane moment neared. I had become reasonably acquainted with some ANC MPs – the result of the daily ritual of tea and scones at 11 am, followed by chicken wings and game pies for lunch outside committee rooms. Ben Turok provided some perspective, as did Mnyamezeli Booi and Jeremy Cronin. But despite their leanings – against and for Mbeki – the general sense in the ANC caucus was that 'the chief' would be able to stave off the Zuma assault in December.

I was in no mood to cap a trying parliamentary year with an ANC conference 30 km outside Polokwane at the Turfloop campus of the University of Limpopo in Mankweng, formerly an apartheid 'bush college'. From the first to the last moment, however, we could see and feel how the country's future was being heaved onto another trajectory. The Polokwane Holiday Inn was chockablock with delegates. But there was an ominous feeling in the air as we were vetted by the NIA at Polokwane International Airport on the eve of the conference, and it turned into nastiness as the gathering got under way.

The tone was set when Mosiuoa Lekota, the defence minister and ANC chairperson (and part of the Mbeki kitchen cabinet), was booed so loudly during the opening plenary session he had to hand over his duties to Kgalema Motlanthe, the secretary general. It was a shocking development and seemed to indicate a new rowdiness, a scruffiness, even a thuggishness in how the ANC conducted itself. Proceedings were regularly interrupted from the floor, with Zumaites from across the country protesting about voting procedures, accredited delegates and collation of results. And that was before even a single policy had been discussed or changes to Strategy and Tactics considered. All the while, Mbeki and Zuma sat on the stage sharing grins and wisecracks.

On the day the election started, delegates were supposed to break into commissions to discuss policy related to issues such as the economy, safety and security, governance, organisation, and so on. But duelling rallies in support of the presidential candidates dominated the day. It was clear that there was no interest in policy among the 4000 ANC delegates – it was all about who would win.

Mbeki's fall was dramatic and clearly unexpected. Sitting among delegates, surrounded by confidants including the Pahads, Lekota and Mbhazima Shilowa, the president's face turned ashen when the results came. I was 20 or 30 metres from him when Dren Nupen, who oversaw the election on behalf of an outside agency, announced that Zuma had won convincingly – 2329 votes to 1505. Startled, Mbeki appeared to age in an instant. He stared at the stage while behind him bedlam broke out. The winning faction were on their feet, stomping on the floor and dancing on tables, chanting, 'Zuma, Zuma, Zuma!' The new leader made a grand entrance onto the stage, laughing and smiling as the vanquished faction sat among the ordinary delegates, trying to make sense of their defeat.

Mbeki managed that awkward, fake smile of someone trying to

convince others he was coping. He even gave a quick thumbs-up to journalists gawking at him. Lekota sat on the edge of his seat with a pained smile on his face – he and Shilowa were to lead a breakaway party the following year. Shilowa couldn't get a word out. Gert Oosthuizen, Mbeki's deputy minister of sport and an early National Party convert to the ANC, clutched a pack of cigarettes in the VIP area: 'It's a disaster, I don't know what to say.' Mbeki quickly left the sweaty and heaving marquee where the raucous delegates were now celebrating wildly and was whisked away to his lodgings in Magoebaskloof. Legend has it that he told anyone within earshot, 'They're going to destroy the country.'

At the press conference that followed, Mbalula, a man-child in every sense of the term, bounced around the university cafeteria like a black, green and yellow rubber ball. 'I told you we were going to win,' he crowed to all and sundry. Mbeki was never going to beat Zuma, Mbalula gushed. Shortly afterwards he handed the reins of the ANCYL, one of Zuma's most effective mobilising formations, to a youngster from Limpopo, Julius Malema.

Mbeki wasn't wrong about the change in leadership. Zuma's tenure at the helm of the ANC and the country was utterly and indisputably disastrous. But he was Mbeki's gift to his party and country. Mbeki, for all his democratic yearnings during the struggle and his charm in the approach to the 1994 rainbow moment, was an authoritarian. He piloted the cadre deployment resolutions through the ANC's 1997 national conference and ensured changes to statute so they could be implemented. He centralised state power in the Presidency and crafted the ANC in his image.

When the revolt came, as it always would have, he was too isolated and removed from the rank and file to respond to the challenge. Mbeki bequeathed Zuma and his ANC to South Africa and with them a retreat from any chance the country had to modernise and undo the legacy of apartheid. Because with Zuma's ANC came a dramatic increase in corruption and criminality in tandem with an equally precipitous decline (and in many cases a collapse) of the state and infrastructure.

Tim du Plessis, at the time editing *Rapport*, thought that even though Zuma was an undesirable choice to lead the ANC and eventually the country, the centre would hold. 'By that time people were thoroughly tired of Mbeki. He was paranoid, isolated himself, and the only communication from him were those newsletters which, when you got them, you thought to yourself, "God, what is this guy doing in the dead of night, writing these? What is he smoking, what is he drinking?" There was a sense of relief when it was over because everything came to a standstill while they were fighting among themselves: the party, the country, everything.'[6]

The Polokwane putsch by Zuma and his coalition of the wounded propelled people such as Gwede Mantashe, Malusi Gigaba, Tina Joemat-Pettersson and Bathabile Dlamini into positions of power and influence. And South Africa continues to suffer under the consequences of their misrule. 'And that's the irony of the Mbeki era. So many good things but also so many things that went wrong and that we're still struggling with today,' says Du Plessis.[7]

15
Staying out of jail

THE OVERTHROW OF THE MBEKI REGIME signalled the start of an era in which South Africa gradually, then dramatically, declined – and in many instances collapsed. The rise of Zuma, a largely uneducated Zulu nationalist and inherently anti-democratic polygamist, also represented the ANC's sharp retreat from the slivers of idealism it sometimes proclaimed.

Mandela's stated purpose was to foster reconciliation and to start building a unified nation on the debris of apartheid. And the ANC, initially, seemed to agree with his chosen path. Under Mbeki, who became fixated on fundamental transformation based on a new nationalist fervour, the ANC understood the party needed to fuse with the state. With Zuma's election as leader, however, the ANC's transformation from an anti-apartheid liberation movement into a parasite invading its host was completed.

This parasite systematically and shamelessly withdrew and redirected public resources for its own corrupt benefit. It constructed a national network of patronage affecting and afflicting every level of government, every state entity and every state function. And it could do so because of cadre deployment, the system designed by Mbeki and Joel Netshitenzhe that seamlessly injected ANC cadres into the body politic. Chief Justice Raymond Zondo would later find that 'the ANC under President Zuma permitted, supported and enabled corruption and state capture'.

Zuma's ANC took a sledgehammer to the principles of good governance, transparency, accountability and participatory democracy – all codified in the Constitution. The party rode roughshod over the ideals of those who fought for and believed in a new democracy and the rule of law. It oversaw the disintegration of infrastructure, local government and the economy. Zuma's coterie of enablers assisted him in auctioning the country's interests to the highest bidder and set back the democratic project by at least three decades. In a period spanning a decade, Zuma used the foundation laid by Mandela and Mbeki to threaten South Africa's future as a going concern.

Political instability became part of national life after Zuma's ascension to the top of the ANC, and 2008 saw bitter conflict between those who still supported Mbeki and the new dominant faction. The build-up to the Polokwane conference was a harbinger of what was to come as every institution of state became embroiled in the split between those who supported Zuma and those who supported Mbeki. After Zuma's victory, deployed ANC cadres quickly fell in line – but Mbeki wasn't about to leave quietly.

Two days after the conference, the media was called to the presidential guest house next door to Mahlamba Ndlopfu, the president's Pretoria residence in the Bryntirion estate. In the late afternoon sun on the mansion's back lawn, he announced a new board at the SABC, the public broadcaster. It was a routine appointment based on recommendations from Parliament's portfolio committee on communications after an interview process, and shouldn't have caused much of a fuss. It was his first encounter with the media since his humiliation in Polokwane and I asked the first question: 'Mr President, it has now been a couple of days since Mr Zuma was elected president of the ANC. How do you feel?'

I don't remember his exact answer but he responded in the manner you'd expect. He respected Zuma as leader of his party and they would continue to work together closely as they had in the past. But there was clear tension in his voice and it was obvious that the battle wasn't over. His associates and supporters were already talking about fighting a rearguard action against Zuma and using the state and Parliament to force the coming Zuma government into a straitjacket.

Reaction to Mbeki's SABC announcement came thick and fast.

Zwelinzima Vavi of Cosatu called for an urgent meeting of the alliance partners, denouncing Mbeki's decision to appoint the board on his own and saying he needed to understand that ANC delegates voted for change at Polokwane.[1] The SACP called it 'factionalist', saying the board had been appointed by 'past ANC leaders' and would be 'illegitimate'.[2] Mantashe, the former NUM general secretary who was catapulted into the powerful position of Zuma's secretary general, urged calm.[3]

The set-to emphasised the fault lines that were on full display ahead of Polokwane. The SABC was frequently accused of being manipulated by the Mbeki faction before delegates voted, and there was a clamour from the Zuma faction that the broadcaster should be depoliticised. Mbeki's decision to make the appointment within days of losing his position as head of the party convinced the Zumaites he was going to continue doing as he pleased without consulting the alliance partners.

Zuma's personal history will not be lost on any reader who has reached this point in the book, so it will suffice to recap it in broad strokes. Born in rural KwaZulu-Natal in 1942, he grew up in the east coast's rural hinterland and had no formal schooling. 'I never went to school but I educated myself. I'm proud of that,' he later said.[4] His father was a policeman and his mother a domestic worker. He joined the ANC in 1958 and the ANC's armed wing four years later. Arrested in 1963, he was imprisoned for ten years on Robben Island, and on his release he went underground before going into exile in 1975. He was stationed in Swaziland, Lesotho and Zambia and rose to the top of the ANC's intelligence structures.

He was one of the first exiles to return to South Africa after the unbanning of the ANC on 2 February 1990 and was part of the ANC negotiating teams at Codesa and the Multi-Party Negotiating Forum. After 1994, the ANC deployed him to KwaZulu-Natal, where he was the member of the executive council (MEC) for economic development before becoming deputy president of the ANC and the country.

Zuma represented the 'dark side' of the ANC and it was this side that gained the upper hand after Polokwane, says journalist Max du

Preez, who knew Zuma during the latter years of exile: 'I ran into him twice in Lusaka before 1990. My first impression was that he was a jovial, polite fellow, but after conversations with others of the ANC-in-exile realised he was a semi-literate Zulu traditionalist and leader of the ANC's murderous internal security machinery. With his return in 1990 I was given the repeated assurance from his senior comrades: he is our head Zulu; we must tolerate him. But there can never be talk of a senior leadership position.'[5]

Tim du Plessis says the De Klerk government's original lead negotiator, Gerrit Viljoen, told him he liked Zuma. 'He understands our people. The Afrikaners and the Zulu understand each other. And Jürgen Kögl [a political fixer in the 1990s] told me that after he, Zuma and Mbeki met Constand Viljoen [the former SADF chief who joined other retired generals in forming the Afrikaner Volksfront in 1993] and the group of right-wingers who were opposed to the transition, Zuma told him driving away from the meeting that he liked Viljoen. "I like this man, these are our people," he said.'[6]

Zuma was an almost accidental ANC leader. He seemed content to scratch around KwaZulu-Natal as an MEC, pursuing his polygamous lifestyle while enjoying the largesse of Schabir Shaik. Unfortunately for him, the Shaik clan became the target of an investigation by the Directorate of Special Operations (DSO), colloquially known as the Scorpions. In 1999, Mbeki said the government was planning to establish an elite crime-fighting unit to curb organised crime and corruption. Finally operational in January 2001 and housed in the NPA, the Scorpions consisted of project teams led by prosecutors and assisted by investigators and analysts.[7] By combining their efforts, the best possible case could be prepared before it was taken to court.

The Scorpions were located in the NPA precisely because of this model – and because the police were riven by internal corruption and hampered by a severe lack of trust from society. The best investigators and analysts were recruited – including some from the police – and the sharpest prosecutors were seconded to the DSO. Members drove fast cars emblazoned with the red-and-white Scorpions emblem and started nailing organised crime kingpins at a rapid rate – often headlining television news bulletins with high-profile arrests or convictions.

The Scorpions had a significant impact on crime-battered South

Africans' psyche in their first four years, an Institute for Security Studies researcher found in 2004. 'The DSO investigation into the arms deal concluded by the South African government in 1999, and its investigation of the role of the deputy president in this deal, upped this public profile considerably,' she wrote.[8]

The DSO became the most reviled – and feared – institution of the state among senior ANC leaders, being outside the police and therefore less vulnerable to political interference – and because of its vast resources and focus on corruption. In the turbulent period between 2005, when Mbeki dismissed Zuma and Shaik was found guilty of corruption and fraud, and 2007, when Zuma became ANC leader, the whole criminal justice system became politicised. Every law enforcement agency was drawn into the governing party's internal conflict as the factions battled for control of the state and its resources. Mbeki relied heavily on an old exile comrade, Jackie Selebi, who was national police commissioner, and the police crime intelligence division. Zuma had an ally in Arthur Fraser, the head of domestic intelligence at the NIA.

The extent to which the criminal justice system fell victim to the ANC's internal conflict is perhaps best exemplified by Mbeki's decision on 24 September 2007 to suspend the NDPP, Vusi Pikoli, due to the 'breakdown in the working relationship' between Pikoli and the justice minister, Brigitte Mabandla.[9] It was all a ruse and there was no inkling of a poor working relationship between them. In fact, Pikoli had informed Mbeki and Mabandla that the DSO was about to arrest Selebi on charges of corruption. This was too much for the president, who needed Selebi's support before the Polokwane conference. Pikoli and the DSO's investigation into Selebi's links with a drug kingpin, Glenn Agliotti, was thwarted at every turn by Selebi, Mbeki, the state and the ANC.[10]

The DSO became a target for the Zuma faction because it was running the continuing investigation into the arms deal and Zuma's role in it. But even worse for Zuma, it uncovered information of a corrupt relationship between Shaik and Zuma that went way beyond the arms deal. If it went to trial, the whole Zuma revolution could be derailed. The Scorpions and the NPA therefore became political opponents of the Zuma faction.

In 2006 and 2007 the DSO came under regular attack, accused of being an example of Mbeki's abuse of state institutions to prevent Zuma becoming president. The strategy was to relentlessly attack the credibility of the DSO and whip up public support against it. Zuma was held up as the victim of an institution gone rogue, as a leader who was being targeted unfairly, and the DSO was depicted as a law enforcement body abusing its powers. This strategy – of attacking statutory bodies and debasing the constitutional and legal order – was later regularly used by Zuma during his years of destruction.

The ANC cadre deployment policy did not help the DSO's cause. The NPA was established in 1998, replacing the previous system of provincial attorneys-general, who oversaw prosecutions. The first NDPP was Bulelani Ngcuka, an ANC MP and deputy chairperson of the National Council of Provinces. He was married to Phumzile Mlambo-Ngcuka, a minister in Mbeki's cabinet. Ngcuka's job was to build a new organisation out of the disparate system of provincial prosecution offices, but he could never extricate himself from his loyalty to the party – and he made crucial errors that gave Zuma succour.

In August 2001, he rejected a recommendation by the prosecution team investigating the arms deal that Zuma's home and offices be searched at the same time as Shaik's premises.[11] Two years later, he rejected a recommendation that there was enough evidence to prosecute Zuma on charges of corruption.[12] He only told the prosecutions team on the day that he made the announcement to the public, famously declaring that 'despite there being prima facie evidence of corruption' the NPA will not prosecute Zuma.[13] But the investigation did not end there, and with Ngcuka's departure in 2004 the team continued looking into Zuma. Even after Mbeki suspended Pikoli in September 2007, the Scorpions team led by advocate Billy Downer continued to piece together evidence and prepare their case.

On 29 November 2007, shortly before the ANC's Polokwane conference, the prosecutions team met advocate Mokotedi Mpshe, who was acting in Pikoli's position. It was agreed that charges should be reinstated against Zuma, racketeering charges should be added and the case should be enrolled at the high court in Durban.[14] Four days later, a draft indictment was forwarded to Mpshe and a report was shared with Mabandla. But Mpshe did not want to charge Zuma yet, telling the DSO team he preferred to wait until 2008 because 'he did not want the NPA to be seen to be responsible for Mr Zuma failing to be elected as ANC president'.[15] Leonard McCarthy, head of the Scorpions, was furious. He spoke to Ngcuka (who had left the NPA years earlier) about Mpshe's decision and these conversations were recorded by the NIA in its investigation into the Special Browse Mole Report. Fraser weaponised the recordings and allegedly handed them to Michael Hulley, Zuma's lawyer, and the NPA.[16]

The movement to get Zuma elected president of the ANC comprised varied interests. There was a faction in the ANC that believed Mbeki and Mandela had sold out and that the new dispensation needed to be radically changed. Many among them were criminals, eyeing rent-seeking opportunities and seeking to extract as much from the state as they could. There were the ideologues in the SACP, who wanted the ANC to move away from what they perceived as Mbeki's neoliberal policies, and the unions, which cried out for a future under socialism. The young cadres, or 'the youth', detested Mbeki and his studious bookishness. They still wanted a full-scale revolution.

And Zuma? He just wanted to stay out of jail. But the price South Africa would have to pay for his impunity was the destruction of the criminal justice system.

16

The counter-revolution

JACOB ZUMA WAS ELECTED PRESIDENT OF THE ANC ON 18 December 2007. Three days later, Leonard McCarthy called Billy Downer and instructed him to get his team ready. And on 28 December a summons was served on Zuma. Letters to him and French arms company Thales (which was charged alongside Zuma) told them their criminal trial would commence on 4 August 2008.[1]

This set in motion events that would have enormous repercussions for the rule of law, the independence of the NPA, the functioning of the criminal justice system, institutions such as SARS and the entire democratic project. Hoping to bludgeon judges, officers of the court and the public into submission so Zuma would never be prosecuted or go to prison, the ANC launched an assault on the rule of law, telling the public the courts were part of the 'counter-revolution' and Zuma was the victim of a political conspiracy. It claimed judges were tainted, that they would never be able to act impartially, and repeatedly attacked the NPA as part of the sinister forces bent on destroying the 'revolution'. The ANC pitted the rule of law against South Africa's citizens in service of one man.

This sustained campaign established a culture in the ANC which made the criminal justice system a legitimate political target. The ANC saw the rule of law as a hostile political player and treated it as such. The courts, judges, the NPA and prosecutors became political opponents who were singled out for protest action, demonstrations and personal attacks from the governing party and its alliance partners, and it became increasingly difficult for the system to function. The ANC's tactic of debasing the judiciary normalised broad disdain and rejection of the rule of law in society. It would eventually lead to serial impunity for Zuma and his criminal network and a weakening of the judiciary and the NPA. Judges became afraid to reject Zuma's cynical legal strategy, and after the NPA backed off it was refitted and disfigured to become one of his biggest allies. The ANC inflicted debilitating damage on the criminal justice system.

In January 2008, the ANC's new leadership started to put together a plan to save their president from prosecution. The NEC appointed a task team to investigate the arms deal and to compile a 'detailed and factual report' – even though there was already a lengthy report from the joint investigative team (described in Chapter 6) and the charge sheet against Zuma.[2] The team was led by Kgalema Motlanthe, the ANC deputy president. He was assisted by Mathews Phosa, the treasurer-general, Zuma devotee Lindiwe Sisulu, Naledi Pandor, SACP veteran Jeremy Cronin, former SANDF chief Siphiwe Nyanda and former minister and ANC deputy secretary general Sankie Mthembi-Mahanyele. Also on the task team was Cyril Ramaphosa, then a popular member of the NEC.[3]

Gwede Mantashe, the SACP and NUM veteran, took to his new job as ANC enforcer with gusto, saying the task team needed to 'locate' the charges and the case against Zuma. And he quickly signalled his Stalinist beliefs, declaring that 'the ANC is the party that leads government. There's no division between government and the ANC.'[4] The ANC was clearly not going to let the law run its course. Phosa (around the same time he told me to 'fuck off' when I asked him about Chancellor House) lashed out at the DSO's 'Hollywood-style' prosecutions – a favourite criticism of the Scorpions. Zuma, he said, would fight the case 'with every sinew in his body'.[5] Zuma and his legal team, for the most part led by his attorney, Michael Hulley, and advocate Kemp J Kemp, would launch innumerable court actions and applications over the next decade or more as they sought to keep him out of prison. But more than that, Zuma used his position as head of state to weaken law enforcement, insert accomplices into leadership positions and undermine trust in the judiciary.

Motlanthe's subcommittee, advised by Professor Sipho Seepe, an academic, Paul Ngobeni, a lawyer and senior University of Cape Town official, and the former head of the Special Investigating Unit, Judge Willem Heath, decided on cynical and damaging tactics. The ANC wanted the arms deal and everything related to it dead and buried, and Zuma off the hook. And it decided on a broad strategy to achieve its goals. It would cast Zuma as a victim and build a campaign around the 'unfairness' of the investigation into him. It would help Zuma's legal team with ammunition to use against the NPA in an application to ensure a stay of prosecution. And it planned to use the fallout after justices from the Constitutional Court accused a Zuma-aligned judge, John Hlophe, of improperly interfering in the court's affairs around Zuma, to show that the courts were tainted.[6]

It would also attack the credibility of the NPA, the judiciary and Parliament, thereby undermining the trustworthiness of three institutions vital to a constitutional democracy.[7] Seepe, who operated in Sisulu's orbit for years alongside Ngobeni, said the NPA was not independent and that public opinion should be considered when deciding Zuma's fate – a clear intimation that if the courts did not acquiesce and let Zuma off the hook, there would be hell to pay.

The courts were the ANC's second big target. Seepe said they were 'corrupted', with a line of attack also focused on Chief Justice Pius Langa and Deputy Chief Justice Dikgang Moseneke, who were accused of not being impartial.[8] As for Parliament, the 'brains trust' advising Motlanthe's subcommittee argued that the legislature must be instructed to shut down all investigations into the arms deal. 'We must look at the lessons we should learn from the whole saga to make sure it is not repeated,' Seepe said.[9]

In July 2008, Mantashe accused the judiciary of being an element of 'counter-revolutionary forces' seeking the destruction of Zuma and the ANC. Hlophe became a lightning conductor in the ANC's eagerness to attack the courts. An investigation was launched into his attempts to sway justices of the highest court to favour Zuma – but he was called out by fellow judges and an investigation was launched. But Mantashe leapt to Hlophe's defence. 'This is psycho-logical preparation of society so that when the Constitutional Court judges pounce on our president we should be ready at that point in time,' he said. 'Our revolution is in danger; we must declare to defend it till the end.'[10]

❖

The tale of ANC misrule will soon move past events in the period of the ANC's Polokwane conference, but in analysing present-day crises it is clear that almost all of them can be directly traced to the years immediately before and after Zuma's elevation to ANC leader. It is therefore important to detail how the foundation of the Zuma ANC's doctrine of lawlessness and grand corruption was constructed.

One of the most trumpeted resolutions at Polokwane was a decision to 'dissolve the Scorpions' in line with the constitutional directive that South Africa was to have a single police service.[11] As we have seen, ANC luminaries hated the DSO for prosecuting MPs embroiled in the notorious Travelgate scam. But it was the pending prosecution of Zuma that really angered ANC delegates, who resolved to smash the DSO, scatter its members into the ranks of the police and transfer all resources and skills to the SAPS. There was palpable hostility from ANC leaders and members towards the Scorpions. This was despite a judicial commission of inquiry, established in 2005 by Mbeki in response to the clamour from Zuma-aligned factions, finding there was nothing unconstitutional about the DSO falling under the NPA and that the need for the Scorpions remained as compelling as on the day it was founded.[12]

The assault on the NPA and DSO commenced almost immediately after the Polokwane conference. At a meeting of Parliament's portfolio committee on justice on 26 February 2008, McCarthy and the DSO leadership were accused by Yunus Carrim, the ANC chairperson, of spying on political leaders and acting outside their mandate.[13] He was supported in this by ANC MPs on the committee who questioned the constitutionality of the DSO's mandate and accused it of illegal intelligence-gathering operations. McCarthy and his team were forced to defend the DSO, and opposition MPs accused Carrim and his colleagues of 'building a case' against the Scorpions – something the chairperson strenuously denied.[14] The ANC attack on the Scorpions came as the DSO reported to Parliament a stellar conviction rate of

81 per cent in the previous financial year, as well as asset recoveries totalling hundreds of millions of rands.[15]

What the ANC was doing was precisely what opposition law-makers were claiming: its caucus was starting to lay the groundwork for the disbandment of the Scorpions. It had to find a way to translate the party's resolution into the legislative process, then create the legal context that could withstand scrutiny beyond merely a party resolution. Carrim, a smart, senior SACP leader, eagerly and enthusiastically led the campaign. The Zuma-led ANC ensured that Mbeki's cabinet adopted two draft bills in May that would see the dissolution of the Scorpions, and a parliamentary ad hoc committee was convened two months later.

It was during a press conference before the legislative process to consider the SAPS Amendment Bill and the NPA Amendment Bill – which engineered the dissolution of the DSO – that the ANC's ruthlessness in attacking good governance and the rule of law came into full view. Returning from the Polokwane conference to the press gallery in Parliament, the only issue reporters focused on was the future of the Scorpions. So, on Wednesday, 30 July 2008, a cold and wet winter's day in Cape Town, a stuffy committee room in Parliament's 120 Plein Street building was packed as Carrim and Maggie Sotyu, ANC MP and chairperson of the parliamentary portfolio committee on safety and security, told the media they would co-chair an ad hoc committee to consider the two Scorpions bills. By then Zuma had already launched two high court applications to stop his prosecution and the ANC's strategy of divide and destroy was starting to become evident.

During question time, Carrim and Sotyu were asked about the public consultation process on the bills. After all, the role of Parliament wasn't to rubber-stamp the whims of the governing party – or so we believed. A bill becomes law only after an extensive public consultation process, thorough deliberations in committee, various reading debates in the National Assembly, then debate and a vote. Only then, after the National Assembly has adopted it, is it sent to the president for assent. But what was unfolding with the Scorpions bill was anathema to a constitutional democracy. The ANC was steamrollering through a partisan political process initiated by a faction of the party at its national conference.

Sotyu let the mask slip: 'It is over! It is over! The Scorpions will be disbanded, they will be, they will be,' she shouted in answer to questions. She and Carrim were cut from the same cloth and exhibited unquestioning loyalty to the movement. Carrim argued that the DSO was one of the reasons for the 'low-intensity civil war' in the ANC and that it acted outside its mandate, taking cases it shouldn't. And then came the clincher, for Carrim and many others wanting to give the dissolution of the Scorpions a veneer of respectability: 'There was a strong view that the Scorpions were being used to settle political scores within the ANC. Moreover, through the Scorpions' preliminary statements, aggressive media profiling of investigations in progress and media leaks, some people's constitutional rights to a free trial were being undermined and innocent people were being besmirched,' he said, clearly referring to Zuma.[16]

The Zuma ANC had now laid the groundwork for impunity. It attacked the judiciary and the NPA, built Zuma into the embodiment of the revolution that had to be defended, and co-opted the national legislature into destroying the country's best chance of stopping corruption. South Africa's sharp descent into the era of patronage, grand corruption and lawlessness had begun.

17
Interregnum and overthrow

IF CADRE DEPLOYMENT WAS A KEY POLICY TOOL for the ANC to gain complete control over the state and society, the assault on the rule of law was a crucial intervention to ensure the party retained command. Nominally, the ANC said it believed in the supremacy of the Constitution, respected the judiciary and believed in the independence of the prosecuting authority. Even Zuma, shortly before being elected at Polokwane, spoke about upholding the Constitution. But there was always a caveat: respect for the rule of law and the separation of powers meant impunity. It meant law enforcement agencies should respect the party and its leader; they were above the law and not to be sparred with.

Speaking at Wits University in December 2007, Zuma told his audience the constitutional order could unravel if the rights of individuals were trampled on. 'Our citizens need to maintain careful watch to ensure the separation of powers such that the executive can never exercise undue influence over the judiciary and Parliament. I say this as I believe that turning a blind eye to abuses of state power, no matter how small or insignificant they may appear, will eventually result in the unravelling of our system and the undermining of our rights as shareholders in our democracy,' he said.[1]

Zuma's statement made it look as though he was guided by a moral or civic duty towards good governance, or that he possessed an awareness of how to maintain a fragile constitutional democracy. There was nothing of that. At Wits, Zuma spoke out of self-preservation, as he so often did. He did not refer to 'separation of powers' or the undermining of citizens' rights because of honestly held convictions about the rule of law. It was purely because he felt threatened by the arms deal investigation and had to attach nefarious motives to it to garner popular support. Zuma was desperate to stay out of jail.

How much damage the ANC's devilish ploys did to judges, courts, prosecutors and law enforcement would become clear only much later. But in the years immediately before and after the Polokwane conference, Zuma became the totem around which the enablers of state capture congregated. Not yet in executive power, Zuma and his acolytes doubled down on efforts to convince the public he was the victim of dastardly and illegal machinations of the state machinery under Mbeki to prevent him becoming head of state.

Zuma had to become the embodiment of the freedom struggle; the symbol of the revolution that had yet to be concluded. If the state was striking at Zuma, it was striking at the revolution. And that meant the Scorpions, the NPA and the courts were against the people. Only if the public, the ANC's rank and file, believed that could attacks on the credibility of the country's legal foundations work. They had to be convinced that the state and its institutions were being abused to target Zuma, that those institutions were in opposition to the democratic dispensation and that they could not be trusted. The ANC achieved this in spades.

Zuma, Gwede Mantashe and the rest were impatient. They were in office at Luthuli House but Mbeki remained head of state and wielded considerable power from the Union Buildings. Gear remained the government's macroeconomic framework, directed by the detested finance minister Trevor Manuel, and Mbeki continued to direct foreign policy and travel the world on his Boeing Business Jet in his quest to be remembered as a statesman of global repute. Tension between the two centres of power – Pretoria and Johannesburg – simmered and every NEC meeting became fraught with debate about resolving the matter.

This debate had been central to the Mbeki/Zuma standoff, with the party eventually deciding its leader should automatically be the head of state.[2] Others saw this as a way to undermine the authority of a sitting president, arguing that there had been no issue when Mandela was president and Mbeki ANC leader – why would there be a problem with a similar arrangement between Mbeki and Zuma?[3]

On Tuesday 9 September and Wednesday 10 September 2008, Yunus Carrim and Maggie Sotyu's parliamentary ad hoc committee held public hearings into the future of the Scorpions. Although there was a raft of submissions in support of the DSO by civil society, academics and opposition parties, the ANC and its alliance partners hammered on the Scorpions' alleged illegal intelligence-gathering capabilities, its 'Hollywood-style' operations, political interference and the need to strengthen the police – a fig leaf if ever there was one.

Buti Manamela, the leader of the SACP Young Communist League (later a deputy minister under Zuma and Ramaphosa), told MPs the DSO had 'lost credibility' and was 'riddled with apartheid diehards'.[4] John Jeffery, an ANC MP who also became a deputy minister under Zuma and Ramaphosa, lashed out at the DSO and its 'intelligence-gathering activities'.

But Carrim was the ANC's main battering ram. With him at the helm of the parliamentary process, the end of the Scorpions was a foregone conclusion. 'The way the DSO had conducted its work had given rise to legitimate perceptions, particularly within the ranks of the majority party and its voters, that senior ANC politicians had received undue attention from this unit as against other aspects of organised crime,' he said.[5]

Listening to the process unfold in the stinkwood-panelled Old Assembly in Parliament, where apartheid premier Hendrik Verwoerd had been assassinated 42 years earlier, I was struck by the ANC's intransigence. Carrim led the committee with aplomb, sticking to meeting times, involving parliamentary and state law advisers and giving the opposition enough time to state its case. But there was no way through. And Carrim was the quintessential deployed cadre: loyalty to the party, first and above all. On 30 January 2009, Kgalema Motlanthe, the caretaker president after Mbeki's ouster, signed the two amendment bills into law, and dissolved the Scorpions.

153

❖

Two days after the ad hoc committee met, everything changed. On Friday, 12 September, Judge Chris Nicholson delivered a blow at the high court in Pietermaritzburg that not only knocked the stuffing out of the NPA but emboldened the Zuma faction to remove Mbeki in what amounted to a coup d'état. Nicholson found the NPA's decision to prosecute Zuma on corruption charges invalid and made wide-ranging findings of serious political interference in the prosecution process by members of the executive.[6] He also agreed with Zuma that there seemed to be a conspiracy related to the timing of charges.[7]

Nicholson made 'scathing observations' about the motivation for the prosecution and the political influence on the process, pointing his finger straight at Mbeki, justice minister Brigitte Mabandla and former NDPP Bulelani Ngcuka.[8] 'Is it really possible that the president did not know?' asked Nicholson, referring to his finding that there was political interference.[9]

The judgment was a political earthquake. It gave the Zuma faction everything it needed to remove Mbeki and take power, confirming what it had been telling its supporters all along: that state institutions were being manipulated and used to wage a political campaign – and the sitting president was behind it. The judgment was political gold and it wasn't only the Zuma faction who jumped at it like a lion to red meat. Helen Zille, the DA leader, said Mbeki 'clearly violated the Constitution' and the party's parliamentary leader, Sandra Botha, said the DA would table a motion of no-confidence in the president.[10]

Outside court, an elated Zuma sang as thousands of supporters cheered. He repeated his claim that he was the victim of a political conspiracy and added that he was a 'wounded warrior'. 'When I sat in court, I remembered one of my learned friends saying he was [as] sober as a judge. Indeed, this judge was sober,' Zuma said, to laughter. 'My view is, today's judgment will help South Africa.'[11]

Zuma was always surrounded by supporters, singing and dancing with him outside court as he took aim at the constitutional order. Mantashe was a constant, as were Zwelinzima Vavi and Blade Nzimande. Kgalema Motlanthe regularly appeared, as did Fikile Mbalula, and eventually Julius Malema too. 'Chris Nicholson is not a counter-revolutionary judge,' Mantashe said. Find in Zuma's favour and you're a good jurist, was the message. 'The problem in this country is [President] Thabo Mbeki and his people … We don't want him,' said Malema. Vavi: 'Today we feel absolutely vindicated. We want to see who are the rapists of the judicial system.' And Nzimande completed the trio: 'We are happy for Msholozi [Zuma's clan name] and we did say we would support him until the end.' Jessie Duarte, the ANC spokesperson and a vindictive apparatchik, called the judgment a 'victory for justice and the Constitution'.[12]

Zille, who succeeded Tony Leon as leader of the opposition in 2007, believed the country's foundations to be under threat after a meeting with the president in which he opened up to her: 'It showed me then what the war between him and his opponents was like and that it was a war over controlling the institutions of state. It was a war over controlling the police. It was a war over controlling the prosecuting authority. Because all of these institutions of state were seen as proxies in the political war.'[13]

After a week of intense speculation and behind-the-scenes manoeuvring, the ANC NEC met at a decrepit old Transnet training facility, Esselen Park, on the East Rand. The only issue on the agenda was the future of Mbeki, who cancelled a visit to the UN Security Council in New York to remain in South Africa. Zuma, Mantashe and the rest of the Zuma faction wanted him out, and pronto.

On Friday, 19 September 2008, news started to filter through to the media contingent overnight – cloistered in a clubhouse away from the hall where the NEC was meeting – that Mbeki supporters were starting to wilt and his sacking was a fait accompli. 'Earlier on that critical Friday, reports emanated from the meeting telling of tough debates … The voices of reason which pleaded that Mbeki be allowed to complete his term, perhaps bringing the election date forward, were drowned out by the angry voices of the night. Even the proposal that he should be allowed a month or so to complete some of his critical commitments of state was shot down,' wrote Frank Chikane, Mbeki's director general. 'In the end, the *ngoko!* ['now!'] chorus won the day.'[14]

On Saturday morning, 20 September 2008, an ANC delegation met Mbeki at Mahlamba Ndlopfu. Motlanthe and Mantashe told him the party had decided to 'recall' him from his position as president and that he must tender his resignation as soon as possible. There was to be no time for pleasantries or a winding down of the cabinet's affairs. Mbeki enquired how the ANC wanted to manage the transition, specifically how he could finalise immediate tasks. Chikane said the message came back 'to say that the president could not continue with any of his responsibilities, particularly the international commitments'.[15] It was a complete humiliation.

In a statement, the ANC sought to reassure the country that changes in executive office would not lead to instability: 'We wish to assert to you that our most important task as a revolutionary movement is the stability of our country and the unity and cohesion of the ANC. Our movement has been through a trying period and we are determined to heal the rifts that may exist. In the light of this, and after a long and difficult discussion, the ANC has decided to recall the President of the Republic before his term of office expires. Our decision has been communicated to him. The formalities are now subject of a Parliamentary process and, we can assure you, will take place in a way which ensures smooth running of government.'[16]

Mbeki was instructed by the ANC to stick to the deadlines it determined, which necessitated the immediate dispatch of a letter of resignation to the speaker of Parliament, Baleka Mbete, and her reply that he would cease to be head of state the following Thursday. In an address to the nation on Sunday night, Mbeki denied interference in the unfolding process involving Zuma – but confirmed he would be resigning his office because he was 'a loyal member of the ANC'.[17]

On Monday, 22 September 2008, I rushed to the press gallery in the National Assembly to get to my regular seat in the front row. At 2.16 pm, Mbete called the meeting to order and a moment of silence for prayer or meditation was requested. Then she announced that she had received a letter from Mbeki and proceeded to read it into Hansard, the parliamentary record. He highlighted his government's achievements and reiterated that his oath of office informed all his actions as president, before saying that the ANC had decided to 'recall' him from office. It was a short letter and a copy of that day's minutes –

which I have kept – shows that by 2.19 pm the business of the house had moved on to notice of motions. The ANC benches were bare on that day, the opposition quiet. Everyone knew a Zuma presidency was seeded with the possibility of disaster.

On Wednesday another bombshell burst as news filtered through that Trevor Manuel had resigned as finance minister. Shares on the JSE tumbled and the rand fell sharply against the dollar.[18] Apart from Mbeki, Manuel was one of the most maligned figures among the Zuma faction. His commitment to strict fiscal discipline, his eschewing of party dogma and the high regard in which he was held abroad and by the private sector made him a natural enemy of the anti-intellectual and anti-constitutional Zuma group.

But almost immediately he indicated that he was willing to serve in a new cabinet, his resignation merely a formality to give the president-designate, Motlanthe, the freedom to choose his own cabinet. But it was a shot across the bow, too, to show Zuma and his cronies that governing and statecraft are not for the faint-hearted. Political stability and trust are the currencies governments deal in and they could ill afford some populist cleaning out of the stables, was the message. Prudent fiscal and monetary policies were non-negotiable, regardless of who was president.

Manuel left the NEC at Esselen Park early on Friday to prepare for meetings at the UN in New York: 'I got a call from a colleague on the NEC – it was about 1.45 in the morning and he said, "We recalled Thabo." Nothing to do, I asked my two protectors to pick me up at 6 am and my secretaries to be in the office by 7 am. I got there, typed my letter of resignation, told my immediate staff what I was doing and had my protectors deliver it to Mahlamba Ndlopfu. When they got there, Gwede as SG of the ANC and Kgalema as deputy president of the ANC were there waiting to see Thabo, and my letter was handed to the butler. And by the time Thabo came down to see them, he must have had the letter in hand. It wasn't antics, it was just straightforward. I serve at the pleasure of the president.

'I went back to Esselen Park and I gave a copy of that letter to … JZ. And they said, "No, you must withdraw it." And I said, "No, I can't withdraw it, I can't, I can't. In fact, you should encourage all ministers to do the same so that there isn't factionalism." Later that day I had left for the States and they had called all ministers and asked them not to resign, and then there was a bit of a break and some ministers only resigned on the morning that Kgalema was being elected. They had already flown to Cape Town and that then created a bit of a vacuum and they needed to find people to fill those spaces.

'Jabu Moleketi was deputy minister of finance and resigned that morning and Nhlanhla Nene came in as deputy minister. He had been chairing the portfolio committee. Geraldine (Fraser-Moleketi, Jabu's wife and sister of spymaster Arthur Fraser) resigned as minister of public service and administration. And Richard Baloyi, who had been chairing the portfolio committee, was appointed to replace her – a disaster of note. Aziz Pahad resigned and they appointed Fatima Hajaig – you might not even remember her – as deputy minister [of foreign affairs].'[19]

Motlanthe was elected and sworn in as the country's third democratic president late in the afternoon of Thursday, 24 September. There was no pomp and ceremony, no lavish banquet. Motlanthe was to be a caretaker president, head of state in name only, the country governed by committee from Luthuli House until the next election. He had no mandate and no agency. But Mbeki was out and that's what the Zuma faction wanted.

Motlanthe delivered short remarks in the banquet hall at Tuynhuys, next door to the National Assembly, as guests enjoyed snacks and cocktails. In the gallery, looking down on the newly minted President Motlanthe, MPs, diplomats, senior bureaucrats and an assortment of deployed cadres, the police band struck up Stevie Wonder's 'I Just Called to Say I Love You'. The Casio synthesiser almost buckled under pressure from the enormous police officer's hands on the keyboard. South Africa was about to buckle under Zuma.

Manuel says the period immediately after Mbeki's removal was a battle – then the financial crisis broke. 'Within days of the recall of Thabo Mbeki, Lehman Brothers collapsed and so the world spun into that recession. It was the most unbelievably difficult time, because you didn't have the wherewithal to convene as you used to convene and have the trust between people to be able to take things forward, so it was a very, very difficult period.'[20]

❖

Postscript: On 22 October 2008, a month after Mbeki had been hounded from office, Judge Nicholson granted the NPA leave to appeal his judgment. In a statement, the prosecuting authority said: 'It is important that certainty and finality is established on this matter in order for the NPA to make a decision in the main criminal case.'

18
Normalising Zuma

SOUTH AFRICA IN THE POST-MBEKI, PRE-ZUMA era was a strange place. Reporting from Parliament felt like a welcome Prague Spring as committees suddenly sprang into life and MPs fearlessly tackled thorny issues while seemingly opening space for debate. Kgalema Motlanthe was a dour character, clearly uneasy in the role of head of state, and made no secret of his caretaker status.

Analysts and commentators started arguing that perhaps Zuma wasn't such a philistine after all. Maybe he should be given a chance because he seemed to connect easily with the common man. He appeared to understand people's frustrations and wasn't as aloof as his predecessor, was the argument. But he also had the support of the ANC and its alliance partners and he was clear that not much would change under his leadership. Motlanthe said as much in his first address to Parliament, confirming that government policies 'will not change' and that 'policy belongs to the collective. It doesn't belong to any individual and it is not for any individual to change those policies.'[1]

Zuma criss-crossed the country as the face of the ANC election campaign in 2009. In KwaZulu-Natal, the campaign was worryingly tribal, with the party telling its supporters that in electing the ANC and Zuma, South Africa would be getting a Zulu monarch.

There was an exodus of ministers from the cabinet after the Zuma takeover. Mosiuoa Lekota, the ANC's former chairperson who was jeered at Polokwane, as well as Aziz Pahad, Deputy President Phumzile

Mlambo-Ngcuka, Alec Erwin and Ronnie Kasrils informed the ANC they weren't available to serve in a new cabinet.

At the end of 2008, Mbhazima Shilowa, the Gauteng premier, and Lekota led an ANC breakaway party named Congress of the People, drawing several relatively high-profile ANC members and former UDF leaders, such as Gertrude Shope and Thozamile Botha. The new party performed well in the following year's general election before rapidly fading and eventually becoming a nonentity.

But Zuma's ANC was firmly in control. The NEC united behind its leader, and with Parliament taking instruction from Luthuli House the only remaining challenge was to deal with the corruption charges and to ensure Zuma was able to lead the country into the May 2009 general election before becoming president. The goal always remained the same: the political and legal system had to submit before Zuma.

On 12 January 2009, four months after Mbeki was overthrown, the Supreme Court of Appeal overturned Judge Chris Nicholson's devastating judgment. In a unanimous decision by a full bench of five judges, the court found Nicholson overreached in an 'incomprehensible' judgment. He shouldn't have, and couldn't, make any findings on political meddling, Judge Louis Harms wrote: 'It makes no sense to strike them [the findings of political meddling] out at this late stage of the proceedings. The damage has been done. This does not mean that the order of the court below should stand. Most of the allegations were not only irrelevant but they were gratuitous and based on suspicion and not on fact. The excuse for including them was unconvincing, especially in the light of the disavowal of any intention to rely on them.'[2] It meant that the charges against Zuma remained in force and he had to respond to them. Mbeki welcomed the judgment but by then it didn't matter.[3] Nicholson was the stick the ANC used to chase him from office and there was no going back.

One of Nicholson's main findings was that Zuma should have been allowed to make representations to the NPA before a final decision about charging him was taken. On 10 February 2009, his legal team forwarded written arguments to the NPA, and at a meeting ten days later it dropped a bombshell. It was in possession of secret recordings which it claimed proved the existence of a politically driven conspiracy at the NPA to charge Zuma and prevent him from becoming president.[4]

These became known as the 'spy tapes' and Zuma's lawyers, Michael Hulley and advocate Kemp J Kemp, held nothing back.

They told Mokotedi Mpshe, who had been appointed acting NDPP the previous year after Mbeki suspended Vusi Pikoli, that the tapes revealed how Scorpions boss Leonard McCarthy manipulated the timing of the charges against Zuma.[5] This, they argued, was to undermine his chances of becoming ANC president – and when he did so, McCarthy quickly moved to reinstate the charges. What was even worse, Hulley argued, was that McCarthy abused the resources of the NPA and the DSO to 'source negative intelligence' about Zuma.

If the NPA did not drop the charges, was the threat, Zuma's team would apply for a permanent stay of prosecution in the high court and would hang out the prosecuting authority's dirty linen in public. Zuma would tell the country that the NPA was involved in a political campaign, that the DSO's head was the ringleader and that the motive was to stop Zuma from becoming party leader and president.[6]

Two of Mpshe's deputies, including ANC and struggle veteran Willie Hofmeyr, were dispatched to listen to the tapes. The NPA was spooked, Mpshe especially so. On 1 April 2009, Mpshe, Hofmeyr and the senior leadership decided to give in to Zuma – but also not to tell prosecutor Billy Downer and his team until shortly before a public announcement. The next day, Downer and his team sent the umpteenth memorandum to their bosses explaining why Zuma's representations should be rejected and why they believed they would win a trial. But on the morning of 6 April, Mpshe called Downer and his team to a meeting and told them he was dropping the charges against Zuma.[7]

Mpshe then explained his decision at a press conference, including publishing details of the spy tape conversations between McCarthy and Ngcuka. Mpshe called it an 'intolerable abuse' of power and blasted McCarthy for using the DSO to manipulate Zuma's prosecution for 'extraneous' purposes.[8] But crucially, he did not say that the prosecution was tainted or that Zuma was innocent and did not have a case to answer.[9] Mpshe, Hofmeyr and others never considered the merits of the case against Zuma, arguing that the spy tapes were enough to quash the charges based on McCarthy's alleged abuse of process.

Transcripts of the tapes reveal crass and sloppy discussions between McCarthy and Ngcuka about the timing of the charges against Zuma, delivery of court papers and Mbeki's defeat at Polokwane. But they did not discuss the merits of the case against Zuma or go into detail about the investigation, the evidence or how the case was constructed.

At worst, McCarthy was guilty of negligence in sharing operational thoughts with a former NDPP – but at first blush that day it did not appear as if he and Ngcuka conspired to cook up evidence or manipulate an investigation. Even Mpshe acknowledged that the prosecution wasn't affected. As DA leader Helen Zille was to point out, the decision to charge Zuma was taken by Mpshe, not McCarthy or Ngcuka.[10] Practically, the discussions between the two men amounted to nothing.

Seven years after Zuma became a target of the arms deal investigation, six years after Ngcuka announced that he was not charging Zuma despite 'prima facie' evidence against him and four years after Mbeki fired him as deputy president, Zuma was finally cleared. His survival was the product of a coordinated, aggressive and sweeping mass political campaign driven by interest groups ranging from the ideological to the criminal. It entailed a mass-based populist offensive targeting individuals and state institutions, anchored in revolutionary rhetoric and casting the rule of law and constitutionalism as antagonistic to the transformation of post-apartheid society. And it involved the whole of the ANC's leadership, its allies and deployed cadres in institutions of state.

Julius Malema, who succeeded Mbalula as leader of the influential ANCYL in the winter of 2008, was one of the campaign's most visible agitators and attack dogs. Not only did he threaten murder and violence, he articulated what many in the ANC believed: they wanted Zuma, no matter what. 'If Jacob Zuma is corrupt, then we want him with all his corruption. We want him with all his weaknesses. If he is uneducated, then we want him as our uneducated president,' Malema said on 21 February 2009.[11]

Threats of violence became a regular theme of Malema's defence of Zuma, best exemplified by a speech at an ANCYL Youth Day rally in 2008: 'Let us make it clear now: we are prepared to die for

Zuma. Not only that, we are prepared to take up arms and kill for Zuma.'[12] He repeated this on numerous occasions and was later joined by Zwelinzima Vavi, who said: 'Because Jacob Zuma is one of us, and he is one of our leaders, for him we are prepared to lay [down] our lives and to shoot and kill.'[13]

The violent rhetoric of Malema in particular, supported by leaders such as Vavi, was never denounced by Zuma and contributed to a climate in which opposing Zuma (or advocating for the independence of the NPA) was akin to rejecting 'the revolution'. And rejecting the revolution was akin to treason.

It was a wildly successful campaign and paved the way for Zuma to be sworn in as president on 9 May 2009. Zille, in her first election campaign as DA leader, was wary of Zuma, whom she called 'a charming traditionalist'. The party's campaign centred on the dangers a Zuma presidency held for the country but its 'Stop Zuma!' slogan proved to be deeply polarising and racially divisive. 'Zuma was overwhelmingly popular among black South Africans,' she later said.[14]

The desire and compunction from many in the media and civil society to excuse Zuma's glaring shortcomings and clear criminal intent, and to advocate for a type of Zuma reset, became a notable phenomenon. Many resigned themselves to the fact that Zuma would be president and sought to rationalise this by searching for reasons why he should be given a shot at leading the country. Even then, much of this rationalising seemed illogical. At best, it was the function of a severe mischaracterisation of Zuma and a willingness to ignore what the ANC was clearly becoming. At worst, it amounted to shameless attempts by many to ingratiate themselves with the new political elite.

How big a part did the media play in downplaying the threat of the ANC and normalising Zuma? Writing in the American magazine *Newsweek*, analyst Eusebius McKaiser and American journalist Sasha Polakow-Suransky declared that 'South Africa will survive Zuma', arguing that fears of capital flight, economic mismanagement, hyperinflation and 'tyrannical government' were 'overblown'. South Africa's institutions would be able to withstand Zuma and his party's 'worst impulses' and were 'likely to resist a single, possibly corrupt, demagogic politician'.[15] It was a stunning misjudgement.

Time put Zuma on its cover, declaring 'The surprising promise of Jacob Zuma'. It said his presidency was supposed to 'spell disaster … but has started well'.[16] Zuma hadn't shied away from problems and had replaced disastrous cabinet ministers such as Manto Tshabalala-Msimang at health, wrote Alex Perry. 'The President has also expanded accountability … "We are too strong. Such support and power can intoxicate the party and lead you into believing that you know it all…" ' Zuma said.[17] It was a generous and optimistic appraisal in the face of mounting evidence to the contrary.

South African media, too, seemed keen to 'contextualise' Zuma, and much analysis was centred on perceived racism or racial slights, especially in the DA's warnings that Zuma was bad news. *Business Day* editor Peter Bruce and the newspaper's political editor, Karima Brown, roundly rejected Zille's bare-knuckle attacks on Zuma. Bruce called the 'Stop Zuma' campaign 'a major blunder' and said it was 'so disturbing I cannot even write about it'.[18]

Brown, who frolicked with ANC leaders and later wore ANC regalia at a party rally,[19] slammed the opposition parties' position that the election 'was some kind of moral referendum on issues of leadership…' And she claimed that warnings about the ANC and Zuma amounted to 'Zumaphobia', that they were 'scare tactics' and designed to 'whip up minority fears about an ANC victory'.[20]

In *Sowetan*, analyst Steven Friedman said that the DA seemed to have 'some kind of cultural problem' with Zuma.[21] Even business royalty signalled acquiescence. Raymond Ackerman, the Pick n Pay supremo, said South Africa should 'forget' about Zuma's corruption case and show some patriotism. 'Let's put all the politicking behind us. I don't care what party anyone belongs to; it is vital for us to back our president. It is what every country should do. It is important to show loyalty to one's country. It is important to get rid of cynicism, let's put that aside.'[22] Respected academic and analyst Xolela Mangcu wrote in *Business Day* that Zuma should be 'given a chance after the intolerance of Mbeki'.[23] Large swathes of the country, and many of the intelligentsia, fell into line behind Ace Magashule, the ANC strongman from the Free State, who advised that 'in church they sing they will follow Jesus wherever he goes. That's how we should be about Jacob Zuma.'[24]

❖

When ANC support in the May election declined from 69.69 per cent to 65.9 per cent, it lost the fabled two-thirds majority needed to amend the Constitution on its own. Analysts interpreted Mandela's presence at Zuma's inauguration on a cold Pretoria day as symbolic of the former president's blessing, a new beginning.

'Today, as I take this solemn oath of office as the fourth president of the Republic of South Africa, I do so deeply conscious of the responsibilities that you, the people of our country, are entrusting in me. I commit myself to the service of our nation with dedication, commitment, discipline, integrity, hard work and passion,' Zuma said, without a hint of irony, in his inaugural address. Never before or since in democratic history has someone lied so brazenly. He had no consciousness of what it meant to be the head of state of a young democracy, with a modern economy but cursed with deep poverty and inequality. And he would exhibit nothing of the dedication and integrity he so flippantly identified as the core characteristics of a president. In corrupting the government and state and abdicating his responsibilities to the Gupta family, Zuma revealed his utter lack of commitment to the rule of law. And he certainly was not known as a hard worker.

The ANC, however, was primed and ready for life under a man it painted as a victim, a martyr, the physical embodiment of the struggle against apartheid, of anti-racism and of impunity. The party and Zuma appeared bulletproof. Writing for Independent Media, staunch Zuma supporter Zweli Mkhize rejected claims of corruption against him, lauding his reputation as 'an honest and caring person, and a committed leader'. He added that Zuma's 'passion' for rural development, education and fighting crime was 'legendary'. Zuma, said Mkhize (who would later be forced to resign as minister of health after a corruption scandal), 'may turn out to be one of our finest presidents'.[25]

Zuma turned out to be not only one of the worst leaders in the democratic era but one of the worst the country has produced in any era.

19

Incompetents, fools and lawfare

ZUMA WAS NEVER A DEEP THINKER ABOUT GOVERNMENT and policy. In the years during which I sat in the press gallery in Parliament, listening to oral questions and State of the Nation addresses, it was clear that Zuma relied on his wit and charm. He was unable to engage in debate or discussions on complicated matters such as the economy, foreign policy or development. He was mostly comfortable when talking about intangibles like nation-building, reconciliation or race. He had a terrible grasp of detail and a habit of simply laughing off serious issues or matters of constitutional significance.

His first cabinet, which members of the media were extensively briefed about in the first few months of his presidency, reflected his lack of focus and his total devotion to the ANC and the alliance. Everyone was represented and everyone who supported him against Mbeki was rewarded. It was a giant executive of no fewer than 62 ministers and deputy ministers, a whole host of new ministries and departments and half a dozen renamed departments. The biggest move was his retention of Trevor Manuel, but as the newly created minister in the Presidency responsible for the National Planning Commission (NPC), a body the ANC copied straight from the Chinese Communist Party.

Manuel was the most experienced and longest-serving finance minister on the planet at the time, and greatly respected by international markets and institutions. The country's steady economic progress was put down largely to his strong leadership and the establishment of a culture of excellence at the National Treasury and SARS. Under his stewardship, the country enjoyed a period of consistent GDP growth and steady (but slow) decline in unemployment. He was by all accounts primarily responsible for establishing a culture at the Treasury that maintained strict fiscal discipline and led to the financial stability and predictability capital craved.

The Mbeki-Manuel partnership delivered the first budget surplus of the democratic era in 2007, the result of planning and deep policy debates in the cabinet and between the president and his finance minister. 'This was one of the biggest inflection points and it's not often spoken about,' says Manuel. 'In 2007, around the time of the Medium-Term Budget Policy Statement [the MTBPS, or the mini budget, tabled in October], we started arguing that we needed a surplus. We needed to run on a surplus because all the signs we were picking up suggested there were problems brewing in the global economy. The wheels would come off.

'I think in my 13 years as finance minister, perhaps those were the most intense policy discussions we ever had. First in cabinet, twice ... two virtually full days ... and then with the president just one-on-one. I was resolute about needing this surplus, and for everybody on the centre left it is viewed almost an article of faith that developing countries can't run on a surplus. The president was actually a lot more sanguine about that issue eventually, because there was a debate that we had at various points.'[1]

Manuel refers to discussions with Mbeki about Karl Marx and *Das Kapital* and his contention that public debt is bad for a developing economy. 'You know, when you debate issues with Thabo Mbeki and you discuss the classics and so on, he doesn't need a hell of a lot of persuasion. By the time we got through that discussion there had been fundamental disagreements, policy disagreements on this issue. But at 3.30, 3.45 in the morning, he said to me, "Okay, it's okay." By the time I got into the cabinet room two days later, the mood had turned and he had managed ... you see, things don't happen by accident. They need to be managed, and so he had managed the opposition, and so cabinet supported it.'[2]

In February 2008, shortly after the Polokwane putsch, Manuel delivered perhaps his most famous budget speech – but also his most difficult. He knew he didn't have a lot of support in the party and he had to explain why the Treasury was running a surplus; in effect, why the extra money was not being ploughed back into the country. Before delivering the speech, he recorded it in the SABC studios in Parliament in front of a green screen, pretending to be a weatherman delivering the news of impending storms. And in the National Assembly, with his 'weather report' on the screen, he was able to explain how South Africa planned to traverse the impending storms and gales of a global economy in crisis.

'That weather report was actually the basis for the surplus, because there was going to be a problem in the global economy. There was a build-up of debt, a build-up of derivatives, and we needed to protect ourselves. Gear was a big moment, yes, but that shift into surplus was fundamentally important. It was important because it took a lot of persuasion for the Treasury and intellectuals in the Treasury to persuade the rest of government that it was the correct thing to do at the time. But it only worked because there was a head of state who was interested, who was involved, who listened, who engaged, who took his cabinet along. I don't know that those things are happening any more.'[3]

Despite this, Manuel remained an ideological enemy of the Zuma faction, who rejected the policies and macroeconomic framework of Gear. Manuel was considered one of their prime enemies but his procedural and symbolic resignation in September 2008 made it clear to Zuma and his kitchen cabinet that they couldn't get rid of him altogether – and that they needed to replace him with someone palatable to the high priests of international finance. The solution was to move Pravin Gordhan, a trained pharmacist and major underground figure during the struggle, from SARS to the Treasury.

Analysts believed Gordhan to be a sound choice. He had turned SARS into a world-class tax collector, an organisation whose efficiency and ethos was admired and studied internationally. 'I was called to the presidential guest house on the night before the inauguration, and everyone waits in a lounge before you get called in. And when it was my turn, he [Zuma] told me, we want you to take the finance job. Whilst I understood some of the fiscal stuff, having worked with the Treasury people and being accountable to Gill Marcus and then

Manuel and [Jabu] Moleketi, I had to go in there and learn. Lesetja Kganyago was the director general at the time and you had a very experienced set of hands there. Kuben Naidoo, Andrew Donaldson and a couple of others.

'And then came the impact, literally after two months, of the financial crisis with officials telling us we're going to be R50 billion short on the revenue side. But what the Manuel era had done was reduce debt quite substantially, so debt to GDP was, what, 22 or something per cent. There was a slight surplus at the end of the 2008 financial year, so they were saying we've got space. So, there is a narrative that you see among some of the detractors which says the debt started piling up during that period. Of course it did, because globally there was this debate about austerity versus fiscal stimulation. And we chose the latter.'[4]

The move to the NPC meant Manuel's political career was effectively over. Despite the authority that supposedly cloaked the commission, it was designed as an expensive and elaborate exit vehicle for Manuel, who had to lead the legislative process to establish it, determine its mandate, convene its members and finally compile a long-term planning document. Which was then shelved by the Zuma government.

Asked whether he could have seen himself serving under Zuma as finance minister, Manuel doesn't hesitate. 'No. No.' He had to navigate a torrid period between Mbeki's removal and the 2009 election, during the short period of Kgalema Motlanthe's caretaker presidency. When the ANC finalised its lists for the election, Manuel refused to sign a nomination form. Gwede Mantashe, the ANC's secretary general, convened a meeting between the three. 'And I said there is no way that I can return as minister of finance. And I noticed how happy Zuma was. I solved a problem for them.'

Manuel clearly managed his expectations as planning minister for Zuma's government. He surrounded himself with smart people, enjoyed the intellectual nature of the NPC's work and served on various international bodies. Once he handed the report to Zuma, 'I didn't need to bother him again. I didn't need to have a lot of contact with him, so my expectations weren't let down. The NPC proposals were adopted by the ANC conference at Mangaung in 2012 and we knew we had some runway to be able to do this. But not a hell of a lot was done with implementation ...'[5]

Manuel had served under every president since 1994 and found the differences between Zuma and his predecessors stark. 'In the individual relationships between a head of state and ministers, inasmuch as the cabinet collective is important, the right of access to a president is fundamentally important in the way a government runs. And with previous presidents, I got to know their habits. If you wanted to speak to Madiba, he would say, "Can you come for breakfast at 6.45?" and it's quite basic. It's pap and coffee, but you have time to talk. There was an intimacy that worked. When you wanted to talk to Thabo it was always inevitably at night, after 9 pm, and then you could have as much time as you needed. But it was always guaranteed if it was one-on-one time that you needed, or if it was a smaller group of three ministers or something like that, that time was always available. Kgalema didn't mind talking to a minister at lunch and it was good to be able to talk and eat, and so on.[6]

'But when you pulled up at Mahlamba Ndlopfu or Genadendal [the presidential residences in Pretoria and Cape Town] when JZ was president, Lakela Kaunda [Zuma's chief of staff] would always say, "Minister, go at 8 pm this evening." And then it's like pulling into the parking lot of a mall, there are so many cars there. And you just get put in a room somewhere. You are put in a room and you have to wait your turn, and you don't actually know ... it's one of those curious things that the butlers take you and they say, "Okay, minister, the other rooms are full, go upstairs to that or that bedroom and please wait." And on two occasions I waited, and the president came and he said he's very tired. And you spent all that time waiting and you never got to talk to him.'[7]

Zuma's first cabinet, in hindsight, revealed the direction he was headed. It was brimful of the unqualified and incompetent. But they were all deeply loyal party hacks who would play key roles during the years of state capture. The cabinet was also fully representative of the vested interests that helped Zuma escape prosecution and engineered his installation as party leader and head of state. And it represented the ANC's ideological commitment to the primacy of the state in society. Tim du Plessis, editor of *Beeld* when Zuma was elected president, says: 'That impulse to have the state control everything was always there. There was a short period after he became president where some people thought he must be given a chance. If he's clever, he would appoint smart people around him. But he wasn't clever, he was crooked. And he appointed crooks around him.'[8]

With economic policy such contested terrain, Cosatu and the SACP were rewarded with two economic ministries. Ebrahim Patel, a leader of the Southern African Clothing and Textile Workers' Union, was given a new-fangled ministry called economic development, which was to 'focus on economic policymaking', Zuma said. And Rob Davies, a senior SACP member, was handed the Department of Trade and Industry. This meant that economic policy, which used to be run from the National Treasury and the Presidency, was now divided between three departments, as well as the Presidency and to a lesser extent Manuel's NPC, which also considered policy. It was an untenable situation but one that was to become a hallmark of the ANC: appoint various ministers or executives to focus on the same problem. It was to lead to policy confusion, turf wars and intractable problems.

Zuma dished out ministries like he did gifts to friends. Blade Nzimande, his loyalist SACP general secretary, was rewarded with the ministry of higher education, a new department after education was split. Incredibly, Fikile Mbalula, the fatuous former ANCYL leader who until then had shown no aptitude for anything beyond shouting into a microphone at a Zuma rally, was made deputy minister of police. His minister was Nathi Mthethwa, the party's former chief whip in Parliament, who ably helped subjugate the legislature after Polokwane. Bathabile Dlamini, the leader of the ANC Women's League and a staunch, hysterical supporter of Zuma – despite his misogynistic and problematic relationship with women – was made deputy minister of social development. She would later wreak havoc as a full minister in the same department.

Tokyo Sexwale, one of the most prominent beneficiaries of black economic empowerment (his consortium made billions of rands in

2004 when it became the empowerment partner of Absa) and a Donald Trump-like figure, was handed the renamed Department of Human Settlements (formerly housing). Yunus Carrim, the Scorpions' executioner, also received his just deserts. He was appointed deputy minister to Sicelo Shiceka in the Department of Cooperative Governance and Traditional Affairs, the former department of local government. Malusi Gigaba, Mbalula's flamboyant and slippery predecessor as ANCYL president, was elevated to deputy minister of home affairs.[9] 'We reiterate that we will not tolerate laziness and incompetence, and that we will emphasise excellence and achievement from the cabinet and the public service,' Zuma said as he announced his executive. 'With these objectives in mind, I am confident that the new structure of government will enable the state machinery to speed up service delivery.'[10]

Gordhan says he was largely left alone to run the country's financial affairs between 2009 and 2014. Growth slowed, recovered slightly to 3 per cent 'and then deteriorated again, never to recover. But the 2009 to 2014 period was also one where one began to become aware of state corruption in provinces. We intervened in Limpopo, invoking Section 100 of the Constitution [which gives the national government control over a provincial government], and the guys still haven't forgiven us for that. There was a different Section 100 applied to the Free State, particularly in relation to the R2 billion or R3 billion road contract that they were messing up. I remember going to cabinet any number of times talking about how much the public sector was paying for bottled water, or computers, or whatever the case might be. And I was frank in some of those situations, saying that the population will pick up that these kinds of corrupt activities are taking place. But it was nothing on the scale of the Guptas.'

Another emerging theme from Zuma's first appointments was the securitisation and further politicisation of the state. Being an old spy and carrying the scars of his battle against Mbeki, Zuma understood that he needed to control four departments without any threat of resistance or independence: intelligence, justice, police and defence.

The National Intelligence Agency became the State Security Agency (SSA) and Siyabonga Cwele became the minister of state security. The change in name also entailed a change in mandate to that of providing security to the state, instead of providing intelligence information to the government of the day. The SSA later became one of the most corrupted government institutions, totally beholden to ANC politics and factional strife, with spies, networks, money and resources pushed into the service of Zuma and the party.

The Department of Justice, which oversaw the NPA, became the province of party luminary Jeff Radebe, who kept a tight leash on the prosecuting authority. Lindiwe Sisulu, daughter of Walter, a gentleman of the struggle, became minister of defence and military veterans, but she was nothing like her illustrious father. She was an unashamed disciple of Zuma, notorious for her expensive taste in clothes and the antagonistic way she submitted herself to parliamentary oversight. Even ANC MPs despised the way she saw the SANDF as her personal plaything and treated lawmakers with derision.

From the start, Zuma made sure he had direct control over the security services, with intelligence and the prosecuting authority being key to his survival. He wanted to know who was plotting against him and he wanted to stay out of jail. On 25 November 2009, he appointed Menzi Simelane as the new NDPP and head of the NPA. A former director general of justice, he replaced Mokotedi Mpshe, who acted in the position when Vusi Pikoli was suspended and eventually removed. While Simelane was clearly unfit for office, his lack of honesty and obvious subservience to Zuma made him the perfect candidate for the new president.

In a report by Frene Ginwala, the former speaker of Parliament who led a commission of inquiry into Pikoli's fitness to hold office, Simelane was excoriated as dishonest and conniving, having made up evidence against Pikoli and been driven by 'personal issues'. Much of his oral testimony, she said, 'I found in many respects to be inaccurate or without any basis in fact and law. He was forced to concede during cross-examination that the allegations he made against Adv Pikoli were without foundation.'[11] Simelane did Zuma's bidding at the Ginwala commission and did all he could to sink Pikoli. She saw through the ruse and said so. But despite the Public Service Commission recommending that Simelane should face a disciplinary hearing, Radebe declared him ready for deployment and Zuma made it official.

Simelane's appointment set the ANC's pattern of deployment under Zuma. It sought individuals who were loyal to the party above all else, and their primary task was to safeguard the interests of the party and individuals such as Zuma. Whereas under Mbeki and Mandela, the ANC feigned fealty to the Constitution, due process and rationality, it jettisoned this almost completely during the Zuma era. Appointments, or deployments, were glibly made in the obvious interest of Zuma, his faction or the party. Zille says she had to fight hard after Zuma's election to convince her party that challenging decisions by the ANC-in-government was a sound tactic. The DA, she said, went to court repeatedly and at great cost to prevent state capture, 'the practice of powerful politicians turning supposedly independent institutions of state into political instruments to pursue their own agendas, protecting their allies, prosecuting their enemies and enriching themselves.'[12]

This strategy became known as 'lawfare', a programme of serial litigation by the DA and civil society organisations such as retired Justice Johann Kriegler's Freedom Under Law, the Helen Suzman Foundation and others. They sought to challenge decisions by the government and the state in the absence of proper parliamentary oversight and the dramatic weakening of institutions. 'We had underestimated the extent of this rush towards litigation. The degradation of state institutions began relatively slowly. But by the end of the decade, a parallel state with compromised heads of security and law enforcement agencies, including the revenue service, was revealed,' Judge Dennis Davis and advocate Michelle le Roux wrote later.[13] Lawfare was not ideal because it showed how constitutional systems of governance and accountability could fail if bad actors such as Zuma and the ANC purposefully set out to subvert it. 'Vigorous contests in court' came to define the Zuma era.[14]

The DA immediately challenged Simelane's appointment in the Pretoria high court. He had shown that he neither 'understood nor respected' the principle of prosecutorial independence, Zille said. 'We believe advocate Simelane is not a fit and proper person. He does not believe in the independence of the judiciary. It [the NPA] will merely become an extension of the ANC.'[15] The Simelane saga was one of the first cases of lawfare during the Zuma era. It took more than two years for the DA to eject Simelane from office in a battle that went from the high court to the Supreme Court of Appeal and finally the Constitutional Court. The apex court set aside Simelane's appointment by Zuma and agreed with the appeals court that it was 'irrational' and 'unconstitutional'.[16] While in office, he wreaked havoc. He stopped the seizure of assets suspected of being the proceeds of arms deal bribes, one of the last criminal investigations into the scam;[17] and he attempted to restructure the NPA and disband the Specialised Commercial Crime Unit, one of the authority's most successful units after the dissolution of the DSO.[18]

After Simelane's court-enforced exit, Zuma moved advocate Nomgcobo Jiba into the position of acting NPA head. Vindictive and scheming, Jiba had been charged internally with dishonesty, unprofessional conduct and bringing the NPA into disrepute. She was suspended in 2007 for 'what appeared to be a personal and political vendetta' against a colleague, advocate Gerrie Nel, who investigated disgraced police chief Jackie Selebi. Like Simelane, she proceeded to do significant damage to the NPA, and all seemingly in service of the president and his party. During her years as acting NDPP and deputy, the organisation became toxic with racial division and faction fighting, deeply politicised and wholly subservient to the interests of Zuma.

The NPA was answerable to his government, Zuma said: 'The NPA reports to government; it's not a thing flying in the sky on its own – unconnected – and there are decisions ... that have implications and that's why we have a department [of justice].' Command and control over prosecutions was what Zuma wanted, and that's exactly what he got.

20
Creeping authoritarianism

MY COLLEAGUE LIZEL STEENKAMP AND I WERE USHERED into President Jacob Zuma's outer office at Tuynhuys in Cape Town on a sweltering February afternoon in 2011, shortly after he delivered his third State of the Nation address to a joint sitting of Parliament. We had been granted an interview with the president, and Zizi Kodwa, the former ANCYL spokesperson then seconded to the Presidency, was tasked to chaperone us.

It was the same office where I had an informal tête-à-tête with Thabo Mbeki some years before but the room looked much different. The bookshelves behind the desk were empty and old oil paintings and Africana on the walls had been replaced by black-and-white images by the veteran press photographer Alf Kumalo. Zuma was approaching the halfway stage of his term of office as head of state and the ANC was preparing to elect new leaders the following year. Zuma remained locked in battle with the DA about the NPA decision to drop corruption charges against him. He was opposing a high court application to review the decision and to get access to the record of the NPA's decision-making process. The ANC had also become increasingly divided, chiefly because of Julius Malema and his youth league's militancy at the party's midterm conference, the NGC, the previous year.

The ANCYL, with the backing of the SACP and Cosatu, had started to push the ANC towards nationalisation, which Malema and his cohorts believed held the key to economic freedom for the poor and downtrodden. Debate raged about the repercussions should it become ANC policy, and the consequences for the country if mining and banking assets were seized. The party under Zuma, driven by frustration with a free media exposing corruption and dysfunction, felt increasingly threatened. At the NGC in Durban the party held fierce discussions about a so-called media appeals tribunal, a body to be regulated by Parliament (in effect, politicians) and which would hold journalists and the media accountable. In effect, the ANC wanted to license journalists, something completely at odds with the Constitution. The ANC was not comfortable with the media, just like it detested a strong opposition calling out poor performance in Parliament.

Zuma's first term of office saw a range of bills introduced that sought to continue the quest for dominance of the 'Polokwane victors'.[1] After an amendment to the Broadcasting Act in 2008, which enabled Parliament to fire the SABC board, Zuma's government introduced a Broadcasting Amendment Bill that appeared to overhaul the SABC's operations but in fact enabled the state to interfere with the broadcaster's mandate. Activists warned it could neuter media freedom and give politicians enormous influence.[2]

But controlling the SABC was one thing; independent media was something altogether different. In March 2010, new minister of state security Siyabonga Cwele tabled the Protection of State Information Bill. A previous version of the bill had been withdrawn under Mbeki after civil society complained that it would have serious repercussions for media freedom. But the Zuma government's redrafted version doubled down, wanting to classify almost everything it deemed in the interests of national security and introduce heavy punishment if the law was broken. This was ostensibly to negate the influence of 'information peddlers' and threats of espionage[3] but the real targets were whistleblowers and the media. Zuma's ANC wanted control even in areas of society that cadre deployment was unable to reach.

The judiciary was another target. In an interview with Independent Media in 2009, Zuma exhibited his authoritarian impulses – and his lack of insight into how the legal system works – when he spoke with derision of the Constitutional Court: 'If I look at the chief justice of the Constitutional Court, that is the ultimate authority, which I think we need to look at ... because I don't think we should have people who are almost like God in a democracy ... you can have a judge of whatever level making a judgment [and] and other judges ... saying it was wrong ... And therefore we have to look at it in a democratic setting; how do you avoid that?'[4]

Across Zuma's whole period of office, his government regularly lost in the courts – and the president and his party hated the judiciary for it. In 2011 alone, the Polokwane victors suffered significant setbacks as the courts ruled against ANC factional interests, including a court challenge to ensure the independence of the Hawks, the new police unit that replaced the Scorpions; a decision that enabled the investigation into delinquent Western Cape Judge President John Hlophe to continue; the Supreme Court's judgment on Menzi Simelane; and its decision to hear an appeal in the Zuma corruption matter.[5]

In November 2011, the cabinet announced it planned an 'assessment' of the Constitutional Court,[6] and in an interview the following year Zuma said: 'We want to review the [Constitutional Court's] powers. It is after experience that some of the decisions are not decisions that every other judge agrees with ... You will find that the dissenting [judgment] has more logic than the one that enjoyed the majority. What do you do in that case?' Ominously – and tellingly – he added: 'Judges are influenced by you guys [the media].'[7]

As we walked into Zuma's outer office in Tuynhuys for the February 2011 interview, there was nothing obviously devious or ominous about the president. Surrounded by a host of assistants and aides, Zuma was welcoming and gregarious, urging us to sit wherever we wanted and offering drinks. There was no sign of a corrupted president who was systematically re-engineering the state to his and his party's benefit. Although benign on the surface, the interview gave deep insight into Zuma's statist and dangerous impulses. The president was clearly a wounded man who harboured deep resentment.

He was not prepared to denounce the loud calls for nationalisation, arguing that it was simply a debate taking place in the governing party. 'How do we wipe it off the table? We have to find ways to consider it, we can't wish it away,' he said.[8] He explained that, even though during the transition to democracy the ANC agreed that nationalisation was not a workable policy in a free market system, many in the party believed it was the answer to poverty and inequality. 'The outcome of this debate must be founded on realities, not simply on what people feel about the matter.' And he wasn't concerned about the impact it was having on the economy, dismissing market reaction. The debate shouldn't spook investors, he said. 'They must do what they always do: invest!'[9]

He remained adamant that the South African Democratic Teachers' Union (Sadtu), a close ally severely criticised for its members' poor performance, would not be censured despite the destructive effect it was having on the education of millions of children. 'You can't do that [ban unions from the education sector]. It would be autocratic. The question is rather: how do you manage this space in a democracy where everyone is free to do what they want?'

But it was the idea of limits on media freedom that elicited the most passion from Zuma: 'The way in which you [the media] interpret your rights is part of the problem we have with you, isn't that so? How far do your rights to express opinions about others go while we also have the right to privacy? We must draw a line so that my rights are acknowledged and respected. It is too important.'[10] He was supportive of the ANC's proposal for a statutory media appeals tribunal. 'Everything is regulated in some form or another. Even Parliament is regulated. In fact, there is nothing that is not regulated.'[11]

Zuma did not have a philosophy or ideology guiding him. Mandela had a set of principles and beliefs, while Mbeki was an unabashed ideologue. Zuma had no big plans and no big ideas. He was in it for himself first, and for the ANC. Yes, he adhered to the ANC's central policy positions like those articulated in Strategy and Tactics and the tenets of the National Democratic Revolution. But to him, it was mostly gobbledygook. Zuma wanted power, access and control of law enforcement – principally to thwart the arms deal investigation.

His government's actions in the initial stages of his presidency did, however, confirm fears that many who normalised him in 2008 and 2009 tried to downplay as 'overblown'. After the ANC took full control of the state after the implementation of its doctrine of cadre deployment and prime loyalty to the party in 1997 and 1998, it handed this machine to Zuma. And he supercharged the network of cadres, inserting his people everywhere.

The president, as many knew, was bereft of hard and fast ideals or morals – except self-interest. And it shone through during that interview in Tuynhuys. He wasn't perturbed in the slightest by the nonsensical and damaging calls for nationalisation; what mattered to him was that it gave Malema the platform he craved, and since the ANCYL leader was one of his strongest supporters, that was enough. It was the same with Sadtu, whose foray into politics became its main preoccupation. Sadtu has been a blight on the education landscape for years, destroying children's chances of better lives with politicking and a refusal to hold its members accountable. Again, Zuma was non-committal, and if anything declared himself a supporter. No surprises that the union, one of the biggest Cosatu affiliates, was an ardent Zuma ally.

It was also abundantly clear that if he could, he would come down hard on press freedom, freedom of speech and the media in general. Investigative journalists had been recording his every doubtful move since he was identified as a person of interest in the arms deal. And since then, through his rape trial, his comments about HIV and Aids, the news that he impregnated the young daughter of Orlando Pirates chairperson Irvin Khoza and the ongoing corruption investigation, the media had interrogated him. Zuma, who never deviated from his persona as a tribal chief and was never able make the transition to a democrat and a constitutionalist, furiously rejected the scrutiny. If he believed in anything, then, it was in party-led state control over everything, including the judiciary, the media and Parliament.

Zuma was re-elected ANC president at the party's elective conference in Mangaung in December 2012. He beat off a challenge from Kgalema Motlanthe, his deputy, who launched a symbolic campaign despite the overwhelming odds against him. Even though the ANC's grip on the state had never been stronger, the demons of factionalism and powermongering unleashed by the Zuma-Mbeki conflict roamed freely in the organisation. Internal conflicts often spilt into the public environment, with assassinations in KwaZulu-Natal spiking as ANC councillors vied for elected positions.[12]

Malema established himself as part of a new breed of ANC politicians, the so-called 'tenderpreneurs', who used their proximity to the governing party and the state to extract rent from the public sector. Tenderpreneurs seemed rampant as the public sector fell prey to a network of patronage, all seemingly connected to the ANC. Beyond his allegedly criminal dealings (SARS also launched an investigation into his tax affairs), Malema became increasingly problematic for the ANC leadership, who did not take kindly to his violent rhetoric, insulting language and anti-constitutional rants. He was suspended from the party in 2012 and expelled the following year.

Malema and his party, the Economic Freedom Fighters (EFF), germinated in the bosom of Luthuli House. The ANC tolerated Malema and his stormtroopers' outlandish threats and violence for years and the EFF became a quasi-fascist, ethno-nationalist formation, drenched in militarism and spouting anti-democratic and anti-constitutional rhetoric. Malema, who once declared that he would 'die for Zuma', became one of the president's avowed enemies and the EFF a vehicle for his political entrepreneurship and rage.

Even though Zuma won a clean victory at Mangaung – his whole leadership team was elected without shots being fired – there was increased unhappiness in some quarters about the direction the party and the country was headed. Cosatu's Zwelinzima Vavi, who once also declared he would lay down his life in defence of Zuma, was the first to break ranks when he warned about the dangers of 'tenderpreneurism' and of the government turning into a 'predatory elite'. 'If the current trajectory continues, the entire state and society will be up for sale to the highest bidder,' he said.[13] The country's political direction was subjected to 'wild zigzagging' and a 'powerful, corrupt, predatory elite combined with a conservative populist agenda to harness the ANC to advance their interests' had emerged under Zuma.[14]

What was plain to observers outside the party was starting to become visible to some on the inside. Poor leadership, worsening governance, a rise in crime and corruption, and policy malaise were suppressing progress, growth and development. Motlanthe's challenge was a direct function of unease in some quarters with the president's erratic behaviour and poor grasp of policy. Motlanthe and others did not approve of the country's direction under Zuma's leadership and the president was under increasing pressure.

The Supreme Court of Appeal ordered the NPA to give the DA all records on the decision to drop corruption charges against Zuma.[15] And the *Mail & Guardian* revealed that his multimillion-rand homestead at Nkandla, KwaZulu-Natal, was being built with public money – even though he had told Parliament it was financed by his family.[16] A blatant lie. He also exacerbated the country's already tight fiscal position after the 2008–2009 global financial crisis when he 'bought off' opposition in the unions with exorbitant and unaffordable wage increases for teachers, health workers and the public service in 2010.[17]

There were other indicators of South Africa's slide towards kleptocracy. From about 2011, a flurry of media reports appeared about the Gupta family and their close relationship with Zuma. It seemed that the family, who launched an ANC- and Zuma-aligned newspaper, *The New Age*, in 2010, had an inordinate amount of influence on the president and his executive. Zuma was transforming the ANC into an inept government, a party driven by greed and criminality, and presiding over the rise of a vast network of resource extraction.

Pravin Gordhan, the finance minister, followed events surrounding Nkandla and the emerging Gupta family but did not get into the weeds of the matter: 'I didn't get into the detail because there were other ministers – like the ministers of police and public works – who were dealing with it. I did my job. And the worst manifestations [of Zuma's corruption] weren't yet clear.'[18]

PART FOUR
DESTRUCTION

21
The accomplice

CYRIL RAMAPHOSA MADE A SPECTACULAR RETURN to frontline politics at the ANC's elective conference in Mangaung in December 2012 when he was catapulted into position as the party's deputy president. Although he had been out of mainstream politics for 16 years, he remained an ANC loyalist and had stayed in touch with the tribulations of the organisation during the Mbeki and Zuma eras. His election was a boon for Zuma, whose poor first term as party leader meant he needed a credible and respectable second-in-command. Ramaphosa fit the bill perfectly.

Since leading the ANC negotiating team during the transition, Ramaphosa had quietly harboured ambitions for high office. Despite his disappointment when Mbeki was elevated to the deputy presidency in 1994 and eventually the presidency, Ramaphosa never abandoned his dream. He remained popular and was elected to the NEC at party elective conferences in Mahikeng, Stellenbosch and Polokwane.

His reintroduction into politics came in 2010 when he was appointed Manuel's deputy at the National Planning Commission, the body ostensibly tasked with plotting South Africa's long-term strategic future. After the Polokwane putsch he was elected chair of the NEC disciplinary appeals committee that paved the way for Julius Malema's expulsion from the party. His business successes – as one of the ANC's senior deployees in the private sector, he became a billionaire – informed his image. He was seen as someone who understood private enterprise and was respected by capital and the market. That meant his election as ANC deputy president was useful to the Zuma leadership team, who were perceived to be hostile to the private sector while maintaining and encouraging an almost intemperate devotion to the ANC.

Ramaphosa would not have been elected without the spadework of the faction that orchestrated his addition to the Zuma slate before Mangaung. This happened despite the uproar over the Marikana massacre four months earlier, when 34 mineworkers were shot dead by police after violence erupted at platinum miner Lonmin's operations near Brits in North West. Ramaphosa was a director and shareholder of Lonmin and lobbied the government vigorously to intervene when violence during an illegal strike spiralled out of control. His enemies, notably Malema, accused him of siding with the capitalists against the workers, and many considered him an accomplice in the killings. But slate politics was powerful and criticism of his role at Marikana couldn't prevent his election.

While he was finding his way back into politics, Ramaphosa played the role of unctuous and often gushing deputy to Zuma with conviction. Because he was not yet deputy president at the Union Buildings – Kgalema Motlanthe occupied that position until the 2014 election – his role was limited to organisational matters and he took to it with gusto. 'Talk time is over, we want action and action man Jacob Zuma is going to make sure that this country moves forward. Right now, our "Mr Action", Jacob Zuma, is very committed,' he told an ANC cadres forum weeks after the Mangaung conference.[1] Describing Zuma shortly after his election as a 'strong president', Ramaphosa said he 'has led from the front. What he has done that is most outstanding and prominent in my mind is delivering to the nation the NDP [National Development Plan].'[2] He also praised his leader's 'political maturity' in being able to work with those who opposed him at Mangaung while still striving for party unity – something Zuma, Ramaphosa, Gwede Mantashe and others continued to prize above everything else. 'The sermon of unity will continue. The seeds were long planted. And President Zuma continues watering the tree of unity.'[3]

With his election as deputy president, Ramaphosa became

chairperson of the deployment committee and held that position for the next five years. The committee was one of the most important and powerful bodies in the organisation because it oversaw almost every senior government and state appointment. And Ramaphosa presided over it during the most destructive period in democratic South Africa's history. He was assisted in his duties by 15 other NEC members, as well as Jessie Duarte, the venal deputy secretary general. In achieving ANC hegemony over society, theirs was the most important job in the party. But they proved to be toxic to the interests of the country.

The committee's job was to execute the ANC's cadre deployment policy, which said 'key centres' of authority fell within its purview. These included the cabinet, the entire civil service, premiers and provincial governments, legislatures, state-owned enterprises, independent statutory commissions and bodies, agencies, boards, institutes, ambassadorial appointments and international organisations and institutions.[4]

The policy was introduced to 'deepen the hold of the liberation movement over the levers of the state'[5] and its success enabled Zuma and the ANC to dispatch legions of party apparatchiks – some criminal, many incompetent – to every outpost. It had a profoundly destructive effect at every level of government, with no state body, institution or agency untouched. Although the decline in the quality of the public service began under Mbeki's large-scale infusion of party automatons into the public sector, the Zuma era saw the widespread destruction and collapse of work ethic, performance, culture, governance and a shared sense of civic duty.

Under Mbeki there was a deliberate project of transformation to achieve certain ideological goals. But under Zuma, supported by party structures such as the NEC, the NWC, the top six leaders and the deployment committee, the ANC merged criminal interests and patronage networks with the state it controlled. That led to systemic malfunctions in service delivery across the state and rampant corruption and rent-seeking.

When he took over the deployment committee, Ramaphosa heaped praise on Zuma, saying that while Mandela 'delivered freedom' and

Mbeki 'stabilised' the country, 'Zuma has actually delivered a blueprint for the future.' He was all in and said he would do his damnedest to ensure the president's plans succeeded: 'I am also going to play a key role in helping that plan to be implemented. I don't think it is too ambitious. It is doable because it has the levers that we can put our hands on and make sure that it is implemented, and what that plan will spawn is economic growth, job creation, and it will also help in so far as economic empowerment is concerned.

'We need to go for renewal and to this end we have developed the decade of the cadre. The decade of the cadre also means that we have got to inculcate the most outstanding values and ethics among the members of the ANC. The education that they will be exposed to during this period is meant to chisel out precisely all those very bad tendencies. I know it is going to happen. We are going to get some of the best attributes coming through from our cadres, who will have total commitment to their service of South Africa. I believe we can do it.'[6] And what a decade the cadres proceeded to have with Zuma and Ramaphosa in charge.

The ANC and its deployment committee regularly and rapidly made significant changes to the executive leadership teams and boards of parastatals such as Eskom, Transnet, the Passenger Rail Agency of South Africa (Prasa) and the SABC. These changes – including appointing chief executive officers and chief operating officers – were key to capturing the institutions because they put governance in the hands of individuals beholden to the Guptas or other criminal networks bent on extracting as much money as possible.

The ANC also decapitated the leadership of SARS and gutted its ability to combat organised crime, disbanding efficient anti-corruption units, introducing a culture of internal persecution, removing experienced professionals from their jobs and compromising the state's ability to collect revenue. The party leadership's role in destroying SARS was nothing short of criminal. The same pattern repeated itself at the NPA, which Zuma kept under his heel in his eternal quest to evade accountability for corruption and fraud. Zuma, the ANC and Ramaphosa's deployment committee made a series of appointments to ensure the NPA remained pliant and dormant. Three times Zuma appointed an NDPP and three times the court found the appointments to be irregular and unconstitutional. The ANC simply did not stick to principle and the law.

But the deployment committee went even further, considering judgeships and involving itself in judicial appointments, which meant certain appointments to the bench were the direct result of extra-constitutional processes driven by factional interests at Luthuli House.[7] Ministers went to the deployment committee to motivate for senior appointments in the civil service and were often sent packing if Ramaphosa's team was unhappy with the proposed candidate. The committee always made sure its candidate was eventually appointed and insisted that it should be notified first whenever senior positions were about to be vacated or advertised.[8] The party 'is where the power resides', Ramaphosa said.[9]

Ramaphosa's arrival on the sixth floor of Luthuli House, where the senior leadership had offices, coincided with the ANC abandoning all pretence to good governance. The organisation, with Mantashe in his second term as secretary general, was in thrall to Zuma, who became completely beholden to the Guptas. The ANC also reprised its reprehensible tactic of attacking the credibility of constitutional bodies as an investigation by the Public Protector into Zuma's Nkandla homestead was progressing, launching vile and personal attacks on the incumbent, advocate Thuli Madonsela. It was the age of madness.

But Ramaphosa seemed oblivious to what was happening, even as 'hundreds' of newspaper articles appeared detailing the metastasis of the Guptas' sprawling criminal network in the government and state.[10] There were stories about government contracts, pressure on civil servants to grant tenders, attempts to take over mining operations. For Ramaphosa 'there were signs', he said – but the ANC didn't act.[11]

Mantashe's response was perhaps the most telling. During his decade as secretary general, no one did more to protect Zuma and defend the ANC in the face of clear criminality and corruption. Alongside Zuma and Ramaphosa, Mantashe is responsible for the misrule and collapse the country has experienced since 2007. When investigative journalists started publishing tales of ANC corruption and the Guptas' state capture network, he dismissed them out of hand. The ANC, he said, analysed the reports and concluded they were 'racist'.[12] That was the reason why multiple – and credible, the state capture commission later found – reports were ignored by Mantashe. Amid unfolding anarchy in the country and party, with Zuma and his handlers in the middle, Mantashe said the party leader had nothing to answer for. 'Did the president take us into his confidence about the relationship between [him] and the Gupta family? I'm not sure if that is necessary,' he told browbeaten journalists.[13]

The origin of state capture and the Guptas' role in it has been widely traversed and analysed but it is worth noting that when Ramaphosa returned to politics, the family and their activities were already the subject of much scrutiny. In August 2011, while Ramaphosa served on the NEC, a meeting was devoted to discussing the role the Guptas played in party and government affairs and the impact it had on the organisation. It was at that meeting that Fikile Mbalula made a tearful statement that he had to hear from one of the Gupta brothers about his imminent promotion to minister. According to Trevor Manuel, who was minister in the Presidency at the time, Mbalula said he was summoned to the Gupta compound to be congratulated on his imminent posting. This means that Mbalula, too, had an existing and prior relationship with the Guptas, and according to Manuel it proved Zuma had abdicated his responsibilities to the Guptas.[14] What was worse was Zuma's unfazed reaction. Mbalula's 'emotional outburst' made no impact on the president.[15] It didn't bother Ramaphosa either, although some in the NEC were 'startled'. Nothing was done about the matter and life went on as normal.[16]

The Guptas' involvement with the ANC and Zuma started even before the Polokwane conference. They were introduced to the party by Mbeki confidant Essop Pahad, and before the conference ANC leadership hopeful Tokyo Sexwale and businessman Lazarus Zim went into business with the family.[17] The Guptas made their private jet available to Zuma during his campaign and Sahara Computers, one of their companies, sponsored an internet cafe at the conference.[18] Later, they appointed Zuma's twins, Duduzane and Duduzile, to the board of one of their companies, investigative journalist Pieter-Louis Myburgh says in his audit of the family empire, *The Republic of Gupta*.

He details how the family quickly branched out into mining, scoring a series of lucrative deals. An SSA intelligence report was circulated on their influence on the appointment of ministers and the awarding of government tenders, but it was suppressed when three senior intelligence officials were forced out in 2011. All at the behest of Zuma.

Much of this, at the time, was being reported on by investigative journalists and the Sunday newspapers but it didn't stop the Guptas flaunting their influence and proximity to power through their loss-making media properties, *The New Age* newspaper and ANN7 television news channel. Those outfits were unapologetic about their affiliation: they were unabashed Zuma supporters, unflinchingly took the ANC line and were furiously opposed to so-called 'white monopoly capital' and 'the Stellenbosch mafia' who were supposedly running the country.

But the landing at Waterkloof air base on 30 April 2013 registered off the charts as far as audacity and a sense of power and entitlement by the Guptas was concerned. The landing of a Jet Airways Airbus A330-200 that disgorged more than 300 passengers for a garish Sun City wedding left the ANC seemingly aghast. Mantashe issued a strong statement saying the ANC 'demands' an explanation: 'The African National Congress will never rest where there is any indication that all and sundry may be permitted to undermine the republic, its citizens and its borders.'[19] Zuma offered no response. Pravin Gordhan says 'many ministers' received invitations to the wedding: 'It came in a fancy box, if I'm not mistaken. By then the rumours about the Guptas were flying and we said, "Be careful, keep your distance." I just said I'm not going, end of story. A number of cabinet colleagues didn't go … but some did.'[20]

A subsequent investigation by the SANDF identified Bruce Koloane, chief of state protocol at the international relations ministry, and an air force officer, Colonel Christine Anderson, as the culprits who allowed the Gupta plane to land at Waterkloof. But, as Koloane and Anderson would later argue, the pressure to allow the landing came from 'Number One' – and colloquially, 'Number One' was the president. Koloane was rewarded with an ambassadorship. Anderson resigned.

Zuma, rightly, has been identified as the most important enabler, facilitator and participant in the state capture saga. He was, after all, the deeply compromised head of state (remember his corrupt relationship with Shaik) who eagerly opened the gates of the Union Buildings for the Guptas. But it was the ANC's culture, ethos and structures that allowed it to happen. Not only did the party allow it, it also encouraged the Guptas and a myriad of other networks of corruption to take root and flourish. And in this, Ramaphosa and Mantashe played central roles: Ramaphosa as head of the deployment committee that sanctioned innumerable placements, deployments and appointments; and Mantashe as the powerful secretary general who defended his party with bombast and bent logic.

The ANC allowed misrule and criminality to be normalised after the Polokwane moment. Its extended organisational structure in the state was abused to deploy corrupt cadres into positions of influence and authority. After the Mangaung party conference, a marked decline in ethics and morals, compounded by the weakening of law enforcement and a growing sense of impunity, opened the floodgates for mass corruption and the destruction of governance on an unprecedented scale.

22
Covering for corruption

WHAT DID CYRIL RAMAPHOSA THINK when he stepped into the deputy president's office suite at the Union Buildings in Pretoria on 25 May 2014, shortly after the election? The ANC had been in power for 20 years but it was clear to anyone with a beating heart that the Zuma presidency was headed for abject disaster. Scandal upon scandal had unfolded over the previous couple of years and the ANC had become a staffing agency for party kleptocrats and corrupt cadres. Ramaphosa's arrival at the top table of ANC politics in 2012 coincided with the unfolding drama of Nkandla, and by the time he was deployed to the government two years later the controversy had engulfed the party.

Under the erratic leadership of Zuma's government and an ANC engineering the state to serve its own sectarian needs, South Africa was starting to show significant signs of strain. Real GDP growth slowed markedly from 2014 onwards, compared to the halcyon days of Manuel and Mbeki when it grew by 5 per cent for three consecutive years.[1] After the global financial crisis in 2008, established macroeconomic policies and sound fiscal and monetary management helped the country weather the storm.

But by 2014, GDP growth had collapsed to 1.7 per cent, followed by 1.3 per cent in 2015 and a lamentable 0.3 per cent in 2016.[2] Unemployment, always stubbornly high, started its upward march from 2008's 22.6 per cent to reach 25.5 per cent in 2014.[3] In 2007, before the Polokwane putsch, a dollar was worth R7.05. In 2014, it cost

R10.84.[4] Under Manuel, the country ran a budget surplus in 2006–2007 and 2007–2008, but by 2014–2015 increased spending, notably on higher public sector wages, opened a budget deficit of 4.5 per cent. Manuel helped to reduce government debt from almost 50 per cent of GDP shortly after the fall of apartheid to 26 per cent in 2008–2009. But by 2014–2015 it had ballooned to 46.6 per cent.[5] The country was not in good shape and Zuma and his party were determinedly steering it in the wrong direction.

So, what was Ramaphosa thinking? He desperately wanted to be president, and the bitterness of his rejection by party elders before the 1994 election never quite left him. Despite this, he remained as loyal a cadre as anyone, as his continued presence on the ANC NEC testifies. And when Zuma's people came calling in 2012, he was ready. It surely played on his mind that ANC tradition dictates that the deputy eventually succeeds the president, and that his dream of becoming head of state was within his grasp. He just had to grin and bear the remaining period of Zuma destruction and try to avoid the shrapnel.

And that, it seems, is exactly what Ramaphosa decided to do. He attached his name to Zuma's as deputy party leader, lending credibility to the ANC, then proceeded to prop up the Guptas' most important surrogate. Ramaphosa never planned to, and never did, take any principled position in direct contradiction and opposition to Zuma.

Pravin Gordhan was removed as finance minister after the election, and the way it was done showed the contempt in which Zuma held him: 'I was kept waiting in the lounge at the presidential guest house until four or five in the morning after we were called there the previous evening. It was just Lindiwe Sisulu and I who were left. He had to decide where the hell I would go. And he told me that he was sending me to local government, I can go and have fun there. But I was surprised at being moved. I think, however, that by that time the Gupta operation had started and I was an obstruction to them. My replacement, Nhlanhla Nene, met the Guptas ten times … sorry, I don't forgive him for that. I was his minister and he never told me.'[6]

In March 2014, six weeks before the election, Public Protector Thuli Madonsela released her report into the Zuma homestead at Nkandla – and it was damning. She found that Zuma benefited unduly from multimillion-rand upgrades funded by the taxpayer and contravened the Constitution and the executive ethics code by not taking reasonable steps to stop irregular expenditure on his private residence; his personal architect was even employed on the project. The visitor centre, swimming pool, extensive paving, cattle kraal and chicken run were clearly not security upgrades and part of the cost had to be repaid to the state, the report found.

If the Nkandla issue had by then turned into a farce, it would become a tragedy in subsequent years. Zuma had surrounded himself with a praetorian guard of toadies – ANC deployees who slavishly defended him against all criticism and all logic. Apart from Gwede Mantashe, surely the most hard-baked party ideologue of them all, he had a range of ministers and parliamentarians who had no qualms about defending the indefensible. Ministers such as Thulas Nxesi (public works), Jeff Radebe (justice) and Nathi Nhleko (police) and MPs including Mathole Motshekga and Cedric Frolick cast their dignity aside and became frothing crusaders in the cause of Zuma.

And in the two years after Ramaphosa became deputy party leader, the ANC mounted an unprecedented assault on the office of the Public Protector and its incumbent that represented a clear attack on the constitutional order. Mantashe led the charge, repeatedly attacking Madonsela's reputation and credibility and undermining the authority of the Public Protector. In the months before the final report was released – and as snippets of the preliminary document distributed to affected parties were leaked – Mantashe accused her of inserting herself into the political process, finding the innocent Zuma guilty in the court of public opinion and playing a political game.[7] 'It is a political report and we will treat it as such,' he said shortly before it was released.[8]

The vitriol was stepped up after the report's release. Mantashe accused Madonsela of interfering in the general election by giving 'ammunition' to the opposition.[9] The ANCYL 'noted' the report 'with sheer disgust', called it a 'kangaroo court' and said Madonsela 'compromised herself to the bone'. The ANC chief whip in Parliament, Stone Sizani, added that 'she has overstepped the mark' and that her report 'contained political overtones'.

Attacks on Madonsela were also launched by Naledi Pandor, a career minister and party loyalist; Lindiwe Sisulu, who would later also

197

attack the judiciary; and Jessie Duarte, who had a reputation as baleful and shrill. Kebby Maphatsoe, the leader of the Umkhonto weSizwe Military Veterans Organisation (his embellished service to the struggle was also questioned in later years), declared that the Public Protector was controlled by the CIA. Collen Maine, the ANCYL president after Julius Malema's expulsion, went further, claiming Madonsela 'is a CIA agent ... behaving like a popcorn'.[10]

The ANC's tactics after the release of the report were made clear on day one. Radebe, who had served in every cabinet since 1994, addressed a press conference rubbishing Madonsela and her findings. 'The private house of the president was built by the president and his family. The retaining wall, cattle kraal and culvert, fire pool and water reservoir ... are all essential security features which ensures physical security and effective operation of security equipment,' he claimed. This contradicted the Public Protector's findings and signalled the government's intent to subvert the authority of her office. Radebe also said Zuma had a bond on the property, which wasn't true.

Ramaphosa, on the verge of becoming deputy president of the country, didn't seemed perturbed and wasn't going to challenge the guy who had given him a political lifeline. 'There was no corruption, nothing to do with Nkandla was unlawful. The "fire pool" is not even as big as an Olympic swimming pool,' he said two days before the report was released. And once it was out, he defended Zuma. 'We are saying that the integrity of the president remains intact and that this president has the ability and know-how to lead our government and South Africa going forward,' he told a gathering in Port Elizabeth.

In the two years between becoming deputy leader of the ANC and being appointed deputy president, Ramaphosa assumed offices and leadership positions whose decisions and machinations were central to the state capture project and the unfolding culture of state corruption. First, he was appointed to chair the ANC deployment committee. With the deputy presidency came the job of leader of government business in Parliament, which meant he directed the affairs of government ministers in the legislature, including liaising with the speaker's office about ministers' performance. They were also accountable to him when it came to their appearances in the National Assembly to answer questions.

In December 2014, Zuma appointed Ramaphosa to head an inter-ministerial committee overseeing attempts to turn around ailing parastatals. More importantly, he also oversaw a so-called 'Eskom war room' in the Presidency whose sole focus was the escalating crisis at the state-owned electricity utility. From these positions – not to mention his perch as number two in the national executive and cabinet – Ramaphosa could have directed significant human resources and capital to prevent grand corruption and ensure improved performance and accountability.

Although Ramaphosa would later say that 'many' of the most egregious appointments during state capture were made by Zuma without input from the deployment committee, and that it was often bypassed,[11] his and Mantashe's testimony at hearings of the Judicial Commission of Inquiry into Allegations of State Capture contradicted this. The deployment committee, they said, was a vitally important and central organ of the party that played a crucial role in executing deployment policy in line with the National Democratic Revolution. 'The party is where the power resides,' Ramaphosa said, referring to how government and state appointments were made and how ultimate accountability worked.[12] It was formalised into a structure of the NEC consisting of senior party leaders who met regularly and interacted with ministers and other office bearers about a whole range of appointments.

Ramaphosa and Mantashe furiously defended the rights of the deployment committee and its role in how state and government appointments are made. And both have defended the 'necessity and importance' of the committee's work, describing the body as 'a critical party structure'.[13] Cadres approved for deployment accepted on the express understanding that they were 'beholden to the decisions of the structures of the party', which meant that even though someone might be a mid-level bureaucrat, democratic centralism dictates a loyalty to the party and its programmes first and foremost.[14]

According to Ramaphosa and Mantashe, the committee had to be involved in any appointment in the government, the state, para-statals, government agencies or any other body that would assist the revolutionary movement to strengthen its grip on the 'levers of power' and to 'entrench' it.[15] The party's cadre deployment policy remained a 'fundamental policy' of the ANC when Ramaphosa became chair of the deployment committee at the end of 2012. Similar structures dictated key appointments at provincial and municipal levels.[16]

Decisions of the deployment committee appeared to be final, as per the party's guidelines. Deployees in the government and the state had to adhere to committee instructions, with sanctions threatened should they not do so: 'Decisions of the organisation, after appropriate consultation with the individual cadres, are final and the breach of this policy shall constitute a serious offence to be considered by the appropriate structure.'[17] Mantashe, who did not serve on the deployment committee, saw the deployment policy as reminiscent of how communist East Germany or the Soviet Union functioned, with democratic centralism as determined by the ANC at the core.[18]

Ramaphosa's years in charge of the deployment committee coincided with the worst excesses of the state capture project. In later years, the party leadership would never denounce the policy of cadre deployment and would insist that it was acceptable and proper, despite ample evidence to the contrary. In fact it vigorously defended it, as Chief Justice Raymond Zondo would later comment, even as Ramaphosa attempted to distance himself from the Zuma years.

But the facts of what happened during the Zuma era are clear: appointments in the public sector were used to repurpose the state and the government in service of networks of patronage and organised crime that aimed to extract as much rent and resources as possible for purposes of enrichment. Cadre deployment became the vehicle for these networks, with the ANC providing the ideological cover for its implementation. And Ramaphosa – alongside Zuma – was intimately involved.

23

The crucible of capture

DURING RAMAPHOSA'S FIRST YEARS BACK IN POLITICS, the project of grand corruption and state capture led by Zuma and enabled by the governing party accelerated. The Nkandla scandal provided clear insight into how easily the ANC jettisoned adherence to the law when it attacked and maligned the Public Protector and co-opted Parliament. Under Zuma, the ANC and its government would not be bound by a higher set of values, as Mandela had hoped, existing only to retain political and executive power so that it could protect its networks of patronage. The ANC thrived because of these patronage networks, which gave the party access to resources and made the political elite wealthy. And no one would be able to break them, especially since they were led by the president of party and state.

In these years of heightened corruption – it reached its zenith in 2017 – Ramaphosa witnessed all the major scandals, upheavals and revelations. Later he would acknowledge that state capture was organised and systemic, was conducted by networks inside and outside the state colluding with one another, and included the manipulation of laws, rules, regulations and processes of government.

He admitted to having been intrigued by Fikile Mbalula's statement in 2011 about the Guptas' influence on cabinet appointments (see Chapter 21). He explained that the family's commandeering of Waterkloof Air Force Base in 2013 was another 'signpost' that something was amiss. And he said the dismissal of Nhlanhla Nene as finance minister in 2015, and the subsequent dismissal of Pravin Gordhan as finance minister in 2017, were two more markers on the path to complete capture.[1] These markers, he said, should have spurred him and others into action. They didn't, he claimed, because the grand scheme wasn't that apparent.

But he also read the plethora of reports by investigative journalists at the time, claims by whistleblowers, revelations by the Public Protector and other institutions, and court judgments. Much of it 'startled' him but the full picture – despite large swathes of it being painted daily in bright colours on newspaper front pages – wasn't clear. And, he would protest, 'one could not immediately join the dots'.[2]

It seems highly unlikely that Ramaphosa did not see what was happening. He was at the apex of the system and helped direct operations. But Gordhan, a cabinet minister since 2009, also says the total picture became clear only in 2017 when the trove of Gupta emails was leaked and when the 'Betrayal of the Promise' state capture report by a group of academics was published. 'The report enabled me to locate my own experience from 2015 within a conceptual framework,' says Gordhan.[3]

State capture – the process of institutionalised corruption involving the Zuma-Gupta axis – and the government failure and fraud that flowed from capture and cadre deployment, were the product of planning and organisation. Chief Justice Raymond Zondo later called it a political project. And political projects are planned, led and executed by individuals who wield power in political organisations.

Zuma's initial objective after being installed as party leader and head of state was not to orchestrate networks of patronage but to subvert the rule of law and stay out of prison. As president of the country, with vast executive powers, he was adept at gaming the system and expertly set about reconfiguring the state on the back of the governing party's deployment theology in which the ANC was the centre of power, not the government. Zuma appointed acolytes at the NPA, dismantled SARS with the help of deployee Tom Moyane, ensured the installation of a bully at the Directorate for Priority Crime Investigation when Berning Ntlemeza took over and orchestrated SSA spies thanks to the positioning of allies Arthur Fraser and Thulani Dlomo. He was in complete control, able to appoint whomever he wanted into whatever position he chose.

But, despite his lightly checked executive authority, he remained embroiled in court battles as the DA continued its struggles to access the spy tapes and overturn the decision not to charge him with corruption, fraud and racketeering. On 20 March 2013, shortly after an interministerial committee led by Thulas Nxesi absolved Zuma of any culpability in the Nkandla scandal and a month before the Gupta landing at Waterkloof, the Supreme Court of Appeal agreed with the DA that Mokotedi Mpshe's 2009 decision to withdraw charges against Zuma could be reviewed.[4] And, the appeals judge ordered, the full record of the decision – but excluding the representations made by Zuma and the spy tapes – must be lodged with the court.

Zuma and his legal team had other plans and they instituted what became known as the 'Stalingrad strategy'. It entailed using every available review application, appeal, application for access to a higher court, postponement and anything in between to stop the NPA decision being undone. Years of litigation followed, with the millions in legal fees that Zuma's delaying tactics generated paid for by the taxpayer. Amid the legal war, on 1 October 2013 Zuma appointed attorney Mxolisi Nxasana as the NDPP and head of the NPA.[5] This followed the Constitutional Court ruling in 2012 declaring his appointment of Menzi Simelane invalid and his appointment of Nomgcobo Jiba as acting NDPP (see Chapter 19). Nxasana stepped into a snake pit at the NPA head office in the drab Victoria & Griffiths Mxenge Building in Silverton, Pretoria.

The NPA, cursed by political interference and internal instability since its inception, never recovered from Bulelani Ngcuka's decision not to charge Zuma, the ANC government's culling of the Scorpions and the removal from office of Vusi Pikoli. And in Jiba, the president had a fierce champion who, according to NPA insiders, didn't hesitate to use intimidation and subterfuge to get her way and advance the interests of factions in the organisation. It was exactly as Zuma wanted it: an NPA in perpetual disarray, paralysed and unable to pursue big corruption matters. Nxasana barely lasted two years before he was forced to resign under threat of an inquiry into his fitness for office. Jiba had led a campaign inside the NPA against Nxasana, spreading a rumour that he was on the verge of reinstating charges against Zuma.[6] That couldn't stand and Zuma made his life impossible.

Advocate Shaun Abrahams, who replaced Nxasana, was one of Zuma's most cunning appointees. Between June 2015, when he assumed office, and August 2018, when he became the second NDPP to be ordered from the position by the Constitutional Court,[7] Zuma was secure in the knowledge that the NPA would not act against anyone but his opponents. Abrahams became known as 'Shaun the sheep' for his seeming blind loyalty to the president and shrieking press conferences where he demanded respect for the NPA from detractors. And he played no small part in attempts to cripple and neutralise finance minister Gordhan when he was resisting capture of the Treasury by the Guptas.

❖

SARS was the other major target for Zuma and the state capture networks. Studied by developed nations and academics as an example of how to organise systems of tax collection, SARS was one of the post-1994 success stories.[8] In 2013, it was rated among the top five revenue and customs authorities worldwide.[9] It developed and implemented modern information technology systems such as eFiling that became case studies for other revenue collectors, and supported the government's fiscal commitments thanks to efficient organisational design and strong leadership.

According to Johann van Loggerenberg, a senior SARS executive until 2015, a range of dedicated units within SARS assisted law enforcement agencies 'to control organised crime from a tax, customs and excise perspective'.[10] They were enormously successful in clamping down on illegal money flows and the shifting of millions of rands for nefarious purposes.

Despite South Africans' dislike for paying unto Caesar what he is owed, SARS became extraordinarily successful in communicating how 'cool' it was to pay tax – and it showed taxpayers exactly how their contributions helped to build schools, hospitals and infrastructure. Zuma, as head of state, relied on SARS and its revenue collection prowess – but, as with the NPA, he remained suspicious and threatened. The source of his unease was a team that started out as the special projects unit and became known as the high-risk investigations unit.

Eventually led by Van Loggerenberg, a governance zealot who was uncompromising about the rule of law, the unit dealt with complex and dangerous tax matters related to organised crime.[11] This brought it into direct conflict with the networks of patronage and extraction operating in the state, with the ANC and with Zuma, who had his own tax issues.[12] Van Loggerenberg and his team started clamping down on various syndicates, including those in the tobacco industry, much of which was off the books, illegal and often linked to the governing party.

The assault on SARS, the destruction of its investigations and enforcement capacity and the hobbling of its ability to collect revenue on behalf of the state was one of the biggest injuries done to South Africa during the Zuma years. Moyane, a former prisons service head with no economic or financial experience, was deployed by Zuma as commissioner of SARS in September 2014.[13]

Zondo later commented that what he was told about SARS's excellence 'was no different' from what he heard about parastatals such as SAA, Denel and Eskom, 'each of which were subsequently run down considerably with rampant corruption and state capture'.[14] All of this, Zondo said, happened with the ANC and its government in control. 'Most, if not all, of these entities were led by the chief executive officers and board of directors who would have been approved by the ruling party through its national deployment committee.'[15] And that committee's chairperson at the time was Ramaphosa. In 2024, Thabo Mbeki openly declared that Zuma set out to destroy SARS, the very institution that enabled the ANC to govern.

Moyane set about his Zuma and ANC-mandated task at SARS with gusto. Thanks to the deviousness and collusion of US consulting firm Bain & Company, led in South Africa by a slippery Italian, Vittorio Massone (who invited me to his office at Melrose Arch for a 'chat' about the negative press his company was getting, ordered us expensive salmon then proceeded to browbeat me about the negative press Moyane was getting[16]), Moyane had a document that outlined his first hundred days at SARS. It included the names of executives who needed to be 'neutralised'.

By early the following year, 2015, Moyane had disbanded and replaced the whole of the SARS executive team, driving out experienced and senior executives and finding pliant replacements who toed the line and neglected their oversight functions.[17] He summarily halted the development of SARS's sophisticated information technology systems, blew up its organisational structure and instilled a culture of distrust and fear. Most importantly, he destroyed SARS's established capacity to combat organised crime.[18]

SARS's project management and technical support sub-division, which integrated projects, including those of the high-risk investigations unit, had become a major problem for organised crime and specifically syndicates within the illicit tobacco trade.[19] Between the 2010–2011 and 2013–2014 fiscal years, SARS increased tobacco sector collections from R10.8 billion to R13.1 billion.[20] It also helped the police put drug dealers, drug manufacturers and cash-in-transit heist offenders in prison for tax evasion. But with Moyane's arrival, political and other attacks on the institution increased dramatically, and despite desperate calls from within the organisation to the national commissioner to defend the institution in public, nothing was done.

Adrian Lackay, who had been spokesperson for SARS for more than 11 years and was one of the last senior officials to leave in 2015 after the Moyane purges, went so far as to send a desperate plea to Parliament's standing committee on finance. In the memorandum, dated 25 March 2015, he revealed details about 'matters at hand [that] were being ignored deliberately, adapted to advance a particular narrative and which were used as basis to effectively muzzle, frustrate, victimise and suspend key officials in SARS'.[21] He detailed the sequence of events at SARS since Moyane's arrival, how a false narrative about SARS and its operations was constructed and how law enforcement and intelligence agencies seemed to be complicit in the destruction of the organisation. He also explained the impact on SARS's functions.

Lackay, easily the most diligent, well-informed and honest person I've come across in the public service, had no luck. The chairperson of the finance committee was Yunus Carrim, one of the butchers of the Scorpions and another of those cadres who always supported the faction of the day. He showed no interest in addressing Lackay's concerns, saving SARS or doing proper oversight. The complicity of cadres such as Carrim and Desmond van Rooyen, an ANC MP of low ability and questionable mores who was the ANC whip on the committee, enabled Moyane to destroy SARS. They turned a blind eye while one of democratic South Africa's most celebrated and efficient institutions was devoured by Zuma's lust for corruption. They should be ashamed.

Years later, Carrim offered a limp-wristed response to events involving SARS and Lackay, saying the matters were discussed by the intelligence committee, Lackay was advised that it was a labour matter, and if he had asked Lackay to testify he would have had to invite other role players. 'And with political parties in the committee taking their narrow, self-interested, "point-scoring" positions on these issues, how would we have been able to arrive at independent and fair outcomes?' he bizarrely argued.[22]

Carrim, later promoted to minister of communications by Zuma, was at the centre of two significant crossroads in South Africa's history: he facilitated the destruction of the Scorpions and he ignored the loud and clear cries for help from SARS. The loss of the Scorpions ushered in an era of impunity and broad corruption. The destruction of SARS deprived the country of more law enforcement capability and hobbled the fiscus. History will not be kind to him.

The convergence between rogue intelligence operations, factional ANC interests, organised crime and syndicates, as well as the politically powerful, also became clear during the SARS saga. Intelligence-driven operations, emanating from an SSA repurposed by Zuma to serve his personal interests, led to a series of *Sunday Times* reports claiming that SARS investigative units were conducting illegal surveillance operations targeting, among others, Zuma. Operatives loyal to Zuma – remarkably, they had to swear a personal oath to the president and the minister[23] – concocted tales of illegal activities by the SARS high-risk investigations unit and planted them with sloppy journalists all too eager for a scoop.[24]

The resultant furore gave Moyane the latitude, but more importantly the political cover, to commence his demolition job at the revenue collector.

24

Democracy's worst year

TOWARDS THE END OF 2005, I FOUND MYSELF at a Gauteng ANC networking event at the Sunnyside Park Hotel in Johannesburg. At the time, I was covering the provincial legislature for *Beeld* and spent my days at its home in the old Johannesburg City Hall. Zuma had just been fired as deputy president of the ANC and the party – with Mbeki at the helm – was preparing for the 2006 municipal elections.

Sitting in the hotel ballroom (the building was the official residence of British overlord Sir Alfred Milner after the Anglo-Boer War), the ANC's provincial leadership briefed the media and other interlopers and hangers-on about the better life for all that the party was creating. During dinner, I sat between Thoko Didiza and Naledi Pandor, both ministers. Conversation inevitably turned to Zuma and his prospects for leadership. 'He will never become president, the women of the party won't allow it,' one of them assured me. Both were adamant that senior ANC members and leaders were quite clear about the dangers a Zuma presidency held for the party and the country.

A decade on from that encounter, in 2015 Zuma was the undisputed master of the ANC and head of state. The wrecking ball was in full swing. It was the year Parliament was broken and indisputably put under total ANC administration, in defence of Zuma. It was the year in which the most important parastatals (Eskom, Transnet, Prasa, Denel) were ruthlessly pressed into the service of state capture networks. And it was the year in which external interests, primarily those of the

Guptas, came to bear on the national executive, with the dismissal of the country's finance minister and attempts to bribe his deputy.

On 30 December 2014, veteran journalist Max du Preez, scourge of South African governments whether Afrikaner nationalist or African nationalist, wrote a scathing column in the *Cape Times* headlined, 'Zuma: SA's one-man wrecking ball'. Du Preez did not hold back, berating Zuma and his rule of destruction that was leaving a trail of broken institutions and corruption in its wake. He cited the wholesale purge at SARS and the suspension of Hawks head Anwa Dramat earlier in the year as examples of how the president was repurposing key institutions to suit his agenda. And he made no bones about the emerging anti-intellectualism in the ANC, with Zuma preferring to act as a Zulu chief rather than the president of a modern democracy.

'The golden thread running through his six years as president was his determination to stay out of court [and jail], with more than 700 counts of corruption, fraud and racketeering hanging over his head. In the process he co-opted and corrupted the entire intelligence machinery, the National Prosecuting Authority, the police service and the SABC. Tenderpreneurship blossomed and corruption mushroomed with almost no consequences for perpetrators,' Du Preez wrote. 'It is Zuma Demolition Inc at work.'[1]

The Independent newspaper group's editorial leadership, headed by Karima Brown, who once wore ANC regalia to a party event and was adept at aligning with different factions in the ANC as the balance of power changed, apologised to Zuma after the Presidency complained about references to him and his 'corrupt' relationship with Shaik.[2] Shaik had by then enjoyed five years of freedom after being released on parole in 2009 on medical grounds. He almost immediately returned to playing golf. Du Preez argued that even if Zuma was replaced as president immediately, the damage to the country would take years to rebuild. 'Sounds a bit harsh? Well, I don't think the serious damage this president has inflicted upon our political culture and our key institutions deserves softer condemnation,' he said.[3]

Deputy President Cyril Ramaphosa did not share Du Preez's opinion. 'Mr President … we thank you for being steadfast in your resolve to lead our people despite those who would divert you and detract you,' he said in the National Assembly. 'We thank you for continuing to be strong to lead our people. I wish to thank you, Mr President, for entrusting me with the responsibility as your deputy president, of supporting you in the advancement of your vision and the vision of your ruling party for a better South Africa. I appreciate your wisdom, your guidance and your leadership in the work where you will be leading us.'[4]

Ramaphosa's gushing statement about Zuma's 'steadfast resolve', his so-called 'vision' and 'leadership', is a perfect example of the duplicity and dishonesty that came to define ANC politics. The state of the country in 2015 – democracy's worst year – was dire, its trajectory pointing towards a failing state and the rule of law under extraordinary pressure. Yet Ramaphosa and the ANC were coasting along under Zuma's leadership, maintaining the fiction of a normal, functioning polity while corruption was blossoming and institutions failing. The deputy president's assessment of his line manager came amid the dramatically worsening performance of Eskom, which announced in January that load-shedding was returning due to the poor performance of its generation plants. The year would see the worst levels of power outages in the country's history until then, with 852 hours of load-shedding and more than 1 300 GWh of electricity lost.[5]

The poor performance of Eskom and the lack of reliable electricity supply was starting to have severe consequences for economic growth and employment. Immediately after Eskom announced the severity of electricity constraints and the expectation that the country would see more than 60 days of load-shedding, economists warned of significantly lower growth rates, with expected losses to the economy in excess of R130 billion.[6] Ratings agencies warned of lower GDP growth, the International Monetary Fund cut its forecasts and the National Treasury followed suit.[7]

During the debate following Zuma's annual State of the Nation address in the National Assembly, DA parliamentary leader Mmusi Maimane offered a blistering indictment of Zuma and the ANC government in what was surely one of the best pieces of oratory delivered by a leader of the opposition since 1994. Citing Mandela's vision for a prosperous, just and fair South Africa, Maimane laid into Zuma, detailing the ANC government's assault on institutions, corruption and the escalating Eskom crisis. Everyone except for the ANC, Ramaphosa, Gwede Mantashe and the Guptas saw that Zuma had become the country's biggest liability. And Maimane ripped open the lies and dishonesty about the government and its performance. His speech was commanding and brutal.

'We have, indeed, allowed one powerful man to get away with too much for far too long. This honourable man is in our presence here today. Honourable president, in these very chambers just five days ago you broke Parliament. Please understand that when I use the term "honourable", I do it out of respect for the traditions and conventions of this august house – but please do not take it literally,' Maimane pointedly declared.[8]

Then he looked at Zuma on the government side of the chamber and addressed him directly. It was a big moment, because no one had ever shown this level of scorn towards Zuma, hitherto treated with faux reverence. 'For you, honourable president, are not an honourable man. You are a broken man presiding over a broken society. You are willing to break every democratic institution to try to fix the legal predicament you find yourself in. You are willing to break this Parliament if it means escaping accountability for the wrongs you have done.'[9]

Zuma's 'Stalingrad' legal strategy in trying to prevent the DA from overturning the decision not to prosecute him and from getting access to the spy tapes was still in full operation. Appeals, reviews and counterapplications bogged down the courts in almost every division. He stalled the Public Protector's Nkandla findings, illegally and unconstitutionally farming out a further investigation to a member of his executive. He had no intention of letting the law run its course in either the corruption matter or the Nkandla disgrace.

His government's performance was rapidly deteriorating and state capture was reaching its zenith. Investigative journalists and the media were reporting on it daily and civil society organisations were in the high court trying to ensure accountability and transparency (the Helen Suzman Foundation, Freedom Under Law and the Council for the Advancement of the South African Constitution in particular).

Maimane stuck his finger into the sore: 'For six years, he has run from 783 counts of corruption, fraud and racketeering that have haunted him from before the day he was elected. For six years, this broken man has spent his waking hours plotting and planning to avoid his day in court. In this broken man's path of destruction lies a litany of broken institutions, each one of them targeted because of their constitutional power to hold him to account: a broken South African Revenue Service, SARS, that should have investigated the fringe tax benefits from Nkandla, the palace of corruption that was built by the people's money; a broken National Prosecuting Authority, NPA, that should have continued with its prosecution of the president, without fear or favour; a broken Special Investigating Unit, SIU; a broken Hawks; a broken South African Police Service, SAPS. And so we can go on with the list of institutions President Zuma is willing to break to protect himself and his friends.'[10]

❖

Parliament was one of the institutions that was broken across the knee of Zuma and the ANC. The disgraceful charade that was Zuma's response to the Nkandla report – he waited 148 days then declared his minister of police would determine whether he needed to reimburse the state[11] – contributed to heightened political temperatures.

The pressure exploded into unprecedented violence and hooliganism during Zuma's opening address to Parliament in early February. The build-up to the State of the Nation address was dominated by threats from Julius Malema's EFF that it would disrupt the sitting to demand that Zuma 'pay back the money'. Malema and his red-clad fellow 'fighters' had been ejected from the National Assembly towards the end of the previous year after insisting that Zuma respond to the question of reparations to the state. He refused and was protected by Baleka Mbete, the most servile of speakers.

But on the evening of 12 February, there was a foul mood in the air. The DA caucus, led by Maimane and Helen Zille, arrived dressed in black to symbolise the state of democracy. Malema and his EFF first met in their caucus room in the Marks Building before proceeding to the National Assembly. And in the press gallery, where I sat, we had no cellphone signal – nothing. When proceedings in the chamber started, the various processions entering before the president and speaker, MPs, journalists and guests in the public gallery chanted 'bring back the signal!' It was clear that someone was interfering and preventing journalists from reporting on what was expected to be a raucous sitting.

As we stood in the press gallery, holding our cellphones in the air and chanting, I saw Ramaphosa write a note and a parliamentary messenger deliver it to David Mahlobo, the unknown Mpumalanga politician installed as minister of state security the year before. At first he ignored the piece of paper on his desk, then he read it, stood up and exited the chamber. Minutes later the signal was restored and journalists could again report on events. Mahlobo's spies did not want the outside world to see Zuma being harangued, jeered and embarrassed. Parliament, under Mbete's direction, could cut the feed from the chamber at any moment. But social media and smartphone-wielding journalists were outside the state's control. So, signal-blocking devices had been installed in Parliament, the executive (Mahlobo's department) interfering in the functions of the legislature (Parliament). It was a flagrant violation of the law and the Constitution – confirmed by a later court judgment – and another example of how Zuma's ANC did whatever it pleased to manipulate laws and convention.

As soon as Zuma took to the podium, EFF MP Godrich Gardee stood up on a point of order, asking when the president was going to 'pay back the money'. Mbete, sticking to the house rules, denied the point of order but Gardee was persistent, adding that the EFF wanted to know 'when the money is going to be paid? Is it going to be paid by EFT, cash or eWallet?'[12] Mbete pushed back, ANC MPs stood to defend their leader and Malema responded: 'We want the president to answer a simple question: when is he paying back the money, as directed by the Public Protector? That is all we are asking.'[13] Again the speaker refused the EFF's point of order and things began to spiral out of control.

Sitting in the press gallery, I stared down in disbelief as Mbete and Malema shouted at each other and other EFF MPs leapt to their feet. Hansard records show how everyone shouted at the speaker, with numerous points of order raised, and Mbete responded with instructions of 'order!' She ordered Malema and his deputy, Floyd Shivambu, to leave the chamber, then ordered out the whole of the EFF caucus. But they refused to leave.

Malema clung to the microphone, demanding to know when Zuma would pay back the money, and Mbete issued instructions to security services to remove the EFF. Suddenly, heavies in white shirts marched into the chamber and attacked Malema and his caucus. Water bottles, EFF helmets (they wore red construction headgear in a fake show of solidarity with the working class) and other paraphernalia flew across desks and chairs as the security detachment tried to drag the EFF out. Malema and his MPs, kicking and screaming, biting and punching, resisted.

Malema was grabbed by the testicles and thrown out. Zuma, grinning, sat at the podium, ANC MPs jeered and the DA sat stony-faced while we of the fourth estate delivered images, video and commentary to a shocked nation. Maimane subsequently led his caucus from the National Assembly chamber because the speaker could not confirm or deny that the white-shirted heavies were members of the police – which entailed a grave breach of the separation of powers. The police, after all, report to the executive, not the legislature. Zuma showed little response and merely continued his speech without the DA and the EFF in the chamber. 'Let me start at the point I was interrupted,' he said. 'I was saying that the year 2015 marks 60 years of a historic moment in our history, when South Africans from all walks of life adopted the Freedom Charter in 1955, in Kliptown, Soweto …'[14]

The EFF's methods to extract concessions from Zuma and the ANC forever marked them as political anarchists having no scruples about desecrating an institution like Parliament. But it was Zuma and his party's barefaced flouting of the law and all prescripts of good governance that pushed Parliament and politics to a point of violence. Nkandla and the Zuma corruption matter revealed an ANC that many suspected represented its true nature: anti-democratic, hostile to the rule of law and antagonistic towards constitutionalism.

In June 2015, Sudanese dictator Omar al-Bashir attended a summit of the African Union in Johannesburg. But he was a war criminal and a warrant for his arrest had been issued by the International Criminal Court (ICC). Hundreds of thousands of people had been displaced in his war-torn country and he stood accused of genocide. South Africa, a signatory to the Rome Statute that governs the ICC, was obliged to arrest him. But Zuma's government refused. The high court in Pretoria issued an order compelling South Africa to jail al-Bashir. Advocate William Mokhari, on behalf of the state, told the full bench that al-Bashir was in the country while the matter was being heard. But it was a lie. On the same day the order was made, al-Bashir was allowed to depart from Waterkloof Air Force Base. The judges said it was a 'clear violation' of the order and the Supreme Court of Appeals later called it 'disgraceful conduct'. For the ANC-in-government, it posed no moral or ethical quandary.

The ANC's cadre deployment system was also humming along nicely in service of the party's National Democratic Revolution, Zuma's goals and the networks of patronage embedded in the state. In March, Robert McBride, who headed the Independent Police Investigative Directorate (Ipid), was suspended. He had been investigating corruption in the police and had delivered reports recommending the suspension of several senior officers. He even investigated Riah Phiyega, the national police commissioner, on allegations of corruption. And he cleared top cops who were accused of various concocted indiscretions by police leadership. The pattern was exactly what happened at SARS. But Nathi Nhleko, the police minister who handled the Nkandla debacle for Zuma, wanted to get rid of him. He was 'too independent and too stubborn not to look the other way, which is one of the reasons they wanted me out', McBride said.[15] In April, Anwa Dramat, the Hawks commander, agreed to leave the police after he was similarly suspended in December 2014. He later said he was targeted because he was 'investigating dockets implicating influential people'.[16]

Zuma appointed Shaun Abrahams (see Chapter 23) as NDPP in June, giving him and the ANC renewed control over one of the most important levers of power in the state, the NPA. And Abrahams, in turn, reinstated Nomgcobo Jiba, who acted as NDPP but had been criminally charged over the victimisation of another top Hawk, General Johan Booysen, who faced trumped-up charges instituted by Jiba.[17] In September, Nhleko appointed a strongman, Berning Ntlemeza, as head of the Hawks. He unflinchingly did Zuma's bidding, readily took political instruction and openly targeted the president's enemies.

Over at the SSA, under Zuma henchmen Arthur Fraser and Thulani Dlomo, a network of spies called the principal agent network and the special operations unit had been established, their sole focus to protect Zuma and the state he and the ANC had created. They had access to millions of rands in hard currency – one intelligence operative told me about safe houses where rands and dollars were stacked from floor to ceiling – and weaponry.

The new Eskom management and board, appointed at the end of 2014 by Gupta toady Lynne Brown and loaded with Gupta cronies, also started to deliver. And Zuma interfered directly with the affairs of the company while Ramaphosa was still in charge of the Eskom war room. Four senior executives – including the chief executive – were suspended in March, the chairperson of the board following soon after. In April, Brian Molefe, a favourite of the Guptas and one of the ANC deployment committee's golden boys, was seconded to Eskom as acting group chief executive from Transnet, where he had been in charge for a few years. The capture of Eskom was pretty much complete. Matshela Koko, a devious and dishonest executive who was in on the Guptas' plan from the beginning and suspended with the others to give the move a veneer of legitimacy, also returned. Brown redeployed Anoj Singh to Eskom from Transnet.

As load-shedding increased, leadership and management were destabilised and patronage networks started to extract and steal resources, Ramaphosa remained unperturbed. He called Molefe's appointment 'a shot in the arm for Eskom' and berated those who criticised the parastatal's leadership, adding that the government needed to 'dispel the myth that the people who run parastatals are ill-equipped to do so …' The economy was cratering thanks to load-shedding but Ramaphosa stood firm. In September, in the National Council of Provinces, he declared himself satisfied that Eskom was returning to rude health. He had given sporadic feedback to MPs on his interventions at the utility, always asserting that progress was being made and that a turnaround was in the offing. 'In another 18 months to two years, you will have forgotten that the challenges we have had with relation to power or energy and Eskom ever existed. Be patient. This problem is going to be resolved.'[18] It was a lie.

And just when everyone believed South Africa couldn't be strafed any further, it was. Shortly after 7 pm on 15 December 2015, the Presidency issued a statement. The finance minister had been fired. The bottom was about to fall out of the rand. The cadres were doing their job.

25
Zenith and nadir

LUNGISA FUZILE IS BURLY AND BROAD-SHOULDERED. Often wearing a broad smile, he is smart and knowledgeable and rarely looks anything but neat and eminently presentable. He is an enjoyable conversationalist who laughs easily and listens intently. Fuzile is also a deeply committed South African who took his role in the public sector seriously, and after exiting he continued to be brutally honest about the state of the country.

He was appointed director general of the National Treasury in May 2011, during Pravin Gordhan's first stint as finance minister, and resigned exactly six years later, in May 2017, after Zuma deployed Gupta acolyte Malusi Gigaba as minister of finance. If Gordhan and his predecessor, Nhlanhla Nene, were the public faces of the resistance against state capture, Fuzile was one of the frontline operatives who worked hard to prevent the National Treasury being sacked and plundered. He was part of the cohort of public sector economic stewards who thrived during the department's golden age, before the ANC imposed Zuma on the country.

The Treasury was formed when the departments of finance and state expenditure were merged in 2001. At the time Gordhan, commissioner of SARS, Trevor Manuel, finance minister, and Tito Mboweni, governor of the Reserve Bank, formed a powerful triumvirate under the leadership of Thabo Mbeki, the head of state.[1] Manuel was responsible for macroeconomic and fiscal policy, ensuring the country remained on a sustainable and responsible road to economic recovery. Gordhan was key to the country's post-apartheid recovery and the ANC government's plans for social transformation with the redesign and modernisation of revenue collection. SARS became a world-class institution. And Mboweni showed admirable independence in his pursuit of inflation targeting and protecting the currency while following and implementing responsible monetary policies.

At the Treasury, Manuel set about building a new institutional culture, working with the incumbents and apartheid holdovers to stabilise and improve public finances while introducing a new generation of financial and economic experts to help ensure future prosperity.[2] Brian Molefe was one of them. Before the Guptas corrupted him and long before he was found to have been a crucial role player in the disembowelling of Transnet and Eskom on behalf of external criminal interests, he was considered one of the Treasury's – and indeed South Africa's – best prospects.

A young, black professional who became a role model for many who wanted to enter the public service, Molefe seemingly showed a measure of commitment to the new democratic project when he was deployed to the Limpopo government. But he wanted to work at the Treasury, taking a pay cut to move to Pretoria then making quick progress up the ranks and into Manuel's orbit. Molefe became an expert in provincial finances and was regularly dispatched to right the ship in places such as the Eastern Cape, a province that has never been able to run its finances properly. Apart from Molefe, able economists such as Lesetja Kganyago and Maria Ramos also rose to senior positions, helping to steer the ship of state while preparing for higher office and different postings.[3]

Fuzile told me how he was part of this contingent of public servants who believed in the ability of the state to effect positive change, and how important they believed the work of the Treasury was. It was abundantly clear that, although he was a supporter of the ANC, if not a member, his loyalty was primarily to the Constitution and the national interest. The chance to enter national public service came with the ANC's victory in 1994, and with it the responsibility to implement the governing party's mandate.

But Fuzile was one of that rare breed in the senior ranks of the state who were mindful of the ANC's historical role and present-day responsibilities but unwilling to put party interests ahead of everything else. His responsibilities as director general at the Treasury were enormous. The Treasury is responsible for disbursements to all three levels of government, driving and managing the budgeting process, procurement and borrowing, and overseeing financial management across the state, including at parastatals.[4] It was Fuzile's job to run all of that as the department's accounting officer.

The director general of any department is not a political appointment. Directors general are the state's most senior civil servants and in theory they should be politically non-aligned, professional public officials. But senior appointments were all made after being approved by the ANC deployment committee and the party always expected full loyalty to it. There was no doubt in the minds of the thousands of deployed ANC cadres in the state and the executive that the party was central to their existence and that its interests came first.

In December 2015, Zuma said in public what everyone in the party, state and government already knew: the ANC came before the country. At a provincial party event in Pietermaritzburg, he said: 'I argued one time with someone who said the country comes first and I said as much as I understand that, I think my organisation, the ANC, comes first.'[5] It was a stunning thing for a head of state to say in public, but in practice it was already blindingly obvious that the national interest came a distant second to what the ANC needed and desired.

Frustratingly for the ANC and Zuma, Fuzile was not a typical deployed cadre, and under his watch the Treasury 'became a stumbling block to the erosion [corruption] of due processes in policy and decision-making in the state'.[6] In concert with Nene, Gordhan and other senior officials, he deliberately stopped or delayed decisions 'which would have had dire consequences for South Africa', including piling on massive debt burdens that would have crippled the country for generations.[7] If these decisions – made at executive and cabinet level by Zuma and his ANC ministers, and by party deployees elsewhere in the state, including state-owned enterprises – were followed through, 'the country would most likely have been bankrupt at some point in the future', Fuzile said later.[8]

His job was not only executive and operations officer at the

Treasury but 'chief adviser' to the minister in the execution of his political programme – where, significantly according to Fuzile, it was in accordance with the law.[9] His role, shared with senior technical staff such as Ismail Momoniat (a mathematician who joined the Treasury in 1994) and Michael Sachs (son of Constitutional Court justice Albie Sachs), was to advise the government on how best to finance its developmental goals.

Fuzile and his colleagues worked in by far and away the most efficient, professional and committed government department. They were resolute about managing the country's finances properly, ensuring it did not spend more than it was able to earn and that borrowing was responsible and sustainable. The Treasury was also tasked with protecting the country's financial integrity, and alongside the Reserve Bank it was the most important institution foreign investors and governments considered in gauging the country's health and stability. It was therefore critical that the Treasury and the Reserve Bank remained free of any whispers of corruption and mismanagement, existing in splendid isolation from the ANC's internecine machinations for access to state resources and power.

Under Zuma, however, it became increasingly difficult for the Treasury to sustain its high-level functioning as the systems and processes that guided the government started to fail. There was no proper setting of government priorities, which led to 'everything' becoming a priority.[10] There was no political process to ensure important programmes were prioritised and low-importance projects shelved. Election promises weren't translated into thorough policies. Line-function departments sent the Treasury ad hoc funding requirements that could often not be met outside the budgeting cycle. But Zuma's government also refused to make hard choices and continued to add new programmes with no money available to fund them.

The Treasury couldn't fund the whims of individuals like Nomvula Mokonyane, the minister of water and sanitation, or Bathabile Dlamini, the minister of social development, surely some of the least talented and most dimwitted ANC appointments since 1994 (in 2024, both remained in the corridors of power). The Treasury repeatedly and often said 'no' to funding requests. And this bred resentment. Attacks on finance ministers – Nene, and later Gordhan – during cabinet meetings and in public increased, and a campaign that cast the Treasury as unaccountable and a 'state within a state' prepared the ground for state capture and ANC corruption's assault on one of the final vestiges of good governance.

The objective of Zuma and many of his executive, as well as the Gupta network of extraction and theft, was full control of the Treasury. They wanted to control the budgeting and payment function, to remove limits on government expenditure and to direct contracting and procurement. This would enable unfettered access to resources at all parastatals and facilitate the flow of public funds to tax havens and into the pockets of corrupt cadres.

In hindsight, the audacity with which Zuma and the Gupta network set out to capture the Treasury and the speed with which it happened is breathtaking. Recall that 2015 was the year in which Zuma and the ANC's power and influence over the state peaked. Apart from the judiciary and the fourth estate, the ANC (with the Guptas embedded in its top structure) enjoyed almost complete mastery of society. Parliament was a pathetic adornment trotted out at regular intervals to maintain the appearance of accountability and oversight. Cadre deployment enabled the ANC to attach the state to Luthuli House as the centre of command, with deployees rigidly sticking to Strategy and Tactics in executing the National Democratic Revolution. And state-owned companies were reconfigured and realigned in service of patronage networks. The Treasury was the last frontier.

Zuma wanted South Africa to conclude a deal with Russia for the provision of 9.6 GW of nuclear power. He had always been attracted to Russian dictator Vladimir Putin, who has ruled the country since the turn of the century. Apart from the ANC's historic ties with the Soviet Union – it provided support to the ANC during exile and many party leaders were educated and trained there – Zuma had a fascination with modern Russia. He admired Putin's machismo, the way he dismissed his political opponents and ruled the country as if he were a monarch. Russia was Putin's to rule over and Zuma believed South Africa was his to do the same.

During 2014 and 2015, Zuma's plans to commit South Africa to a nuclear deal with Russia worth trillions of rands started to accelerate. Instructions were given to the Treasury and the Department of Energy to commence with planning, memoranda were signed with various countries and Tina Joemat-Pettersson, the energy minister, emerged as Zuma's key implementing agent. But the Treasury, with Nene as finance minister and Fuzile as director general, was a significant stumbling block. They were patently not supportive of the idea. A nuclear build programme of that size and complexity was foolish and unaffordable. They had also seen what had happened to the mega construction projects at the Medupi and Kusile power stations in Limpopo and Mpumalanga, already behind schedule and way over budget. The projects were points of resource extraction and theft and would never function as they should. Nene and Fuzile knew a reckless nuclear deal would be corruption central – and cripple the country.

So, when Joemat-Pettersson presented Nene with a letter to sign during a visit to Russia for a Brics (Brazil, Russia, India, China and South Africa) heads of state meeting in July 2015, he refused. The letter was addressed to the Russian authorities and was to be presented to Putin during a meeting with Zuma. The South African president wanted 'something' to give to his Russian totem.[11] Although the letter was not an official agreement, the signature of the finance minister would have given it the status of a binding financial commitment by the government.

Joemat-Pettersson, one of the ANC and Zuma's most pliant and lily-livered deployees, revised the letter and again presented it to Nene to sign. Again, he refused. Exasperated, Joemat-Pettersson asked what she should say to the president. Nene replied, 'I don't know,' but explained that he would not sign anything without due process being followed.[12] And signing a letter hastily written by another minister in a hotel in Ufa, deep inside Russia, did not entail proper process.

If the state capture set were looking for an example of obstruction by the Treasury, they had found it. Zuma accused Nene of insubordination and the tide quickly turned against him and his department. David Mahlobo, the provincial politician Zuma made intelligence minister, and international relations minister Maite Nkoana-Mashabane (another empty vessel) became particularly hostile to Nene and the Treasury.[13]

In October 2015, a couple of months after the Brics meeting in Russia, Nene's deputy at finance, Mcebisi Jonas, met Rajesh 'Tony' Gupta at the family's sprawling pile in Saxonwold, across the road from Johannesburg Zoo.[14] Lured there by Zuma's son Duduzane, allegedly a billionaire and Gupta vassal who served on various family company boards, Gupta told him 'the old man' – meaning Zuma – liked him (Jonas) and was going to appoint him finance minister. The Guptas, Tony said, 'are in control of everything: the NPA, Hawks and the SSA. The old man will do anything we tell him to do,' he said, adding that they 'worked' with Molefe and Lynne Brown, the public enterprises minister. And thanks to this, they were protected – unlike Nene, who was going to be removed from his position.[15]

Jonas listened in disbelief as Gupta said the family enterprises earned as much as R6 billion annually from government contracts and work, including from Transnet, Eskom and Prasa. They wanted to increase this to R8 billion and the Treasury, he said, needed to be 'cleaned up'. Who knows what riches awaited the family conglomerate if the Russian nuclear deal had gone through? Jonas later said Gupta offered him a bribe of R600 million that he could 'stash in Dubai' and was willing to immediately pay him R600 000 and asked for a bag.[16] Jonas rejected the offer. But the fact that the Guptas were empowered to try to cajole and strong-arm a deputy minister ahead of his expected elevation to the executive revealed the prime position they found themselves in thanks to Zuma and the ANC. Jonas shared detail of the event with Nene, his line manager, and Gordhan, under whom he had previously served as deputy.

It was clear that the assault on the Treasury was advanced. Around the same time, Fuzile heard that plans were afoot to transfer the Treasury's budgeting function to the Presidency. Zuma, he heard, was 'very unhappy' with how the Treasury managed the budget and claimed it wasn't aligned with the National Development Plan.[17] An NPC official told Fuzile that, during discussions, Zuma seemed to be particularly irritated by the perception that the Treasury was 'treated like the best department'.[18] The president was an economic and numerical illiterate who did not understand the importance of financial and economic stability and the necessity for policy certainty, nor how South Africa fitted into the global economic architecture. He practised an almost tribal form of government where the chief called the shots and detested the West. It all fed into the decay of cabinet systems and processes – and fuelled antagonism towards the Treasury and good governance.

Zuma convened a meeting at the presidential guest house in Bryntirion, Pretoria, on 8 December that included the Treasury, Mahlobo and Joemat-Pettersson, and during which Nene and Fuzile again resisted the nuclear scheme. Zuma was irritated and angry with the Treasury men, Fuzile told me later. At a cabinet meeting the next day, Nene made final requests to ministers in preparation for the following year's budget. But after the meeting he was called to Zuma's office at the Union Buildings and fired. It was a brief conversation and Zuma spun the unbelievable yarn that Nene was to be deployed as head of the regional Brics bank and had been selected for the job because of his seniority.

It was claptrap, of course. Zuma wanted to deploy someone as finance minister who wasn't independent-minded (or bound to the Constitution), someone who would do his and the Guptas' bidding. Zuma, deeply in thrall to the Guptas, had jettisoned all awareness of civic duty and his oath of office. There was simply no commitment to good governance and the rule of law – just an urgency to assist the robber family from Saxonwold to extend their reach beyond cabinet appointments and control of parastatals into the heart of the South African executive.

What of the ANC? What did discussions among the party leadership, the much-vaunted 'top six', entail at their weekly meetings at Luthuli House in Johannesburg? Apparently, not much, because the ANC leadership oversaw the whole process that eventually led to the systematic deconstruction of the state and principles of good governance. They were there right through South Africa's descent – to paraphrase political analyst Justice Malala – from the early 2000s, Zuma's Polokwane victory in 2007, his election as president in 2009 and the subsequent rise of a dysfunctional state beset by corruption and patronage. All of it enabled by the deployment of cadres at all levels of the state. To Zuma, so used to being able to deploy subservient ANC cadres into any position the party wanted, Nene was an unacceptable anomaly.

26
See no evil

NHLANHLA NENE'S DISMISSAL TURNED OUT TO BE the high-water mark of Ramaphosa's vaunted resistance to capture and corruption. Zuma appointed the little-known provincial, Desmond van Rooyen, a backbencher from North West and a member of the standing committee on finance, as Nene's replacement. He wasn't groomed for the position, didn't grow up in the Treasury environment and was an unknown quantity – and therefore a perfect proposition for the Zuma-Gupta axis.

After the announcement on Wednesday evening, the next two days were carnage on the markets. The value of the biggest financial and property shares on the JSE fell by R290 billion. This figure excludes the remainder of the equities market that was also hit by the disaster. Government bonds lost 12 per cent of their capital value, to the tune of R216 billion. The currency depreciated sharply overnight, dropping from R13.40 to R15.40 against the US dollar.[1] It was an abject disaster that plunged the economy into crisis, severely damaged South Africa's reputation abroad as a stable, developing democracy and alerted ratings agencies to the ascendancy of corruption and misrule.

On Friday, shocked by Nene's firing and deeply concerned about the impact on the economy, Gordhan decided to intervene. 'Obviously, as the former finance minister, you're worried and you're thinking about it,' he said. He sent Lakela Kaunda, Zuma's chief of staff, a text message:

Hi Lakela, the situation out there's very tense and full of anxiety.

If I may suggest a well-crafted statement providing reassurance of policy direction might help to calm markets on Monday. Remember that next week the US Federal Reserve will increase rates, that will be a second knock that we will take. A team consisting of SARB [South African Reserve Bank] and NT [National Treasury] and private sector maybe, should be put together to meet investors with the presidency. Think about it.[2]

Kaunda, with a fearsome reputation as Zuma's gatekeeper, responded to Gordhan with 'Thank you, will discuss with them and organise.'

After Van Rooyen's hastily arranged swearing-in at the Union Buildings and his arrival at the Treasury with two Gupta advisers (who immediately started asking questions about paperwork related to a controversial SAA deal), Fuzile went to see Ramaphosa to express his deep concern. The director general feared for the Treasury's future and the deputy president seemed to take his concerns to heart because he consulted his fellow ANC top six leaders, discussing the dangers should Van Rooyen stay in place. He later told the state capture commission that he even threatened to resign if Zuma did not see reason.[3]

After various discussions, including a fraught meeting between leaders of big business and Zweli Mkhize, the ANC treasurer-general, and Jeff Radebe, the senior minister in the cabinet, a decision was made to try to convince Zuma to replace Van Rooyen with Gordhan before the markets opened on Monday. This Ramaphosa and Duarte did on Sunday, four days after Nene was fired.[4]

Kaunda asked Gordhan to report to the Presidency on Sunday evening. At 4.49 pm she texted him: 'Hello, he says he may need to consult you on the latest situation later this evening, maybe 7 pm. Hoping you are in Gauteng. Will check the suitable time.'

Gordhan responded: 'I am around – please let me know before 8 pm.'

She replied: '7 pm.'

'And that's when the whole thing starts. I go up to the Union Buildings on my own ... Kaunda says you can come through now. I walked into the room and it's, "Hello my brother, how are you, my brother? Take a seat. I want you to take this job." I refused it … because I had done some caucusing behind the scenes. I said, "No, but you have people like Jabu Moleketi, Mcebisi Jonas who can do the job, and besides, I'm enjoying local government." He said, "No man, we need you, there's some issues" – he mentioned each of them. I said, "No, Mr President, I have to talk to my wife because I haven't consulted the family on this." From there I got into a corner, I phoned Vani, my wife, but we already knew what was happening, or going to happen. So, I go back and tell him I'll do it but we'll have to deal with Dudu Myeni at SAA and Tom Moyane at SARS. "No, we'll talk about it," he says. And at 8.32 pm is when we started drafting a Treasury statement.[5]

The chaos and bungling with the dismissal of Nene, the appointment of Van Rooyen and the reappointment of Gordhan in a matter of five days set the country on a downward spiral. Try as the Treasury might (Gordhan immediately started engaging with the country's creditors, investors and international multilateral financial institutions), the world was not fooled. The ANC government under Zuma was careening off on a tangent, heading towards disaster. All three international ratings agencies – Moody's, Fitch and Standard & Poor's – adjusted their outlook to negative,[6] citing increased political 'pressure' and risk.[7] After reaching investment-grade status in 2000 and maintaining it throughout the first decade of the millennium, the Nene disaster began a series of adjustments by the ratings agencies that led all three to class South African debt as junk.[8]

The Nkandla saga dragged on until March 2016, when a scathing Constitutional Court judgment that should have led to Zuma's resignation found he had violated his oath of office. 'The president thus failed to uphold, defend and respect the Constitution as the supreme law of the land. This failure is manifest from the substantial disregard for the remedial action taken against him by the Public Protector in terms of her constitutional powers,' Chief Justice Mogoeng Mogoeng said.[9]

The following month, the high court in Pretoria set aside the contentious 2009 decision by acting NDPP Mokotedi Mpshe (see

Chapter 18) to drop the corruption, fraud, money laundering and racketeering charges against Zuma. The judgment said Mpshe's decision was 'irrational' and he should have let the court decide on the relevance of the spy tapes that so conveniently found their way to Zuma's legal team while spymaster Arthur Fraser was at the SSA. There was secrecy around the decision and Mpshe did not share it with the prosecution team, led by advocate Billy Downer.[10] The judgment meant that the head of state had to face 16 charges and 783 counts in terms of criminal and corruption legislation.

During the same period, the Guptas launched a high-profile public campaign after the biggest banks closed their accounts. After accusing the banks of being part of the 'white monopoly capital' suppressing emerging 'black disruptor business and entrepreneurs', the crime family appealed directly to the ANC, Cosatu and other political allies. The cabinet sprang into action. While Gordhan, the minister of finance under whose authority banks fell, was abroad it appointed an 'interministerial committee' under the leadership of Mosebenzi Zwane, the minister of mineral resources, to investigate the closure of the Guptas' bank accounts. Zwane, it later transpired, was appointed to the cabinet by Zuma on the advice of the Guptas. Another no-name provincial, he did the family's bidding in the Free State and was involved in some of the most egregious instances of corruption and capture.

But what was remarkable was the urgency with which the national executive took up the cudgels on the Guptas' behalf. And as Ismail Momoniat, deputy director general at the Treasury responsible for the banking sector, later noted, nothing happened after deputy minister Jonas revealed how the Guptas interfered in executive matters, yet the cabinet was mobilised after their bank accounts were closed. Gordhan was vehemently and vociferously opposed to Zwane's investigation, telling him there was no formal 'interministerial committee', merely a 'task team' without a mandate or a chairperson, and he went to the high court to bolster his position.

The ANC didn't blink. Despite two major court judgments and two major Gupta revelations and developments in the space of a month, the governing party and its leaders maintained the fiction of a functioning organisation and a government executing on its promises. But the truth was far removed from what the party wanted people to believe. The instability at parastatals, including Eskom and Transnet, was fomented in this period and under the watch of Ramaphosa's deployment committee. Heads of institutions were fired and replaced; SARS became a public victim of corruption; and ANC veterans and elected officials openly made claims and accusations of corruption and capture.

Ramaphosa later told the Zondo commission that the state capture networks conducted their business in the shadows, which was why he, as the deputy president, was not immediately aware of what was happening. But events were unfolding rapidly and publicly. And the Guptas weren't exactly shrinking violets or background operators content to cajole, influence and manoeuvre. They were crass, bombastic and open about their command over the state. They owned a newspaper, *The New Age*, and a television station, ANN7, that blasted out their propaganda and plans every day and every hour. Whether it was expected changes to the cabinet or impending appointments to boards, the management of parastatals or attacks on ministers like Nene and Gordhan, the Guptas' intentions were crystal clear. They literally broadcast them. Ministers were summoned to their compound in Johannesburg and they preened during televised ANN7 breakfast events after state occasions like the opening of Parliament or the tabling of the budget.

Investigative journalists wrote about the Guptas' affairs, about government spokesperson Themba Maseko – another committed and honest public servant – who was fired because he defied them, about Jonas's confrontation with Tony Gupta over the finance minister's job. They wrote about the Guptas' influence on appointments in the state, about ministers regularly being 'summoned' to Saxonwold, about the Guptas' knowledge of cabinet appointments in advance, how they extracted support for their business ventures and how they were known to be 'the president's people'.[11] This was all widely known, spoken of and reported on. Ramaphosa's claim that he was unable to draw links between events, that he couldn't identify patterns and trends and that the penny dropped only in May and June of 2017, is simply not credible. The Public Protector, Thuli Madonsela, released her voluminous report into state capture in November 2016, expanding on events at Eskom,

The New Age and many other corruption matters in minute detail.[12] Zuma even went to the high court to try to prevent its release.

Surely, Ramaphosa must have known by then and acted accordingly? A leader who had the courage of his convictions, who believed in democracy and the rule of law, would have been galvanised into action to protect the constitutional order and the supremacy of the law. Heavens, if not that, he should surely have tried to protect the ANC. Instead, he 'was silent' about Zuma's many abuses of power during his second term, his biographer Anthony Butler writes. He bided his time in the hope of succeeding Zuma, in the process conforming to party dictates that held he should never pine for office in public.

Outside the ANC, however, there existed a 'parallel reality', or 'the real world'.[13] In this world, 'corruption was running rampant, state institutions were being dismembered, the economy was falling into crisis and public trust in political leaders was plummeting. In this parallel reality, critics complained, there was no sign whatsoever of Ramaphosa,' says Butler. And this was in the face of the 'merciless' rotation of cabinet ministers and its deleterious effect on governance and Zuma's 'penetration' of intelligence and law enforcement agencies to harass opponents and protect allies from legal action. 'The destruction of public institutions of course was only possible because it served wider ANC interests,' he wrote.[14]

Jonas's claims about the Guptas' interference were swiftly followed by similar allegations by Barbara Hogan, married to Robben Island veteran and Nelson Mandela confidant Ahmed Kathrada (as well as a minister of public enterprises and health), Vytjie Mentor (chairperson of the ANC caucus in Parliament) and Maseko. In its response, the ANC NEC reiterated its 'full confidence' in Zuma and called for Jonas and others to engage in a confidential party investigation.[15] Ramaphosa promised a 'methodical and rigorous investigation.' Nothing happened. There is no evidence – zero – that either Ramaphosa or Mantashe 'ever proactively sought to make even basic inquiries'.[16] In fact, Zizi Kodwa and Jessie Duarte, who spoke for the ANC, launched baleful attacks on newspapers investigating the matter. Kodwa, in a statement that today looks particularly dishonest and shameful, called *Sunday Times* revelations about Jonas and the Guptas 'gossip mongering' and an overzealous attempt 'to portray the leadership of the ANC in general ... as collaborators to fit the fictitious narrative of a Gupta-controlled country'.[17]

But Zuma and the ANC leadership were exactly what Kodwa said: collaborators, with the country controlled by the Guptas. And his statement on behalf of the party shows how deeply compromised they were, how they lied about what they knew and how they misled the country about the depth and the breadth of the rot.

27
Victory for the axis

PRAVIN GORDHAN WAS ENGAGED IN ALL-OUT WAR with Zuma from the moment he stepped back into the Sir Herbert Baker edifice on Church Square in Pretoria that houses the ministry of finance. It was a war launched by the Zuma-Gupta axis to gain control of the national finances and which sought to do so by any means and at any price – even if it meant destabilising the country, upending the constitutional order or sacrificing the republic's economic prospects. It was also a civil war because it pitted ANC leaders against each other.

Gordhan remained – and remains – devoted to the ideals of the ANC, despite the organisation being shown up as corrupt and unable to govern. And against him was Zuma, a struggle figure who rose to become party leader and head of state and who also professed an unqualified loyalty to the ANC's principles. The finance minister, however, was part of a small minority of party leaders who at first firmly but respectfully, and later openly and forcefully, resisted the ravages of the ANC's Zuma-led programme of capture and corruption. The other was Derek Hanekom, who at the time was minister of tourism. Gordhan and Hanekom were the only two who later openly defied Zuma and spoke out against the naked corruption and abuses of power that occurred under his leadership – with the silent agreement of Ramaphosa, Gwede Mantashe and others.

The first incident occurred days after Gordhan's reappointment. 'I was in Cape Town, I was driving on the N2 with my wife a few days before Christmas, and suddenly there's this phone call. "The president wants to talk to you." So, I said, "Hold on, I'm driving." I got off the road, but now the traffic cops have come and they say, "You can't stop here." I said, "I'm talking to the president." There was this Myeni scheme about Airbus and all that rubbish. I said, "Sorry, Mr President, we don't have the kind of money that SAA's going to require, so we can't do it."' (Zuma wanted Gordhan to help Dudu Myeni and SAA, against the Treasury's advice.)

In January 2016, Gordhan led a delegation to the World Economic Forum in Davos and was cornered by Nedbank's Mike Brown and other business leaders. '"We've got to do something about the ratings," they said, and I agreed. So, the week after Davos we called a meeting and about 60 CEOs were packed around the boardroom table at Nedbank. We decided that government, business and labour would go and speak to the international investment community, and people like Jabu Mabuza and Christo Wiese went with us to London, Boston and elsewhere. It grew into the CEO Initiative and we tried to ensure that we all spoke from the same script,' says Gordhan.[1] The *toenadering* was so successful that CEOs joined marches when Gordhan was charged by Shaun Abrahams, Zuma's NPA head.

Zuma's open disdain and sniping antagonism for Gordhan was evident from the start. Shortly before Gordhan delivered his first post-Nene budget speech – surely the most difficult delivered by any finance minister in South Africa's history – Zuma declared Van Rooyen to be the most 'highly qualified' finance minister he had appointed. Critics never took the time to understand the decision, believing that he 'simply woke up' before appointing Van Rooyen, Zuma moaned.[2]

Gordhan says he kept Zuma apprised of his efforts to restore confidence in the economy and government after the Nene disaster: 'He understood in a crude way that you had to keep the business guys happy. But he wanted to carry on screwing the fiscus anyway. There was an element of recklessness with him because the country didn't matter to him, its reputation didn't matter as long as he could dish out things.'[3]

He was operating in a hostile environment in which Zuma had already manoeuvred most state capture actors into position. 'Malusi Gigaba had replaced Barbara Hogan as minister of public enterprises, and people like Gwede Mantashe for whatever reason were quite insistent on getting Siyabonga Gama in at Transnet. But frustration isn't quite the word to describe my feeling back then because it implies that you are lost. We weren't lost. We knew we were involved in a serious situation. I could have left, said, "Bugger this, here is my letter of resignation." But it was about the national interest.'[4]

Days before Gordhan tabled the budget, a three-page letter signed by Berning Ntlemeza, the apartheid-era strongman Zuma had appointed to lead the Hawks, arrived on his desk demanding answers to 27 questions. The questions – related to the SARS investigative unit that Moyane and Mahlobo's SSA made into a 'rogue' unit – were designed purely to disrupt preparations for the budget. The Hawks were ostensibly probing the SARS investigative unit but their real target was Gordhan. In the public domain, the SARS investigative unit was now 'rogue' after Moyane's cleanout at the taxman. And it was under Gordhan that SARS had established its investigative capability. Zuma and his stooges calculated that investigating and eventually charging Gordhan in relation to the 'rogue unit' would neutralise and destroy him, enabling the president to insert another lackey at finance.

Correspondence between the Hawks and Gordhan's legal team was leaked, nameless sources implicated Gordhan in illegal activities and he and the Treasury were repeatedly attacked, mostly in the pages of the Gupta newspaper and those of Independent Media. 'Moyane claimed that there was spying equipment. Nobody ever produced any evidence of spying on Zuma. And then you had ministers Mahlobo [state security] and Nhleko [police] holding a press conference right after a cabinet meeting ... we had finished a cabinet meeting and they went off to have a press conference about their investigation into SARS and me. I said to Lakela, "What is this?" But she claimed not to know,' says Gordhan.[5]

The assault was relentless. Mandla Nkomfe, a former MEC for finance in Gauteng who became adviser to Gordhan, says the situation developed into a 'full-blown battle'. 'He [Gordhan] would always say, "Okay, you must anticipate how they are going to respond." It was like a real battle. But it was not like he was just waiting to be charged,' Nkomfe says. Gordhan had survived worse and he was not intimidated by the head of state and the leader of his party. 'We are activists, man, and we survived apartheid and we survived the security police. I didn't give a shit if it was the president. That's where your moral fibre comes up, or your political fibre. And if you want to f*** me around, I'm going to challenge you wherever I can, however I can. But it was tough [inside the ANC], it was tough. Derek led a process once in the NEC and you had what, probably 15, 20 speakers all saying [to Zuma], "You should go. You should go." There were other comrades who also understood what was going on.'[6]

In a statement, Gordhan declared: 'There is a group of people that are not interested in the economic stability of this country and the welfare of its people. It seems they are interested in disrupting institutions and destroying reputations,' adding that there was 'no reason' to investigate him.[7] The Hawks kept harassing the finance minister – even while he was abroad on a roadshow trying to calm the frayed nerves of investors and creditors – and demanding that he answer their spurious questions. He refused. Ntlemeza was adamant. 'As for the minister suggesting that the Hawks had leaked the letters and should call a press conference and talk about the matter at hand, we would like to set the record straight as well, that had the minister, like any law-abiding citizen, complied with our letter and provided answers, we would not be where we are today. This is neither a talk show nor a soapie. We are mandated to investigate without fear, favour or prejudice,' the Hawks hit back.[8]

As rumours of the finance minister's imminent arrest began circulating, Gordhan and the Treasury issued an unprecedented statement imploring the public 'to protect the National Treasury staff, who have diligently, honestly and skilfully served the national interest to the best of their ability'. It was remarkable – a serving minister of finance, under siege from his own president, with no cover from his party, trying to stabilise the battered economy, desperately rallying the public to his defence. 'The statement, importantly, said we were prepared to fight the war. That was the point. That we were not going to give up and that they could do what they liked.'[9]

At a press conference, Abrahams proclaimed that 'the time for disrespecting the NPA is over' and even Gordhan would have to face the law. But it was all a charade, part of the Zuma-Gupta axis's assault on good governance and undermining the one part of the state that was still functional – the Treasury. (Abrahams later vacated his office after the high court found his appointment to have been irregular. Gordhan believes he should be charged for abuse of power.[10])

Despite the overwhelming evidence that was stacking up against Zuma and the failures of his government, ANC mandarins continued singing his hosannas. Naledi Pandor, then minister of science and technology, offered a rousing defence of the man, dismissing criticism of him and his government and praising his leadership. Across the years she has displayed a remarkable ability to ignore (or rationalise) abuses, criminality and dishonesty. She has been a valuable member of the ANC executive. 'No amount of vilification of President Zuma and his government will erase these achievements [of Zuma's government], just as hatred of President Zuma will never propel Hon [Mmusi] Maimane [the DA leader] to the leadership of South Africa,' she said during a no-confidence debate in Parliament after the Nene disaster.[11]

Lindiwe Sisulu, another consistent underperformer but perennial cabinet member, was equally ebullient about Zuma, saying he had a 'solid roadmap for the current period that we are in'. Remarkably, at the time, she also said that criticism of Zuma amounted to hatred of him and was a manifestation of 'white supremacy'.[12]

On 1 March 2016, Ramaphosa was one of the 225 ANC MPs in the National Assembly who rejected a motion of no-confidence in Zuma brought by Maimane. The DA leader's exhortation that Zuma had 'sold out' to the Guptas and that he was wrecking the country and its economy found no support on the government benches. Jackson Mthembu, the ANC chief whip, Mathole Motshekga, a veteran ANC leader, and Lindiwe Zulu, a venomous careerist MP, spoke strongly in defence of their president, despite everything that was happening around them.[13]

A month later, Ramaphosa again voted with his party to keep Zuma in office when the DA brought another motion to remove him after the Constitutional Court's Nkandla judgment. Maimane made a direct appeal to Ramaphosa, 'a South African whom I respect and who was key in authoring the Constitution', to vote in favour of the rule of law and remove Zuma from office. The deputy president voted against the motion with 234 other MPs who wanted to keep Zuma in the Union Buildings.[14]

Among the president's most full-throated defenders that day were Mmamoloko Kubayi, considered a Ramaphosa insider whom he promoted to the cabinet, and John Jeffery, the deputy minister of justice under Zuma and Ramaphosa. The motion was 'frivolous', said Kubayi (who was pictured doing her nails while Parliament's Nkandla committee met to absolve Zuma), while Jeffery said Zuma was a president who acted in 'good faith'.[15] The ANC, its leadership, deployed ministers, MPs and other members who occupied positions of power in society – as per the cadre deployment policy – were in lockstep behind their leader. Total mobilisation in defence of one man.

Zuma had been emboldened over the years by his comrades' and colleagues' acquiescence and lack of morality and principles. And he resented the fact that he was forced to insert Gordhan at the Treasury, a significant setback for the Guptas. The family had already achieved enormous success, including helping Tegeta Resources, one of their mining ventures, buy a Glencore-owned coal mine, Optimum, financed by an illegal advance payment to Tegeta by Eskom.[16]

They were also on the verge of disembowelling Denel, the state-owned arms manufacturer, with a deal that would see it form a joint venture with a firm in which a Gupta agent, Salim Essa, was the sole shareholder.[17] The deal would have meant Denel's vast intellectual property reserves being exported to the benefit of the Guptas. Again, a Gupta and ANC deployee, Daniel Mantsha, was in charge.[18] And this was after the family had extracted billions of rands in lucrative contracts from Transnet thanks to their capture of the company's management and board.[19]

It has become a tired refrain, but the ANC's top six continued to ignore blatant warnings about rising and rampant corruption. In March 2016, the Nelson Mandela, Ahmed Kathrada and Adelaide and Oliver Tambo foundations wrote to the ANC executive asking for 'corrective action'. In the same month, 101 former members of Umkhonto weSizwe sent a memorandum to Zuma, Ramaphosa and the rest of the leadership 'expressing concerns about the Guptas'. A month later, a forum of former directors general wrote to Ramaphosa and the cabinet pleading for an intervention. Meetings between ANC leaders and the clergy, business and political veterans also highlighted the scourge of state capture.[20]

'The ANC does not seem to have done anything about these complaints from its own members, nor does it seem to have done anything to protect them in their positions,' Chief Justice Raymond Zondo writes in his final report.[21] There was no serious intervention, no attempt to stop the country's accelerating slide. Ramaphosa believed he should sit and wait, preparing the ground to ensure victory at the ANC national conference in December 2017. But that necessarily meant merely observing as increasing damage was done to the country, the economy and the nation's social fabric. For Ramaphosa, it was evidently a price he was willing to pay.

Early on Monday 27 March 2017, as Gordhan's plane landed at Heathrow Airport in London, a text message from the director general in the Presidency, Cassius Lubisi, flashed onto the screen of his smartphone. It read:

> To: Honourable Minister Pravin Gordhan, and Honourable Deputy Minister Mcebisi Jonas, and Director General Lungisa Fuzile.
>
> Good evening Honourable Minister and Honourable DG.
>
> By order of his Excellency, the President, I have been directed to communicate an urgent message to your good selves. The permission for you to travel to the UK and the USA from 26 to 31 March 2017 has been rescinded with immediate effect.
>
> In that regard His Excellency has directed that I request your good selves to return to the Republic of the South Africa as soon as you receive this message. Further His Excellency has directed that you instruct DG Lungisa Fuzile to accompany your good selves back home.
>
> His Excellency, the President, will be dispatching a formal directive to your respective offices tomorrow morning, 27 March 2017.
>
> With my best wishes, yours sincerely, Cassius Lubisi, director general and Secretary of the Cabinet.[22]

Gordhan was dumbstruck. As was Fuzile. Jonas had not yet left the country. 'So we just let them know that we can't go back immediately anyway because the flights are in the evening. We cleared Heathrow, went to our hotel, showered and we changed our clothes. And that's how we used to work, by the way: you land, you go, you change and you move into a meeting. We went to the venue where all the meetings were to take place, briefed Jabu Mabuza and Nicky Newton-King [CEO of the Johannesburg Stock Exchange] and went straight into meetings with Moody's and Standard & Poor's.'[23]

Gordhan and Fuzile returned to South Africa that night. On 30 March, after days of wild speculation and intense political drama, Zuma fired Gordhan and Jonas as minister and deputy minister of finance. Zuma and the Guptas had tried and failed to bring Gordhan down with smears and bogus charges and found it difficult to isolate him. The ministry of finance was simply too powerful. Zuma had had enough. Shortly before he reshuffled his cabinet, he met the ANC top six and showed them an 'intelligence report' that implicated Gordhan and Jonas in undermining the country with foreign interests. It was obviously bogus and it emerged later that the 'report' was nothing more than screengrabs of WhatsApp messages.

Ramaphosa, in an affidavit, said he told Zuma he disagreed with his decision and would say so publicly. Zuma responded that it didn't matter and that his relationship with Gordhan had broken down 'irretrievably'.[24] Not only that, he wanted to replace Gordhan with Brian Molefe, the Gupta agent deployed first to Transnet, then to Eskom.

In his findings after the inquiry into state capture, Zondo said 'there might not be a lot for which the ANC leadership from 2009 to 2017 may deserve to be credited with regard to their handling of President Zuma as a member and a leader of the ANC, and as president of the country and his relationship with the Guptas, corruption and state capture. But for standing up to Zuma and stopping him from appointing Molefe, they deserve credit. One shudders to think what would have happened to National Treasury had he not been stopped from appointing Molefe as Gordhan's replacement.'[25]

❖

At the risk of disturbing the fast-paced chronology of events, it is worth considering the leadership structures involved at the time. Zuma was head of party and government, assisted by Ramaphosa, his deputy in both and chairperson of the ANC deployment committee, and the party's organisational executives, Mantashe and Jessie Duarte. They were all intrinsically involved in matters of appointment, deployment, removal and dismissal. This always happened in line with party diktat, deployment policy and ANC requirements. Zondo rightly asks why the deployment committee never stopped Molefe's rise, even though his dramatic progress on behalf of the Guptas was always announced ahead of time by *The New Age*. What did the ANC leaders think was happening at Transnet, at Eskom and in government, Zondo asks: 'Did they bother to ask themselves these questions? If they did not, why not?'[26]

In place of Gordhan and Jonas, Zuma appointed Malusi Gigaba, an active Gupta agent and regular guest in Saxonwold, and Sfiso Buthelezi, another unknown provincial politician. They marched into the ministry's offices as Gordhan and Nene were addressing supporters on Church Square. 'It was about saying, "You're not going to scare us. And we will stand up to you. And we will expose you," ' Gordhan says of his response to being fired by Zuma.[27]

Ramaphosa offered limp criticism of Zuma's decision the morning after the cabinet reshuffle, telling the SABC it was 'totally unacceptable' but that he wouldn't resign in protest.[28] Gordhan's dismissal signalled complete victory for Zuma and the Gupta axis. They were in full charge of the state: all state-owned companies, law enforcement, the Public Protector (Busisiwe Mkhwebane replaced Thuli Madonsela and launched a series of orchestrated witch-hunts), the government and now the Treasury. South Africa was in its deepest crisis since 1994. Zondo found that Zuma was 'determined to give the Guptas direct access to Treasury, to hand control to the Guptas before he left office'.[29]

Ratings agencies Fitch and Standard & Poor's downgraded the country's credit rating to junk status. Civil society warned about democracy under siege. There was a countrywide groundswell of resistance against Zuma and his government, with marches in all major centres. But Nomvula Mokonyane, a Zuma praise singer (she hated Gordhan), was unbowed. 'Let the rand fall!' she crowed at a party rally after Gordhan's firing. 'We will pick it up!' This was someone who, while she was premier of Gauteng, asked a company that was found to have been the beneficiary of corrupt government contracts worth billions to supply her with chicken braai packs and Johnnie Walker whisky for festive seasons. The stupidity was breathtaking, the short-sightedness remarkable and the ineptitude galling. There was carnage on the stock market, the exchange rate was torpedoed and investor and business confidence plummeted.

28
Decline and collapse

ON MONDAY, 18 DECEMBER 2017, ANC DELEGATES AT NASREC, the dilapidated old showgrounds in the south of Johannesburg where the annual Rand Easter Show is held, voted for the ANC's new leaders. Cyril Ramaphosa, deputy leader of the party since 2012 and deputy president of the country since 2014, was contesting the party leadership against Nkosazana Dlamini-Zuma, the hugely uninspiring and dour career politician whose campaign was conceived and managed by her former husband, Jacob Zuma. It was called the billion-rand campaign because of the amount spent on bribes, organisation and campaigning. Hundreds of thousands of rands from secret intelligence accounts were withdrawn that morning to ensure some delegates voted correctly, to buy enough alcohol to placate others and to ensure a good time for all after the election.

Ramaphosa's campaign, in which Pravin Gordhan played a key role, was premised on clean governance, a return to the ANC's 'selfless values' of leadership and service, and above all a break with the era of state capture. Even though he was part of it. Dlamini-Zuma, by contrast, was a proxy for Zuma and the corruption and capture grouping in the ANC, the faction that feasted on patronage and extraction networks and the Guptas. She has no constituency of her own and adroitly made the slogans of capture her own: she wanted 'radical economic transformation' to break 'white monopoly capital' and to challenge 'Western imperialism'. The slogans, however, were concocted by a London public relations firm, Bell Pottinger, in cahoots with the Guptas' favourite son (and Zuma's actual son), Duduzane. They were meaningless and dishonest but very nearly worked.

Late on that afternoon at Nasrec, next to the vast dining hall where delegates were treated to dinners of roast beef and chicken, a close colleague and I sat down with one of Ramaphosa's adjutants. He gave us insight into his campaign, the horse-trading that was happening and what Ramaphosa wanted to accomplish if he was elected. It was a wide-ranging conversation covering the period from Gordhan's dismissal earlier in the year to the present. Our source spoke of Ramaphosa's commitment to the rule of law, how he abhorred corruption and how he planned to heal the country.

But I'll never forget his answer when we pressed him about Ramaphosa's actual plans, what he wanted to be remembered for and what he saw as his biggest task. The ANC leadership election, after all, was much bigger than a popularity contest – the successful candidate would become president. And what's more, the depravity of the state capture era meant that if the Zuma candidate – his former wife – won, it would mean a continuation of party-sanctioned corruption. So, what was Ramaphosa's overarching philosophy, his big dream, the main driver of his ambition? 'He doesn't want to be the ANC president under whose leadership the party finally splits …'

I was completely taken aback. Ramaphosa's biggest motivation in running for the party leadership wasn't to rid it of criminals, to launch a programme of reform and restoration in government and state or to focus on the rule of law. It was about maintaining the party above all else.

Ramaphosa won the contest by just 179 votes: 2 440 against 2 261. It was the narrowest margin in any ANC leadership contest since the 1940s. Shortly before the results were announced late that night, he was still smiling and chatting with Zuma, the architect of South Africa's precipitous decline over the previous decade. Ramaphosa could never bring himself to stand up to Zuma, to have the courage of his convictions and to condemn his predecessor's criminality, his venal and cynical ways and his desecration of the Constitution.

Zuma was so reckless that on the day the conference started, and without informing anyone – including his pliant minister of finance

(Malusi Gigaba) and the Treasury – announced free tertiary education for the poor. It was an astonishing display of desperate populism, better suited to a backwater banana republic than to a modernising constitutional democracy. That's how Zuma operated and Ramaphosa kept indulging him.

But the bitter fruits were about to be harvested. The close contest between Ramaphosa and Dlamini-Zuma and the deep division within the party meant that the new ANC leader couldn't have whomever he wanted. And he was cursed with Ace Magashule, one of Zuma's fiercest supporters and one of the most corrupt in the governing party, who was elected as secretary general, the party's most powerful bureaucratic position. I was right in front of Ramaphosa when the announcement came and his face turned ashen, much like Mbeki's a decade before when Zuma beat him. Even on that night it was clear: the ANC was done for.

Ramaphosa has always found working with senior ANC leaders difficult, preferring to defer to them when standing on principle was warranted. The way in which Mbeki seemed to dominate him, and how he repeatedly withered before Zuma, was in marked contrast to how he was able to command the constitutional negotiations while locked in combat with the National Party government. Was he reluctant to challenge Mbeki because of tribal or seniority doubts? Inside the ANC, enemies have always sought to use his background as a Venda against him, charging that he is from a small ethnic minority and therefore cannot be expected to lead an organisation dominated by Zulus and Xhosas. Zuma, of course, used ethnicity as a weapon, brandishing his Zulu nationalistic fervour like a knobkierie and cowhide shield.

As already amply illustrated, Ramaphosa did not resist state capture as he could and should have done. Even in his closing address at Nasrec, after taking charge of the party and ousting the Zuma leadership, he lavished praise on the Guptas' most valuable asset. Zuma was venerated by Ramaphosa, the self-proclaimed champion of clean government. 'I would like, on your behalf, to thank President Jacob Zuma for the ten years he has spent as the president of our movement and for a lifetime of service to the people of this country,' Ramaphosa said. 'It was during your tenure, Nxamalala, and thanks to your vision that the National Planning Commission was established and produced the country's first National Development Plan. This is a framework for economic and social change that will guide our country for many years to come. History will record that it was at your insistence that South Africa expanded its antiretroviral programme rapidly and progressively to be the largest in the world. Through your intervention, we have made great strides in combating the epidemic, many lives have been saved and many infections prevented.'[1]

Ramaphosa may have been right about HIV but the rest was pure revisionism. And then probably one of the most dishonest and grating comments about Zuma from a public platform: 'We cannot close this, the 54th national conference of the African National Congress, without paying tribute to you for your contribution over many decades to the struggle for freedom, democracy and development.' Zuma was a wrecking ball and Ramaphosa refused to condemn him for it. It would come back to haunt him. 'We will miss your jokes, the sweets you distributed to us and the wonderful conversations we have had,' Ramaphosa said.[2] He would miss the sweets Zuma gave him.

Tim du Plessis got to know Ramaphosa during the negotiations and was impressed by how he 'went around the country in his old Toyota' building a base to be elected as the ANC secretary general in 1991. 'And when I interviewed him in his office at Shell House in downtown Johannesburg, I just thought this is one helluva cool dude. He said the right things, he was firm, he wasn't too friendly but he wasn't unfriendly. He answered all my questions in a forthright way. And I got to know him. I saw him with the media and I saw him negotiate while everyone around him was fighting at Codesa. I saw how he operated in that environment and he was impressive. You cannot deny it.

'Leon Wessels [Ramaphosa's deputy during the final constitutional negotiations between 1994 and 1996] told me that this guy knew exactly what he was doing. He knew beforehand where he was going to make compromises and did so without losing face. But the Ramaphosa who won at Nasrec was not the Ramaphosa from the NUM in the 1980s or the guy who led the negotiations at Codesa. It was someone else.'[3]

There was great excitement across the country after Ramaphosa's election as ANC leader. I, too, was optimistic that he was the right leader at the most challenging of times. And he showed promise, within weeks using his position as new leader of the party and incumbent deputy head of state to appoint a new board and group chief executive at Eskom in January 2018. It seemed he was serious about making dramatic changes. Remarkably, he was able to engineer Zuma's ousting in February after sensitive negotiations and, eventually, forceful instructions that he (Zuma) would be removed from office through a motion of no-confidence if he didn't resign.

Ramaphosa swept into office in February 2018, enjoying the good-will of every right-minded South African who yearned for proper governance and the rule of law. In his first address to a joint sitting of Parliament (when he delivered his famous but ultimately empty call to arms of 'Thuma mina', or 'send me'), he again opted to bow before Zuma: 'I also wish to extend a word of gratitude to former President Jacob Zuma for the manner in which he approached this difficult and sensitive process. I wish to thank him for his service to the nation during his two terms as president of the republic, during which the country made significant progress in several areas of development.'[4]

It was another example of the disingenuous nature of the president whom everyone wanted to succeed. Of course, the reality of politics as fraught as that of a divided and broken ANC requires a measure of moral and rhetorical flexibility, so a modicum of respect to Zuma was to be expected. But in hindsight, Ramaphosa went too far and enabled the perpetrators of state capture to normalise grand corruption and institutionalised graft. 'Significant progress in several areas of development'?

Ismail Momoniat, the deputy director general at the Treasury, differs sharply from Ramaphosa. He told then Deputy Chief Justice Raymond Zondo, who chaired the judicial commission of inquiry into state capture, exactly how bad things were: 'Under President Zuma, the erosion of the discipline of prudent decision-making and value-for-money spending, combined with the misdirection of funds, reversed all these gains [of the Mandela and Mbeki years], moving us back into sub-investment grade, but also took some key economic indicators to a level far lower than that which we inherited in 1994.

'The high level of corruption after 2009 has critically damaged our economy and our country, with the commensurate devastating impact on the lives of our people, not least on our education and health systems. We now have a public service [in all three spheres of government] that cannot even deliver the most basic services in most parts of our country.'[5] It is one of the most damning analyses of the Zuma years and Momoniat (or 'Momo', as those at the Treasury referred to him) delivered his statement as deputy director general: tax and financial sector policy at the National Treasury, with 26 years of experience at the time.

Why the optimism about Ramaphosa, then, given what became known later – the dithering, the decline, the destruction? He quickly reshuffled his cabinet, removing some of the most significant Guptaites, including Mosebenzi Zwane, Faith Muthambi, David Mahlobo, Bongani Bongo, Des van Rooyen, Lynne Brown and, surprisingly, Fikile Mbalula. And he brought back Gordhan (to public enterprises), Nhlanhla Nene (finance) and Derek Hanekom (tourism). But he kept Nomvula Mokonyane, Bathabile Dlamini and Lindiwe Sisulu, all of whom were inept, corrupted or both. The return of Nene and Gordhan, however, overshadowed those who survived the axe, and the argument at the time was that he needed some stability while he was cleaning shop.

During an off-the-record meeting shortly afterwards at Doppio Zero in Rosebank, Johannesburg, the Ramaphosa adviser from Nasrec explained that the new president wanted to move with enough speed to demonstrate urgency but not with so much haste that he alienated the party. It was the famous 'long game' argument. The president was going to follow procedure and the law ahead of the 2019 general election. But once the election was over and his party had a new mandate with him at the helm, South Africa would start to see significant change. It all made sense, the evidence supported what he said, and I reported it as such.

Under Ramaphosa's direction, enough funding was set aside and institutional support was provided for the Zondo commission's work. Zondo was given a secretariat, a legal team, forensic investigators, logistical support and the freedom to conduct an unfettered probe into state capture, an indictment of the ANC. The commission heard hundreds of hours of testimony over four years, processed hundreds of thousands of documents and pieces of evidence and produced a report consisting of six parts detailing the extent of ANC-sponsored corruption and Zuma-enabled capture. The commission's report was damning, indicting the party and its leaders as not only complicit in a vast political project that sought to defraud the state but in actively enabling it.

Zondo repeatedly asked, in his final report, where the ANC and its leaders were when the destruction of parastatals, SARS and attempts to capture the Treasury took place. And his findings were brutal: they were accomplices. They refused to act when the proliferation of graft became clear. The ANC led by Zuma, Ramaphosa and Gwede Mantashe could have stopped it in its tracks if it had wanted to. It chose not to do so. It 'closed ranks' and prioritised the continued survival of the party above everything else.

Zizi Kodwa, the ANC spin doctor who was also named in the final Zondo report (Kodwa was charged with corruption in June 2024, resigned as minister, but was returned to parliament as an MP by the ANC), took great offence one day at a hearing of the commission in Parktown, Johannesburg. He often sat quietly at the back, listening to the damning testimony of proven ANC cadres such as Gordhan, Nene, Barbara Hogan, Mcebisi Jonas and others. It was damning of the party, damning of cadre deployment and damning of almost every leader in the organisation. I suggested the obvious to him: that it was a searing indictment of the ANC. He exploded and rejected my assertion, repeating his famous media statement of years before, after Jonas's claims of being offered the finance ministry by the Guptas, that it was a fiction that the ANC was ever 'captured'.

Ramaphosa also instructed Sydney Mufamadi, a respected former cabinet minister and academic, to lead an investigation into the SSA. Commissions of inquiry were launched into SARS (led by retired judge Robert Nugent), the NPA (led by retired judge Yvonne Mokgoro) and the Public Investment Corporation (led by retired judge Lex Mpati). The new president swiftly moved on Tom Moyane at SARS, firing him in late 2018 and replacing him with Edward Kieswetter. And he opened the closed appointment process for a new NDPP, installing advocate Shamila Batohi in February 2019 and promising her complete independence to prosecute without fear or favour.

Initial portents, therefore, were good. Ramaphosa clearly sought to repair the damage to the criminal justice system and did not interfere with investigations or prosecutions. And he initially acted on the commissions' recommendations, following the advice of the inquiries into the NPA and SARS. But there were signs of weakness. Mufamadi's findings, in an explosive document titled High-Level Review Panel on the SSA, were breathtaking. His report revealed a spy agency completely redesigned and realigned to serve the interests of the Zuma faction in the ANC, parallel states run by spies with access to weaponry and millions of rands in cash, off the books and faceless, roaming the country unchecked. Arthur Fraser and Thulani Dlomo were the men in charge and they were still in the state's employ. It was clear that both, ironically, posed not only a danger to the state but to Ramaphosa politically. Yet he never moved on either of them, nor did he launch a reorganisation of the SSA that was so obviously necessary. It was a fatal mistake.

Fraser was moved sideways to become director general of the prisons service, where he used his position to help Zuma irregularly obtain medical parole after he was sent to prison for defying the Constitutional Court. And he was the brain behind Ramaphosa's biggest political crisis: Phala Phala. It was Fraser who deposed an affidavit about the theft of hundreds of thousands of dollars from the president's game farm in Limpopo and the suspicious circumstances surrounding it. It remains unclear how the money was brought into the country, how it came to be put down as payment for the purchase of buffalo (that never left the property) and whether proper channels were followed when the theft was reported. Phala Phala cast a pall over Ramaphosa's presidency, which in latter years lurched from crisis to crisis.

Ramaphosa made a serious mistake in indulging Fraser, a spymaster of some skill and in possession of enough incriminating material on almost every ANC minister currently in office. During his appearance in front of Mufamadi's panel, he arrived with numerous folders and told the panel he had files on everyone in positions of power. He proceeded to keep the panel busy for, allegedly, two days, sharing with them what he knew.

Dlomo, another shadowy but powerful figure, was summoned to the panel from his posting as ambassador to Japan, a reward from

Zuma. When he sat down he simply laughed off any question and even dismissed a personal call from the president, according to sources with knowledge of events. He waltzed out of the session, leaving Mufamadi seething and no one any the wiser about the parallel spy network he oversaw. And spies seemed to have played a significant role in lighting the fire that led to the orgy of violence unleashed on the country in July 2021.

❖

The ANC's worst election results in 2019 – the party's support receded from 62.15 per cent in 2014 to just above 57 per cent – forced Ramaphosa to retreat. His enemies in the party, led by Magashule, were openly trying to thwart his nominal efforts at reform and, as his adviser told me and as stated by Zondo (based on evidence before him), Ramaphosa prioritised ANC unity ahead of anything else. After the release of the Zondo reports, which made recommendations on the role of Parliament, reforms to the criminal justice system, state procurement, parastatals and proposed prosecutions, Ramaphosa's ANC stalled on implementation. In the two years (at the time of writing) since the final Zondo report was issued, few reforms have been enacted and almost no decisive leadership shown to ensure accountability.

Batohi has tried valiantly to resurrect the embattled NPA and to institute prosecutions against state capture actors but deep damage to the organisational culture, coupled with a loss of skills and expertise over the years, meant that no big name has yet been convicted and imprisoned. Magashule, Zwane, Matshela Koko and others have been charged but no one is in jail. The charges against Koko were thrown out of court, to the disgust of the prosecuting team and Andrea Johnson, who led the NPA's Investigating Directorate that seeks to revive the Scorpions. The biggest success has been the work of the NPA's Asset Forfeiture Unit and the Special Investigating Unit, which have managed to claw back a couple of billion rands lost to multinational concerns such as ABB, McKinsey, Bain & Company, KPMG and others for their role in the capture era.

And the Guptas? They remain at large, having fled the country years ago and found refuge in Dubai and India, the NPA powerless to stop them. Says Gordhan: 'I've got a particular experience at SARS which informs me: put people in orange uniforms and see the rest run. But only if people go to prison. Then the risk model changes. Because people become more apprehensive. "Hey, this SARS is going to catch us." If you go back to about 2000, 2001 and look at the newspapers then, we talked about a new system being created that looks like a kind of octopus, it could connect information from everybody. Ivan Pillay and others built up the enforcement capability. I think you built trust in the institution. People came to respect it. We didn't just change the institution, we changed the tax culture in South Africa.'[6]

Ramaphosa is, however, reaping the whirlwind of his party's misrule. The mismanagement and criminality inflicted on the state through the deployment of corrupt and inept cadres is leading to the collapse of many institutions crucial to the survival of democracy and the functioning of the country. Eskom is a site of destruction and criminality, with rent and resource extraction the order of the day. But the country's energy security has also become the site of ideological contestation, with strong factions in the ANC refusing to modernise and adapt to a changing world to ensure a steady and reliable supply of electricity.

Transnet, the logistics parastatal, is also in an advanced state of collapse. Railways don't function, harbours are clogged and unable to handle traffic and business is unable to export goods to earn much-needed foreign currency. 'It's easy to say Durban's port is congested and this rail doesn't work and so on. But the same business guys who are today complaining were absolutely silent then. They were absolutely silent during the capture years and when all this damage was taking place. They didn't mind working with Molefe, at Transnet or at Eskom, and they didn't mind working with Koko and company,' is Gordhan's rejoinder.[7] Events, however, are overtaking the ANC. Ramaphosa's government was forced to seek the private sector's help to prevent collapse, with joint workstreams established to support (and in many cases take over) the functions of the state. By mid-2024, reform of key sectors was driven by a small band of bureaucrats from Operation Vulindlela, a joint team consisting of civil servants in the Presidency and the Treasury, supported by private sector expertise and money.

Du Plessis says there are strong similarities between the ANC today and the National Party at the end of its life: 'Like the National

Party, the ANC has also lost its leitmotif, its reason for existence. It has succumbed to corruption and mediocrity. It was established by men of letters, they were educated, church leaders, journalists, lawyers, and they had a legitimate grievance. Today there is no one left like Nelson Mandela, who read and understood the world, or who spends time with historians and clever people who know how the world is stitched together, or who tries to find a way to progress or to modernise. And let us be honest: under the ANC this country is turning into a failed state. There is no intellectual resilience left.'[8]

The destruction the ANC has visited on South Africa is keenly felt in every sector of society. Briefings with senior figures in the criminal justice system confirm that the damage to law enforcement is deep and seems difficult to overcome. 'You won't believe what we've had to deal with since we started out here,' one senior official told me in an office where, some years before, decisions were taken that shaped the country for the worse. 'State capture networks still function here and we won't be able to really change things unless we move certain senior leaders out of their positions. And that could lead to internal war. We're trying to do what we can, to rebuild with what we've got. But it's going to take years and years. I don't know if we'll last, to be honest.'

Johann van Loggerenberg, one of Tom Moyane's high-profile victims during the purge at SARS, says everyone in positions of influence knew what was happening there but did nothing. He is desperately sad about how he and others were discarded and how SARS lost much of its enforcement capability: 'If only one person had listened. Only one. And investigated a little deeper and stood up. Only one. But I and others were repeatedly violated. Over and over. We moan easily about corruption in the state, about people not doing anything about it. But no one has the guts to admit, "We missed it, we were wrong." Not a single person. You know, I look at the shit that's happening in our country and I know that if I were still working for SARS I'd be working my fingers to the bone to hold every single crook to account.'

Gordhan, over regular breakfasts in Brooklyn, Pretoria, told me about his and other ANC leaders' determination to right the wrongs of the Zuma era. 'But there are still too many crooks inside of government and the ANC. We know that. They know that. And it will take a strong effort to get rid of them. They are still operating as they used to, you know? They're undermining our efforts to fix Eskom, fix Transnet.'

Dawie Roodt, an economist who detests big government and believes the ANC has destroyed everything in its path over the last 20-plus years, calls Gordhan one of the worst ministers the country has had. His stewardship of state-owned enterprises, after being returned to the cabinet by Ramaphosa, is enough testimony of that, Roodt says. Eskom is worse off than ever, Transnet has never been weaker and the proposed sale of a chunk of SAA, the loss-making airline, was a disaster.

But Gordhan is honest, he is not corrupt and he resisted state capture when hardly anyone else did. He told me: 'Firstly, none of us understood the extent of the damage that was done to institutions when the president took over in 2018. Secondly, we thought putting in new boards and CEOs was going to be the panacea for all your problems. Thirdly, once we started digging into some of the institutions, we discovered there were guys, who are still here, who collaborated with Lynne Brown and the rest.'[9]

The economic and corruption mess the country is in has also led to various off-the-books and private initiatives to force the government's hand and drive change. Advocate Paul Pretorius, Zondo's former evidence leader, is deeply worried about the country's fate. 'We did what we could at the commission ... why is nothing happening? Was it all for nothing?' he asked me at numerous meetings. He visited News24's group of investigative journalists in 2023 and spoke passionately about 'state capture 2.0': the rise of organised crime, the inability of the police, Hawks and NPA to tackle crime and corruption in a coherent manner and the apparent lack of commitment by the government to truly break with the capture past. 'It's up to civil society now, it's up to journalists,' he told me once.

André de Ruyter, who tried to tackle the myriad problems at Eskom, explained the ideological constraints within which he was forced to function. He and Professor Malegapuru Makgoba, the Eskom board chairperson, had to address corruption and mismanagement head-on and implement a programme of repair and maintenance while preventing load-shedding that was killing the economy. 'It is quite simply impossible to do so under an ANC government. They are deeply committed to discredited and outdated Marxist ideas of state-led everything. And Ramaphosa? He is just too afraid to take decisions. He should be a country club manager trying to keep the tennis and golf section happy. You cannot function in a modern and globalised world when your world outlook is based on "comrade this" and "comrade that". It simply doesn't work.'

But Ramaphosa is reluctant to draw on the knowledge and experience of individuals available to him. 'I think societies, and especially governments, need councils of elders, and if the elders are going to disagree with each other and have their arguments and agree on a line of march and so on, it allows the governments to minimise wrong decisions, and you can do that without trying to rule from the grave,' says Trevor Manuel, who should have been in the prime of his political career today.[10] Instead, he chairs the board at Old Mutual.

'Of course I want to climb out of my skin with frustration at what's happening sometimes. You know, there's an author and poet who I used quite often in budget speeches and so on, Ben Okri. He delivered the Steve Biko Memorial Lecture at UCT about 12 years ago and there's this wonderful line in there: "It's not often that a people reach a mountain top and descend with a rich vision of a transformed life for all of its people, and then set about realising it. Too often the euphoria gets swept away into an ideology of state. Too often it is squandered ..."'[11]

Why is South Africa in such a poor state? During a dinner with a high-profile academic who leads an influential think-tank at a prestigious university in the United States, the question was put to a table of guests: 'The ANC government has known about all of this for years ... the mismanagement, the corruption and the dysfunction ... why has it failed to act? Look at Eskom ... it is the single biggest source of misery for the South African economy, growth and employment. The problems are known, they have been identified years ago. But still, nothing. And now everything is coming to a head ... all the problems exploding at the same time. What is it?'

In June 2023, I attended an off-the-record briefing in Ramaphosa's office. About a dozen journalists gathered in the cabinet room, just off the presidential office in the west wing of the Union Buildings. The meeting was confidential and I cannot divulge details of what was discussed, the questions we asked nor the answers he gave. The briefing was on background, to explain his government's attempts at structural reform and interventions to accelerate economic growth. His advisers were smart and articulate, clearly passionate about their job.

But after three hours with him and one or two ministers, I started to formulate an answer to the academic's question, and in this I was assisted by my surroundings. The presidential offices are on the second floor of the Union Buildings, right underneath the clock tower in the west wing. The carpets are plush, the surrounds quiet and venerable. The clock chimes every 15 minutes. Aides and valets are ever-present, offering refreshments and sustenance. Presidential bodyguards are present but inconspicuous. And ministers have briefing notes and policy documents at their fingertips.

So why have Ramaphosa and his government not acted with more haste, more urgency, more speed? Why do the interests of the party always outweigh the national interest? It's hubris. The ANC, its leaders and its deployees suffer from extraordinary levels of hubris. After 30 years in the Union Buildings they are soft, imperious, cold and out of touch. They are corrupted.

Conclusion

ON THE EVENING OF 16 FEBRUARY 2018, I was in the press gallery in the National Assembly in Cape Town as the newly elected president, Cyril Ramaphosa, delivered the finely crafted 'Thuma mina' speech after his election as head of state.

Next to me was an Antipodean diplomat who said South Africans could be proud of the way democracy had held up during the previous couple of weeks as Ramaphosa engineered Jacob Zuma's exit from the Union Buildings. After the ANC's national conference at Nasrec, Ramaphosa consolidated his power on the party's NEC and forced Zuma to resign.

Occupants of the press gallery looked down as the judiciary entered the chamber, with the leadership of the armed forces already seated in the gallery below us. The symbolism was not lost on anyone. An independent judiciary and a defence force subject to an elected government. 'There were no tanks in the streets, no mass riots, nothing. Just a peaceful transfer of power,' said the diplomat. Then Ramaphosa delivered a rousing rallying cry, imploring everyone across the country's political divides to join him in reviving the vision of a unified country.

But the sliver of national optimism Ramaphosa's speech sparked was short-lived. His commitment to rescue South Africa from the destruction and deprivation of the state capture era under Zuma extended only as far as the doors of Luthuli House. Because when it came to implementing essential reforms in the ANC, he recoiled.

Apologists point out that Ramaphosa supported the judicial inquiry into allegations of state capture, led by Chief Justice Raymond Zondo, and that he appointed various other commissions and committees of inquiry. There was the Mpati commission into the Public Investment Corporation, the Nugent commission into SARS, the Mokgoro inquiry into the NPA leadership and a 'high-level panel' that investigated the State Security Agency.

The state capture commission produced a six-part, 17-volume report that detailed the role of the ANC and its leadership in the infiltration and collapse of parastatals and government departments. The other inquiries made astounding findings about abuse of power, corruption and the destructive role of cadre deployment. SARS, for example, was gutted by Zuma's all-consuming quest to stay out of prison; the State Security Agency was reinvented to serve the interests of the ANC and Zuma.

But although there was a new executive leadership and a superficial shift in the ANC's commitment to renewal and reform, nothing else changed when Ramaphosa replaced Zuma. The primacy of the movement remained fundamental, and this required party control of all levers of state power, democratic centralism as the main decision-making mechanism and the supremacy of the cadre in society.

Ramaphosa appointed new leaders at the NPA and SARS but he severely curtailed their ability to function as they should when he left the command structures at the SSA, police and other law enforcement agencies intact. This was done to maintain the extensive networks of patronage, rent-seeking and extraction at all levels of the state that support the lifestyles of party leaders and the ANC itself.

Paul Pretorius, the advocate who was Zondo's evidence leader during the capture inquiry, has a hand-drawn flow chart that he uses to explain how the patronage system works. At its heart lies the billions of rands the state spends annually on goods and services. On one side of the procurement budget are political leaders and bureaucrats, on the other the extraction mechanisms.

The key forces Pretorius identifies are failing oversight and accountability, weak law enforcement and a propaganda and disinformation network providing cover. And then there is the role of the ANC: 'Acquiescence, complacency.'

❖

There is merit in the argument that post-apartheid South Africa can be defined by two eras. The first was immediately post-apartheid, when Mandela and Mbeki tried to reconstruct a country fractured by a divided past. Their attempts included the reform of the state and, most importantly, economic shifts that attempted to reduce debt, close the budget deficit, restart growth and reduce unemployment and poverty. Under the partnership between Mbeki and fnance minister Trevor Manuel, almost every metric improved.

The second era, the argument goes, was when systems began to fail under an ANC leadership opposed to modernism and the rule of law. But this would be to dismiss or discount how the period between 1994 and 2007 prepared the ground for the Zuma and state capture era, and how it established the structures and culture – most importantly the cadre deployment system – that paved the way for the destruction of later years.

The Mandela years, in retrospect, were relatively benign. But, like Mbeki, Zuma and Ramaphosa, Mandela had an unhealthy and anti-democratic reverence for his organisation. Fuelled by his desire to be the national unifier but also the party loyalist, he did not act against early signs of criminality and found it easier to support the courts and the rule of law when the fortunes of his party were not at stake.

From 1997 onwards, Mbeki and his leadership were convinced of the need to take full command of policy, implementation and the bureaucracy. When the new leadership took over in 2007, led by Zuma and Gwede Mantashe, the architecture that united party and state was in place. Criminal networks and extraction syndicates – almost always linked to the party – found the system easy to navigate.

Mbeki's intention was not to lay the groundwork for a national mafia but his ideological bent for command and control led to the near ruining of South Africa. It was a function of the ANC's internal culture, forged during exile, and its exposure to totalitarian states that supported the organisation in the fight against apartheid.

For all his managerial prowess and commitment to efficient government, Mbeki was perhaps the biggest enabler of events after the 2007 Polokwane putsch. His presidency was pockmarked by interference in state institutions such as the NPA, and a range of governance failures, including the arms deal, allowed large-scale corruption to flourish. Mbeki's silence on the power abuses in Zimbabwe also affected the way the rest of the world saw South Africa and how many of his compatriots viewed his commitment to constitutional democracy.

The ANC under Zuma, however, undoubtedly imperilled the future of the country. And that is so because the party – with Mantashe, Ramaphosa, Fikile Mbalula and Julius Malema in its leadership ranks – established a culture of impunity and an ethos opposed to the rule of law and constitutionalism.

The ANC had many opportunities to change course. Apart from its electoral decline – it collapsed from 69.69 per cent in the 2004 national election to 40.18 per cent in 2024 – a series of inflection points might have arrested South Africa's retrogression if the ANC had believed in a set of values and principles aligned with the law and common decency.

To begin with, Zuma was a corruption accused. But, to maintain ANC hegemony, the rule of law was attacked as biased and the victim of manipulation – and Western imperialist interests. When the Nkandla scandal escalated and when the Guptas appeared on the political scene, oversight and accountability were destroyed in the service of party unity. Parliament was first co-opted and then destroyed to preserve the movement. Almost without exception, the ANC put its own interests ahead of those of the country.

After Ramaphosa's inauguration in February 2018, most South Africans were relieved that the Zuma era was over. Optimistically, I wrote at the time that 'the ANC's internal resistance wing won the day' and 'our republic is still standing'.[1] Ferial Haffajee, a friend and colleague, wrote, 'On this night, what has been unleashed is a sense of building and not of only opposing. Suddenly, I want to lend a hand, to be sent. I haven't felt that for the past decade.'[2] Justice Malala said Ramaphosa's speech 'was a rallying cry for each and every South African to give of themselves and their talents to a new dawn and a new society'.[3]

The ANC of Ramaphosa, however, remained the ANC of Zuma, and before him Mbeki and Mandela. It is an organisation that exists to attain and maintain political power, led by cadres who are devoted to the cause. And it has become the organisation that provides cover and protection for patronage networks.

Ramaphosa, like Zuma, always chose the ANC ahead of South Africa. He delayed and dropped reform of the spy agency, leaving intelligence networks in place. He retained many state capture accused in the national executive and the party leadership. He was slow to respond to the need for reform in energy, infrastructure and criminal justice.

The ANC might have lost their parliamentary majority in 2024, but cadre deployment will ensure that it maintains its control over the state. The party has, despite evidence of misrule and corruption – and the findings by Zondo – repeatedly said it will not change its deployment policies. And it felt vindicated after the high court rejected an application by the DA to declare cadre deployment unconstitutional (it was later taken on appeal). Trevor Manuel has openly rejected the workings of the deployment committee. 'We should publicly confirm and embrace the correctness of the observations by Zondo. Having done so, we must require the immediate dissolution of the deployment committee as part of the return to constitutionality. We must recognise that there remain individuals who have been placed in senior positions in the public service, key positions in the state and independent institutions and as our representatives abroad, who were irrationally recommended for these positions by the deployment committee.'[4]

After the ravages of the state capture years, the ANC carried on regardless. It turned a blind eye to existential and internal threats and ignored the fundamental questions that grand corruption and capture posed of it and society. Can we afford a party whose super cadres rule over the citizenry and whose leaders undermine constitutionality and the rule of law, destroying systems and the government?

In January 2022, a fire broke out in Parliament, gutting the National Assembly where Ramaphosa had been elected four years earlier. The imported Italian marble, the inlays made of indigenous stinkwood and yellowwood, the leather benches, the speaker's chair with the country's coat of arms, photographs of Mandela's inauguration, artwork, MPs' offices – everything was destroyed.

As results started coming in after the election on 29 May 2024, winter rain lashed down on the overgrowth starting to conceal the wreckage of Parliament, once the home of participatory democracy and the political heart of a nation freed to determine its own destiny.

The symbolism could hardly have been more clear. Under the ANC, it wasn't only the National Assembly that was burnt to the ground and left to rot.

Notes

The Report of the Judicial Commission of Inquiry into Allegations of State Capture, Corruption and Fraud in the Public Sector Including Organs of State (Zondo commission) is cited below as Judicial Commission of Inquiry into Allegations of State Capture'.

Prologue

1 Jan Gerber, 'Ramaphosa insists ANC is on path of renewal, unconcerned about polls showing party below 50%', News24, 4 May 2024, https://www.news24.com/news24/politics/political-parties/ramaphosa-insists-anc-is-on-path-of-renewal-unconcerned-about-polls-showing-party-below-50-20240504.

2 Jeff Wicks, 'OMG-Wagon: Fikile Mbalula's R3 million armoured car linked to Fort Hare graft-accused Anwar Khan', News24, 10 May 2024, https://www.news24.com/news24/investigations/omg-wagon-fikile-mbalulas-r3m-armoured-car-linked-to-fort-hare-graft-accused-20240510.

3 'ANC gunning for outright majority', SABC, 18 May 2024, https://www.sabcnews.com/sabcnews/anc-gunning-for-outright-majority/.

4 Gareth van Onselen, SRF Reports,

Social Research Foundation, 29 May 2024, https://srfreports.co.za/.

5 Ibid.

6 Jan Gerber, 'ANC digs in on Basic Income Grant as survey shows voters still mulling over who to vote for', News24, 23 May 2024, https://www.news24.com/news24/politics/political-parties/anc-digs-in-on-basic-income-grant-as-survey-shows-voters-still-mulling-who-to-vote-for-20240523.

7 Amanda Khoza, '"You will see who the real top dog is": Ramaphosa wraps up ANC's election campaign', News24, 25 May 2024, https://www.news24.com/news24/politics/you-will-see-who-the-real-top-dog-is-ramaphosa-wraps-up-ancs-election-campaign-20240525.

8 Ibid.

Chapter 1: Better than the Nats?

1 'Remarks by Nelson Mandela at Cape Town City Hall', Reuters, 9 May 1994. (Hard copy of original Reuters telex in author's possession.)

2 Interview with the author, 9 April 2024.

3 Ibid.

4 'Remarks by Nelson Mandela at Cape Town City Hall'.

5 Interview with the author, 9 April 2024.

6 Ibid.

7 Stephen Ellis, *External Mission: The ANC in Exile*, Jonathan Ball Publishers, 2012.

8 Ibid.

9 Ibid.

10 Ibid.

11 Ibid.

12 Ibid.

13 Ibid.

14 Ibid.

15 Shelagh Gastrow, *Who's Who in South African Politics, No. 4*, Ravan Press, 1992.

16 Ellis, *External Mission*.

17 Ibid.

18 Ibid.

19 South African President Arrival Ceremony, C-Span, 4 October 1994, https://www.c-span.org/video/?60621-1/south-african-president-arrival-ceremony.

20 Interview with the author, 9 April 2024.

21 Ibid.

22 Ibid.

23 Interview with the author, 10 April 2024.

Chapter 2: Cadres take command

1 Interview with the author, 10 April 2024.

2 Interview with the author, 9 April 2024.

3 Nelson Mandela and Mandla Langa, *Dare Not Linger: The Presidential Years*, Macmillan, 2017.

4 Ibid.

5 Ibid.

6 Ibid.

7 Mark Gevisser, *Thabo Mbeki: The Dream Deferred*, Jonathan Ball Publishers, 2007.

8 Ibid.

9 Ibid.

10 Pieter du Toit, *The ANC Billionaires: Big Capital's Gambit and the Rise of the Few*, Jonathan Ball Publishers, 2022.

11 Mandela and Langa, *Dare Not Linger*.

12 Gevisser, *Thabo Mbeki*.

13 Ibid.

14 Richard Calland and Mabel Sithole, *The Presidents: From Mandela to Ramaphosa, Leadership in the Age of Crisis*, Penguin, 2022.

15 Interview with the author, 9 April 2024.

16 Interview with the author, 30 April 2024.

17 Interview with the author, 10 April 2024.

18 Interview with the author, 9 April 2024.

19 Gevisser, *Thabo Mbeki*.

20 Tony Leon, *On the Contrary: Leading the Opposition in a Democratic South Africa*, Jonathan Ball Publishers, 2008.

21 Gevisser, *Thabo Mbeki*.

22 Anthony Sampson, *Mandela: The Authorised Biography*, HarperCollins, 1999.

23 Gevisser, *Thabo Mbeki*.

24 Sampson, *Mandela*.

25 Ibid.

26 Ibid.

27 Ibid.

28 Tony Leon, *Opposite Mandela: Encounters with South Africa's Icon*, Jonathan Ball Publishers, 2014.

29 Ibid.

30 Interview with the author, 9 April 2024.

31 Gevisser, *Thabo Mbeki*.

32 Du Toit, *The ANC Billionaires*.

33 Gevisser, *Thabo Mbeki*.

34 Sampson, *Mandela*.

35 'Report of the Presidential Review Commission on the Reform and Transformation of the Public Service

in South Africa', The Presidency, 1998, https://www.gov.za/ documents/report-presidential-review-

commission-reform-and-transformation-public-service-south.

36 Gevisser, *Thabo Mbeki.*

Chapter 3: Broederbond in the machine

1 Budget Review, Department of Finance (National Treasury), March 1995.
2 Ibid.
3 Sampson, *Mandela.*
4 Mandela and Langa, *Dare Not Linger.*
5 Du Toit, *The ANC Billionaires.*
6 Interview with the author, 30 April 2024.
7 Ibid.
8 Ibid.
9 Ibid.
10 Ibid.
11 Ibid.
12 Ibid.
13 Ibid.
14 Ibid.
15 Ibid.
16 Interview with the author, 9 April 2024.
17 'Electoral Commission pays tribute to Former Commissioner Stephanus Sebastiaan van der Merwe', IEC statement, 10 March 2023, https://www.gov.za/news/media-statements/electoral-commission-pays-tribute-former-commissioner-stephanus-sebastiaan.
18 Interview with the author, 9 April 2024.
19 Budget Review, Department of Finance (National Treasury), March 1995.
20 Ibid.
21 Interview with the author, 10 April 2024.
22 Interview with the author, 30 April 2024.
23 Budget Review, Department of Finance (National Treasury), March 1995.
24 Ibid.
25 Ibid.
26 Ibid.
27 Ibid.
28 Interview with the author, 30 April 2024.
29 Ibid.
30 Ibid.
31 Du Toit, *The ANC Billionaires.*
32 Ibid.
33 Ibid
34 Ibid.
35 Ibid.
36 Ibid.
37 Ibid.
38 Ibid.
39 Statement by Ismail Momoniat to the Judicial Commission of Inquiry into Allegations of State Capture, 2021.
40 Helena Wasserman, 'Unemployment rate slightly higher, but embattled SA is still creating jobs', News24, 16 May 2023, https://www.news24.com/fin24/economy/unemployment-rate-slightly-higher-due-to-technicality-but-embattled-sa-is-still-creaing-jobs-20230516.
41 'GDP declines in the fourth quarter', Statistics South Africa statement, 7 March 2023, https://www.statssa.gov.za/?p=16162#:~:text=The%20South%20African%20economy%20grew,trillion%20to%20R4%2C60%20trillion.&text=Although%20GDP%20reached%20an%20all,reading%20

of%20R4%2C58%20trillion.

42 Prinesha Naidoo, 'South Africa faces 14th straight primary budget deficit as tax refunds hurt revenue', Bloomberg, 8 May 2023, https://www.bloomberg.com/news/articles/2023-05-08/south-africa-faces-14th-straight-primary-budget-gap-as-tax-refunds-hurt-revenue#xj4y7vzkg.

43 Budget Review, chapter 3, National Treasury, February 2023.

44 'Socio-Economic Survey of South Africa', South African Institute of Race Relations, 2022.

45 'Rand is 50% undervalued, Big Mac index shows', News24 Business, 7 August 2023, https://www.news24.com/fin24/economy/rand-is-50-undervalued-big-mac-index-shows-20230807#:~:text=%22The%20implied%20exchange%20rate%20is,undervalued%2C%22%20'The%20Economist%20says.&text=A%20year%20ago%2C%20the%20rand,2020%20was%20undervalued%20by%2070%25.

46 'Consumer inflation retreats to 5.4%', Statistics South Africa statement, 19 July 2023, https://www.statssa.gov.za/?p=16483.

Chapter 4: Bickering begins

1 Du Toit, *The ANC Billionaires*.

2 Budget Review, Department of Finance (National Treasury), March 1995.

3 Sampson, *Mandela*.

4 Padraig O'Malley, interview with Chris Liebenberg, The O'Malley Archives, Nelson Mandela Foundation, 1995, https://omalley.nelson-mandela.org/index.php/site/q/03lv00017/04lv00344/05lv00889/06lv00955.htm.

5 Ibid.

6 Ibid.

7 Ibid.

8 Budget Review, Department of Finance (National Treasury), March 1995.

9 Du Toit, *The ANC Billionaires*.

10 Sampson, *Mandela*.

11 O'Malley, interview with Chris Liebenberg.

12 Du Toit, *The ANC Billionaires*.

13 Interview with the author, 30 April 2024.

14 Ibid.

15 Ibid.

16 Ibid.

17 Du Toit, *The ANC Billionaires*.

18 Ibid.

19 Ibid.

20 Ibid.

21 Ibid.

22 Interview with the author, 30 April 2024.

23 Ibid.

24 Ibid.

25 Ibid.

Chapter 5: Whiffs of corruption

1 Interview with the author, 9 April 2024.

2 Leon, *Opposite Mandela*.

3 RW Johnson, *South Africa's Brave New World: The Beloved Country Since the End of Apartheid*, Penguin, 2009.

4 Suzanne Daley, 'South Africa Scandal Over "Sarafina" Spotlights Corruption in the A.N.C.', *The New York Times*, 8 October 1996, https://www.

nytimes.com/1996/10/08/world/south-africa-scandal-over-sarafina-spotlights-corruption-in-the-anc.html.

5 Ibid.

6 'Investigation concerning the Sarafina II donor: Public Protector Report', September 1995, https://www.gov.za/documents/investigation-concerning-sarafina-ii-donor-public-protector-report.

7 Daley, 'South Africa Scandal Over "Sarafina"'.

8 Ibid.

9 Leon, *On the Contrary*.

10 Jacquie Golding-Duffy and Justin Pearce, 'So who did pay for the Aids play then?', *Mail & Guardian*, 8 March 1996, https://mg.co.za/article/1996-03-08-so-who-did-pay-for-the-aids-play-then/.

11 Leon, *Opposite Mandela*.

12 Interview with the author, 9 April 2024.

13 Johnson, *South Africa's Brave New World*.

14 Leon, *Opposite Mandela*.

15 Johnson, *South Africa's Brave New World*.

16 Leon, *On the Contrary*.

17 'Allan Boesak convicted', *Mail & Guardian*, 17 March 1999, https://mg.co.za/article/1999-03-17-allan-boesak-convicted/.

18 'Boesak's pardon raises hackles', News24, 16 January 2005, https://www.news24.com/news24/boesaks-pardon-raises-hackles-20050116.

19 Leon, *Opposite Mandela*.

20 'Holomisa has signed his own death knell in the ANC: Tshwete', SAPA, 1 August 1996, https://www.justice.gov.za/trc/media/1996/9608/s960801d.htm.

21 Leon, *Opposite Mandela*.

22 Mandela and Langa, *Dare Not Linger*.

23 Ibid.

24 Ibid.

Chapter 6: The poisoning of the well

1 Gevisser, *Thabo Mbeki*.

2 Calland and Sithole, *The Presidents*.

3 'De Lille Dossier', Corruption Watch, https://www.corruption-watch.org.za/original-arms-deal-whistleblower-testifies/.

4 'Special Review: Selection process of strategic defence packages for the acquisition of armaments at the department of defence', Auditor-General, 16 September 2000, http://www.armsdeal-vpo.co.za/special_items/reports/ag_review.pdf.

5 Ibid.

6 Ibid.

7 Ibid.

8 Ibid.

9 Ibid.

10 Ibid.

11 Leon, *On the Contrary*.

12 Gevisser, *Thabo Mbeki*.

13 Ibid.

14 Andrew Feinstein, *After the Party: A Personal and Political Journey Inside the ANC*, Jonathan Ball Publishers, 2007.

15 Ibid.

16 Ibid.

17 Ibid.

18 Ibid.

19 Leon, *On the Contrary*.

20 Ibid.

21 Ibid.

22 'Pandemonium at Pollsmoor', News24, 24 August 2006, https://www.news24.com/News24/Pandemonium-at-Pollsmoor-20060824.

23 Gevisser, *Thabo Mbeki*.

24 Greg Nicolson, 'Seriti findings a failure: "Inexplicable" for commission to ignore evidence of corruption',

Daily Maverick, 21 August 2019, https://www.dailymaverick.co.za/article/2019-08-21-seriti-findings-a-failure-inexplicable-for-commission-to-ignore-evidence-of-corruption/.

25 Interview with the author, 9 April 2024.

Chapter 7: The house never wins

1 Pieter Mulder, *Kan Afrikaners toyi-toyi?*, Protea Boekhuis, 2008.

2 Ibid.

3 Leon, *On the Contrary*.

4 Ibid.

5 Ibid.

6 Ibid.

7 Ibid.

8 Ibid.

9 Ibid.

10 Ibid.

11 Ibid.

12 Vanessa Banton, 'Obituary: Frene Ginwala: Lawyer, activist, journalist ... and reluctant Speaker of Parliament', News24, 14 January 2023, https://www.news24.com/news24/obituaries/obituary-frene-ginwala-lawyer-activist-journalist-and-reluctant-speaker-of-parliament-0230114.

13 Martin Meredith, *Nelson Mandela: A Biography*, Penguin, 1997.

14 Leon, *Opposite Mandela*.

15 Ibid.

Chapter 8: Total control

1 Interview with the author, 9 April 2024.

2 Sampson, *Mandela*.

3 Mandela and Langa, *Dare Not Linger*.

4 Leon, *Opposite Mandela*.

5 Tim du Plessis and Peet Kruger, 'Mandela verras met groetwoorde, skerp toespraak kap opposisie', *Beeld*, 17 December 1997.

6 Nelson Mandela, 'Political Report of the ANC to the 50th national conference', ANC, 16 December 1997, https://www.anc1912.org.za/50th-national-conference-report-by-the-president-of-the-anc-nelson-mandela/.

7 Ibid.

8 Ibid.

9 Ibid.

10 Peet Kruger, 'Mandela slaai ...

verslag was "die stem van Mbeki"', *Beeld*, 17 December 1997.

11 Tim du Plessis, 'Mbeki-tromslag: Gaan die land in '98 saam marsjeer?', *Beeld*, 19 December 1997.

12 Nick Bezuidenhout, 'Thabo soek nie Nelson se "lelike skoene": Staatsmasjienerie moet transformeer', *Beeld*, 22 December 1997.

13 'Die ANC se NUK', editorial, *Beeld*, 23 December 1997.

14 Interview with the author, 9 April 2024.

15 Zapiro, 'Parp!!' [cartoon], *Sowetan*, 23 December 1997.

16 Leon, *Opposite Mandela*.

17 Ibid.

18 Sampson, *Mandela*.

19 'Swanesang', editorial, *Beeld*, 17 December 1997.

20 Sampson, *Mandela*.

21 Du Plessis, 'Mbeki-tromslag'.

22 Leon, *Opposite Mandela*.

23 Interview with the author, 9 April 2024.

24 Judicial Commission of Inquiry into Allegations of State Capture, Report: Part 6, Volume 2, paragraph 657, p. 253.

25 Judicial Commission of Inquiry into Allegations of State Capture, Report: Part 6, Volume 2, paragraphs 417–424.

26 Ibid.

27 Ibid.

28 Ibid.

29 Judicial Commission of Inquiry into Allegations of State Capture, Report: Part 6, Volume 2, paragraph 517, p. 199.

30 Resolutions, ANC 50th national conference, December 1997.

31 Ibid.

32 Frederik van Zyl Slabbert, *Duskant die geskiedenis*, Jonathan Ball Publishers, 2006.

Chapter 9: Here come the cadres

1 'Strategy and Tactics', ANC, 1997, https://www.anc1912.org.za/50th-national-conference-strategy-and-tactics-of-the-african-national-congress/.

2 Ibid.

3 Ibid.

4 Ibid.

5 Ibid.

6 Ibid.

7 Allister Sparks, *Beyond the Miracle: Inside the New South Africa*, Jonathan Ball Publishers, 2003.

8 Thula Simpson, *History of South Africa: From 1902 to the Present*, Penguin, 2021.

9 Ibid.

10 Ibid.

11 'All Power to the Party: The ANC's programme to eliminate the distinction between party and state, and extend its hegemony over civil society', Democratic Party discussion document, March 2000.

12 Ibid.

13 Ibid.

14 Ibid.

15 'The State, Property Relations and Social Transformation', ANC discussion document, 1998.

16 Ibid.

17 Ibid.

18 Interview with the author, 30 April 2024

19 Interview with the author, 9 April 2024.

20 'The State, Property Relations and Social Transformation'.

21 Cabinet statement, 2 December 1998.

22 'All Power to the Party'.

23 Ibid.

24 Ibid.

25 Ibid.

26 Interview with the author, 9 April 2024.

27 Simpson, *History of South Africa*.

28 Ibid.

29 Leon, *Opposite Mandela*.

Chapter 10: Mbeki takes charge

1 Gevisser, *Thabo Mbeki*.

2 Sparks, *Beyond the Miracle*.

3 Interview with the author, 9 April 2024.

4 Ibid.

5 Ibid.

6 Ibid.
7 Sparks, *Beyond the Miracle*.
8 Gevisser, *Thabo Mbeki*.
9 Leon, *On the Contrary*.
10 Gevisser, *Thabo Mbeki*.
11 William Gumede, *Thabo Mbeki and the Battle for the Soul of the ANC*, Zebra Press, 2005.
12 Ibid.
13 Gevisser, *Thabo Mbeki*.

14 Ibid.
15 Gumede, *Thabo Mbeki and the Battle for the Soul of the ANC*.
16 Ibid.
17 Ibid.
18 Ibid.
19 Ibid.
20 Ibid.

Chapter 11: Re-engineering the state

1 Leon, *On the Contrary*.
2 Thabo Mbeki, 'Statement of Deputy President Thabo Mbeki at the opening of the debate in the National Assembly on reconciliation and nation-building', 1999.
3 Ibid.
4 Ibid.
5 Ibid.
6 Interview with the author, 9 April 2024.
7 Frank Chikane, 'Democratic Governance: A Restructured Presidency at Work', The Presidency, 2001.
8 Ibid.
9 Ibid.

10 Ibid.
11 Gumede, *Thabo Mbeki and the Battle for the Soul of the ANC*.
12 Gevisser, *Thabo Mbeki*.
13 Gumede, *Thabo Mbeki and the Battle for the Soul of the ANC*.
14 Ibid.
15 Ibid.
16 Leon, *On the Contrary*.
17 Ibid.
18 Padraig O'Malley, The O'Malley Archives, Nelson Mandela Foundation, 1990–1999. Cited in Leon, *On the Contrary*.
19 Sparks, *Beyond the Miracle*.

Chapter 12: Failing the big tests

1 Interview with the author, 9 April 2024.
2 Sparks, *Beyond the Miracle*.
3 Leon, *On the Contrary*.
4 Ibid.
5 Ibid.
6 Gumede, *Thabo Mbeki and the Battle for the Soul of the ANC*.
7 Gevisser, *Thabo Mbeki*.
8 Gumede, *Thabo Mbeki and the Battle for the Soul of the ANC*.
9 Sparks, *Beyond the Miracle*.
10 Leon, *On the Contrary*.
11 Ibid.

12 Gumede, *Thabo Mbeki and the Battle for the Soul of the ANC*.
13 Sparks, *Beyond the Miracle*.
14 Gumede, *Thabo Mbeki and the Battle for the Soul of the ANC*.
15 Leon, *On the Contrary*.
16 Ibid.
17 Gumede, *Thabo Mbeki and the Battle for the Soul of the ANC*.
18 Ibid.
19 Ibid.
20 Leon, *On the Contrary*.
21 Ibid.
22 Ibid.

23 Gevisser, *Thabo Mbeki*.
24 Simpson, *History of South Africa*.
25 Sparks, *Beyond the Miracle*.
26 Gumede, *Thabo Mbeki and the Battle for the Soul of the ANC*.
27 Ibid.
28 Ibid.
29 Sparks, *Beyond the Miracle*.
30 Gumede, *Thabo Mbeki and the Battle for the Soul of the ANC*.
31 Sparks, *Beyond the Miracle*.
32 Interview with the author, 9 April 2024.
33 Gumede, *Thabo Mbeki and the Battle for the Soul of the ANC*.
34 Ibid.
35 Interview with the author, 9 April 2024.
36 Amy Roeder, 'The human cost of South Africa's misguided AIDS policies', *Harvard Public Health Magazine*, Spring 2009, https://www.hsph.harvard.edu/news/magazine/spr09aids/.
37 Interview with the author, 9 April 2024.
38 Gevisser, *Thabo Mbeki*.
39 Christi van der Westhuizen, 'Working Democracy: Perspectives on South Africa's Parliament at 20 Years', Open Society Foundation for South Africa, 2014.
40 Gevisser, *Thabo Mbeki*.
41 Ben Maclennan, 'Travelgate: 14 plead guilty', SAPA, *Mail & Guardian*, 16 October 2006, https://mg.co.za/article/2006-10-16-travelgate-14-plead-guilty/.
42 'Donen Report: ANC bosses are not off the hook', amaBhungane, 9 December 2011, https://amabhungane.org/stories/donen-report-anc-bosses-are-not-off-the-hook/.
43 White Paper on the Energy Policy of the Republic of South Africa, Department of Minerals and Energy, 1998. https://www.energy.gov.za/files/policies/whitepaper_energypolicy_1998.pdf.
44 Simpson, *History of South Africa*.
45 André de Ruyter, *Truth to Power: My Three Years Inside Eskom*, Penguin, 2023.
46 Ibid.
47 Simpson, *History of South Africa*.
48 De Ruyter, *Truth to Power*.
49 Ibid.
50 Simpson, *History of South Africa*.
51 'Mbeki: Eskom was right', News24, 21 June 2008, https://www.news24.com/fin24/mbeki-eskom-was-right-20080121.

Chapter 13: Before the fall

1 Adriaan Basson, *Zuma Exposed*, Jonathan Ball Publishers, 2012.
2 Thabo Mbeki, 'Statement of the president of South Africa, Thabo Mbeki, at the Joint Sitting of Parliament on the Release of Hon Jacob Zuma from his responsibilities as deputy president', National Assembly, 14 June 2005.
3 Ibid.
4 Ibid.
5 Adriaan Basson and Pieter du Toit, *Enemy of the People: How Jacob Zuma Stole South Africa and How the People Fought Back*, Jonathan Ball Publishers, 2017.
6 Basson, *Zuma Exposed*.
7 Ibid.
8 Ibid.
9 Brendan Boyle, Zine George, Prega Govender and S'thembiso Msomi, 'Mbeki battles Zuma revolt', *Sunday*

Times, 19 June 2005.

10 Ibid.

11 'ANCYL still supports Zuma', News24, 15 June 2005, https://www.news24.com/news24/ ancyl-still-supports-zuma- 20050615.

12 Vusi Pikoli and Mandy Wiener, *My Second Initiation: The Memoir of Vusi Pikoli*, Picador Africa, 2013.

13 Ibid.

14 Mariette le Roux, 'ANC ordered not to discuss Zuma at NGC', SAPA, *Mail & Guardian*, 30 June 2005, https://mg.co.za/article/2005-06-30-anc-ordered-not-to-discuss-zuma-at-ngc/.

15 Rapule Tabane, 'ANC should be bigger than Mbeki and Zuma', *Mail & Guardian*, 8 July 2005, https://mg.co.za/article/2005-07-08-anc-should-be-bigger-than-mbeki-and-zuma/.

16 Zuma vs NDPP, Constitutional Court of South Africa, Case no. CCT 92/07.

17 Basson and Du Toit, *Enemy of the People*.

18 Ibid.

19 Pikoli and Wiener, *My Second Initiation*.

20 Jacques Pauw, *The President's Keepers: Those Keeping Zuma in Power and out of Prison*, Tafelberg, 2017.

Chapter 14: The Polokwane putsch

1 Tabane, 'ANC should be bigger than Mbeki and Zuma'.

2 Gumede, *Thabo Mbeki and the Battle for the Soul of the ANC*.

3 Interview with the author, 30 April 2024.

4 Interview with the author, 9 April 2024.

5 Pauw, *The President's Keepers*.

6 Interview with the author, 9 April 2024.

7 Interview with the author, 9 April 2024.

Chapter 15: Staying out of jail

1 Angela Quintal, 'Mbeki's SABC board: The war goes on', *The Sunday Independent*, 23 December 2007, https://www.iol.co.za/news/politics/mbekis-sabc-board-the-war-goes-on-383731.

2 'Board upsets SACP', *Sowetan*, 24 December 2007, https://www.sowetanlive.co.za/news/2007-12-24-board-upsets-sacp/.

3 Quintal, 'Mbeki's SABC board'.

4 Karabo Ngoepe, 'I never went to school, but I educated myself', News24, 22 July 2016, https://www.news24.com/news24/i-educated-myself-zuma-tells-pupils-20160722.

5 Max du Preez, 'Die duur prys wat SA vir Jacob Zuma betaal', Vrye Weekblad, 2 February 2024, https://www.vryeweekblad.com/nuus-en-politiek/2024-02-02-die-duur-prys-wat-sa-vir-jacob-zuma-betaal/.

6 Interview with the author, 9 April 2024.

7 Khampepe Commission of Inquiry into the Mandate and Location of the Directorate of Special Operations, February 2006, https://www.justice.gov.za/commissions/2008_khampempe.pdf.

8 Jean Redpath, 'Monograph 96: The Scorpions: Analysing the Directorate of Special Operations', Institute for Security Studies, 2004, https://

issafrica.org/research/monographs-monograph-96-the-scorpions.-analysing-the-directorate-of-special-operations-jean-redpath.

9 'Further statement on suspension of National Director of Public Prosecutions', The Presidency, 1 October 2007, https://www.gcis.gov.za/content/newsroom/media-releases/media-releases/further-statement-suspension-national-director-public-prosecutions.

10 Pikoli and Wiener, *My Second Initiation.*

11 *S vs Zuma and Another*, KwaZulu-Natal High Court, Case no. CCD 30/2018, https://www.saflii.org/za/cases/ZAKZDHC/2019/19.html.

12 Ibid.

13 Ibid.

14 Ibid.

15 Ibid.

16 Pauw, *The President's Keepers.*

Chapter 16: The counter-revolution

1 *S vs Zuma and Another*, KwaZulu-Natal High Court, Case no. CCD 30/2018, https://www.saflii.org/za/cases/ZAKZDHC/2019/19.html.

2 'ANC to report on arms deal', News24, 8 January 2008, https://www.news24.com/news24/anc-to-report-on-arms-deal-20080108.

3 Deon de Lange, 'Mbeki faces arms deal grilling', IOL, 9 January 2008, https://www.iol.co.za/news/politics/mbeki-faces-arms-deal-grilling-385164.

4 'ANC to report on arms deal'.

5 Ibid.

6 Sello Alcock, Stefaans Brümmer, Mandy Rossouw and Sam Sole, 'Triple play to save Zuma', *Mail & Guardian*, 11 July 2008, https://mg.co.za/article/2008-07-11-triple-play-to-save-zuma/.

7 Ibid.

8 Ibid.

9 Ibid.

10 Sello Alcock, Matuma Letsoala and Mandy Rossouw, 'ANC boss accuses judges of conspiracy against Zuma', *Mail & Guardian*, 4 July 2008, https://mg.co.za/article/2008-07-04-anc-boss-accuses-judges-of-conspiracy-against-zuma/.

11 ANC 52nd National General Council resolutions, https://www.anc1912.org.za/resolutions-2/.

12 Khampepe Commission of Inquiry into the Mandate and Location of the Directorate of Special Operations.

13 National Prosecuting Authority Annual Report briefing, Parliamentary Monitoring Group, 26 February 2008, https://pmg.org.za/committee-meeting/8830/.

14 Ibid.

15 Ibid.

16 James de Villiers, 'Yunus Carrim explains the messy disbanding of the Scorpions ... and why it is unfair to attack him', News24, 21 August 2020, https://www.news24.com/news24/opinions/analysis/yunus-carrim-explains-the-messy-disbanding-of-the-scorpions-and-why-it-is-unfair-to-attack-him-20200820.

Chapter 17: Interregnum and overthrow

1 Sabelo Ndlangisa, 'What the Zumafesto holds', *City Press*, 16 December 2007.

2 'ANC debates two centres of power', SAPA, *Mail & Guardian*, 27 June 2007, https://mg.co.za/article/2007-

06-27-anc-debates-two-centres-of-power/.

3 Mukoni Ratshitanga, 'As SA wakes from the Zuma nightmare, there are hard lessons to be learnt', *Sunday Times*, 16 February 2018, https://www.timeslive.co.za/sunday-times/opinion-and-analysis/2018-02-17-as-sa-wakes-from-the-zuma-nightmare-there-are-hard-lessons-to-be-learnt/.

4 Scorpions Closure public hearings: Day 6 & response to public submissions, Parliamentary Monitoring Group, 9 September 2008, https://pmg.org.za/committee-meeting/9602/.

5 Scorpions Closure public hearings: Day 7 & response to public submissions, Parliamentary Monitoring Group, 10 September 2008, https://pmg.org.za/committee-meeting/9611/.

6 *S vs Zuma and Another*, KwaZulu-Natal High Court, Case no. CCD 30/2018, https://www.saflii.org/za/cases/ZAKZDHC/2019/19.html.

7 Michelle le Roux and Dennis Davis, *Lawfare: Judging Politics in South Africa*, Jonathan Ball Publishers, 2019.

8 Ibid.

9 Jan-Jan Joubert, 'Mbeki moet loop! Zuma staan sterk na uitspraak', *Beeld*, 19 September 2008.

10 Ibid.

11 'Zuma: I am a wounded warrior', SAPA, *Mail & Guardian*, 12 September 2008, https://mg.co.za/article/2008-09-12-zuma-i-am-a-wounded-warrior/.

12 Ibid.

13 Ray Hartley, *Ragged Glory: The Rainbow Nation in Black and White*, Jonathan Ball Publishers, 2014.

14 Frank Chikane, *Eight Days in September: The Removal of Thabo Mbeki*, Pan Macmillan, 2012.

15 Hartley, *Ragged Glory*.

16 Statement by the National Executive Committee of the ANC, 20 September 2008, https://www.politicsweb.co.za/news-and-analysis/anc-nec-statement-on-decision-to-recall-mbeki.

17 Liezel de Lange, Pieter du Toit and Jan-Jan Joubert, 'Ek loop, maar … Mbeki ontken inmenging oor Zuma', *Beeld*, 22 September 2008.

18 'Gaan ANC skeur? Trevor se "ek gaan" en "ek's terug" slaan beurs hard', *Beeld*, 24 September 2008.

19 Interview with the author, 30 April 2024.

20 Ibid.

Chapter 18: Normalising Zuma

1 Rajaa Azzakani and Philda Essop, 'Beleid gaan geensins verander – president', *Beeld*, 26 September 2008.

2 'Nicholson failed in his duties', News24, 12 January 2009, https://www.news24.com/news24/nicholson-failed-in-his-duties-20090112.

3 Statement by the Office of Thabo Mbeki, 13 January 2009, https://www.politicsweb.co.za/news-and-analysis/thabo-mbeki-welcomes-sca-findings.

4 *S vs Zuma and Another*, KwaZulu-Natal High Court, Case no. CCD 30/2018, https://www.saflii.org/za/cases/ZAKZDHC/2019/19.html.

5 Ibid.

6 Ibid.

7 Ibid.

8 Statement by acting national director of public prosecutions, advocate Mokotedi Mpshe, 6 April 2009,

https://www.politicsweb.co.za/
news-and-analysis/why-i-decided-
to-drop-the-zuma-charges--mpshe.

9 Ibid.

10 Helen Zille, *Not Without a Fight: The
Autobiography*, Penguin, 2016.

11 Gareth van Onselen, 'Year One:
How Julius Malema destroyed the
NPA's case against Jacob Zuma in
365 days', South African Institute of
Race Relations, 2018, https://irr.org.
za/reports/occasional-eports/files/
how-julius-malema-destroyed-the-
npas-case-against-jacob-zuma-in-
365-days.pdf.

12 Ibid.

13 Ibid.

14 Zille, *Not Without a Fight*.

15 Eusebius McKaiser and Sasha
Polakow-Suransky, 'South Africa
will survive Zuma', *Newsweek*,
27 April 2009.

16 Alex Perry, 'Could Jacob Zuma be
the president South Africa needs?',
Time, 7 December 2009.

17 Ibid.

18 Gareth van Onselen, 'Zuma: How
the commentariat got it utterly
wrong', Politicsweb, 14 June 2018,
https://www.politicsweb.co.za/
opinion/zuma-how-the-commentar-
iat-got-it-utterly-wrong.

19 Marianne Thamm, 'True colours
shining through: Should journalists
be draping themselves in party political colours?', Daily Maverick,
13 January 2015, https://www.daily-
maverick.co.za/opinionista/2015-
01-13-true-colours-shining-
through-should-journalists-be-drap-
ing-themselves-in-party-political-
colours/#.VLUEVCuUdFN.

20 Van Onselen, 'Zuma: How the
commentariat got it utterly wrong'.

21 Ibid.

22 'Ackerman: Give Zuma a chance',
IOL, 27 April 2009, https://www.
iol.co.za/news/politics/ackerman-
give-zuma-a-chance-441557.

23 Xolela Mangcu, 'Give Zuma a
chance after the intolerance of the
Mbeki regime', *Business Day*,
12 March 2009.

24 Henry Cloete and Vicus Bürger,
'Follow Zuma "like Jesus"', *Volksblad*,
19 January 2 009, https://www.
news24.com/news24/follow-
zuma-like-jesus-20090118.

25 Zweli Mkhize, 'Why Zuma is right
man for right now', IOL, 5 April
2009, https://www.iol.co.za/news/
politics/why-zuma-is-right-man-
for-right-now-439168.

Chapter 19: Incompetents, fools and lawfare

1 Interview with the author, 30 April
2024.

2 Ibid.

3 Ibid.

4 Interview with the author, 24 April
2024.

5 Interview with the author, 30 April
2024.

6 Ibid.

7 Ibid.

8 Interview with the author, 9 April
2024.

9 Statement by President Jacob Zuma
on the appointment of the new Cabinet, Government Communications,
10 May 2009, https://www.gov.za/
news/speeches/statement-president-
jacob-zuma-appointment-new-
cabinet-10-may-2009.

10 Ibid.

11 *Democratic Alliance v President of
South Africa and Others*,

Constitutional Court, CCT 122/11, https://www.saflii.org/za/cases/ZACC/2012/24.html.

12 Zille, *Not Without a Fight*.

13 Le Roux and Davis, *Lawfare*.

14 Ibid.

15 'Strong case against Simelane', News24, 11 December 2009, https://www.news24.com/news24/strong-case-against-simelane-20091211.

16 Niren Tolsi, 'ConCourt confirms Menzi Simelane's appointment invalid', *Mail & Guardian*, 5 October 2012, https://mg.co.za/article/2012-10-05-59-menzi-simelanes-appointment-ruled-invalid/.

17 Henry Macdonald and Daniel Nasaw, 'Axe falls on arms probe', *Mail & Guardian*, 19 March 2010, https://mg.co.za/article/2010-03-19-axe-falls-on-arms-probe/.

18 Glynnis Underhill, 'Menzi guts the NPA', *Mail & Guardian*, 7 May 2010, https://mg.co.za/article/2010-05-07-menzi-guts-the-npa/.

Chapter 20: Creeping authoritarianism

1 Van der Westhuizen, 'Working Democracy'.

2 Ibid.

3 'What's wrong with the Protection of Information Bill', M&G Centre for Investigative Journalism, August 2010, https://serve.mg.co.za/uploads/2010/09/01/briefing-note-whats-wrong-with-the-protection-of-information-bill.pdf.

4 Van der Westhuizen, 'Working Democracy'.

5 Ibid.

6 Statement on Cabinet meeting of 23 November 2011, https://www.gcis.gov.za/content/newsroom/media-releases/cabinet-statements/statement-cabinet-meeting-23-november-2011.

7 Ray Hartley, 'Jacob Zuma vs the Constitution: It's a fight to the bitter end', Rand Daily Mail, 7 April 2016, https://www.businesslive.co.za/rdm/politics/2016-04-07-jacob-zuma-vs-the-constitution-its-a-fight-to-the-bitter-end/.

8 Pieter du Toit and Lizel Steenkamp, 'Dis tandekry-probleme: Zuma oor onnies se unies en persvryheid', *Beeld*, 22 February 2011.

9 Ibid.

10 Ibid.

11 Ibid.

12 Niren Tolsi, 'Audits reveal ANC membership numbers soar', *Mail & Guardian*, 17 December 2012, https://mg.co.za/article/2012-12-17-anc-membership-numbers-soar/.

13 'Vavi warns against "predatory elite"', News24, 10 December 2010, https://www.news24.com/news24/vavi-warns-against-predatory-elite-20150429.

14 'Vavi tells of the rise of "corrupt, predatory elite"', *Mail & Guardian*, 28 June 2011, https://mg.co.za/article/2011-06-28-vavi-tells-of-the-rise-corrupt-predatory-elite/.

15 *Democratic Alliance v The Acting National Director of Public Prosecutions*, Supreme Court of Appeal, Case no. 288/11, https://www.saflii.org/cgi-bin/disp.pl?file=za/cases/ZASCA/2012/15.html&query=%20democratic%20alliance.

16 Lizeka Tandwa, 'Timeline of events leading up to Zuma's Nkandla apology', News24, 1 April 2016, https://www.news24.com/news24/timeline-of-events-leading-up-to-zumas-

nkandla-apology-20160401.

17 Anthony Butler, *Cyril Ramaphosa: The Road to Presidential Power*,

Jacana Media, 2019.

18 Interview with the author, 24 April 2024.

Chapter 21: The accomplice

1 Gareth van Onselen, 'The Zuma-phosa Monitor', Inside Politics blog, 11 January 2019, https://inside-politics.org/2019/01/11/the-zuma-phosa-monitor/.

2 Ibid.

3 Ibid.

4 Judicial Commission of Inquiry into Allegations of State Capture, Report: Part 4. Volume 2: President Ramaphosa as President.

5 Ibid.

6 Gareth van Onselen, 'How Cyril Ramaphosa helped deliver Jacob Zuma's failed state', *Business Day*, 10 October 2018, https://www.businesslive.co.za/bd/opinion/columnists/2018-10-10-gareth-van-onselen-how-cyril-ramaphosa-helped-deliver-jacob-zumas-failed-state/.

7 Judicial Commission of Inquiry into Allegations of State Capture, Report: Part 4. Volume 2: President Ramaphosa as President.

8 Ibid.

9 Ibid.

10 Ibid.

11 Ibid.

12 Jan Gerber, 'ANC dismissed first Gupta allegations because its "analysis" found newspapers were racist – Mantashe', News24, 15 April 2021, https://www.news24.com/news24/southafrica/news/anc-dismissed-first-gupta-allegations-because-its-analysis-found-newspapers-were-racist-mantashe-20210415.

13 'Zuma doesn't have to explain Gupta relationship – Mantashe', SAPA, 21 May 2013, https://www.polity.org.za/article/zuma-doesnt-have-to-explain-gupta-relationship-mantashe-2013-05-21.

14 Sarah Smit, 'Manuel: Zuma was unfazed by Mbalula's Gupta appointment claim', *Mail & Guardian*, 28 February 2019, https://mg.co.za/article/2019-02-28-manuel-zuma-was-unfazed-by-mbalulas-gupta-appointment-claim/.

15 Ibid.

16 Judicial Commission of Inquiry into Allegations of State Capture, Report: Part 4. Volume 2: President Ramaphosa as President.

17 Pieter-Louis Myburgh, *The Republic of Gupta: A Story of State Capture*, Penguin, 2017.

18 Ibid.

19 Charles Molele and Maruma Letsoala, 'Gupta saga: Zuma lays low as united ANC vents', *Mail & Guardian*, 3 May 2013, https://mg.co.za/article/2013-05-03-00-gupta-wedding-zuma-lays-low-as-united-anc-vents/.

20 Interview with the author, 24 April 2024.

Chapter 22: Covering for corruption

1 South African Institute of Race Relations, South Africa Survey 2018.

2 Ibid.

3 Ibid.

4 Ibid.

5 Ibid.

6 Interview with the author, 24 April 2024.

7 Gareth van Onselen, 'ANC attacks on Madonsela archive', Inside Politics, https://inside- politics.org/.

8 Ibid.

9 Ibid.

10 Ibid.

11 Judicial Commission of Inquiry into Allegations of State Capture, Report: Part 4. Volume 2: President Ramaphosa as President.

12 Ibid.

13 Ibid.

14 Ibid.

15 Gwede Mantashe, Transcript of evidence at the Zondo Commission. Day 374, 14 April 2021.

16 Ibid.

17 Ibid.

18 Ibid.

Chapter 23: The crucible of capture

1 Judicial Commission of Inquiry into Allegations of State Capture, Report: Part 4. Volume 2: President Ramaphosa as President.

2 Ibid.

3 Interview with the author, 24 April 2024.

4 *Democratic Alliance v President of South Africa and Others*, Constitutional Court, CCT 122/11, 11 October 2019, https://www.saflii. org/za/cases/ZACC/2012/24.html.

5 'President Zuma appoints the NDPP and SIU Head', Statement by the Presidency, 30 August 2013, https://www.gov.za/news/media-statements/president-zuma-appoints-ndpp-and-siu-head-30-aug-2013.

6 Franny Rabkin, 'Zuma had been "intent" on seeing Nxasana leave the NPA, Zondo commission hears', *Mail & Guardian*, 19 August 2019, https://mg.co.za/article/2019-08-19-zuma-had-been-intent-on-seeing-nxasana-leave-the-npa-zondo-commission-hears/.

7 *Corruption Watch NPC and Others v President of the Republic of South Africa and Others* (Helen Suzman Foundation as Amicus Curiae); *Nxasana v Corruption Watch NPC and Others* (Helen Suzman Foundation as Amicus Curiae), Constitutional Court, CCT 333/17 and CCT 13/18, 13 August 2018, https://collections.concourt.org.za/handle/20.500.12144/34592.

8 Adrian Lackay and Johann van Loggerenberg, *Rogue: The Inside Story of SARS's Elite Crime-busting Unit*, Jonathan Ball Publishers, 2016.

9 Judicial Commission of Inquiry into Allegations of State Capture, Report: Part 1. Volume 3. Chapter 3: SARS.

10 Ibid.

11 Lackay and Van Loggerenberg, *Rogue*.

12 Anton Harber, *So, For the Record: Behind the Headlines in an Era of State Capture*, Jonathan Ball Publishers, 2020.

13 'President Jacob Zuma announces appointment of new SARS Commissioner', Statement by the Presidency, 23 September 2014, https://www.gov.za/news/media-statements/president-jacob-zuma-announces-appointment-new-sars-commissioner-23-sep-2014.

14 Judicial Commission of Inquiry into Allegations of State Capture, Report: Part 1. Volume 3. Chapter 3: SARS.

15 Ibid.

16 Pieter du Toit, 'A slick suit and

seared salmon: How Bain leaned on me', News24, 26 September 2018, https://www.news24.com/fin24/a-slick-suit-and-seared-salmon-how-bain-leaned-on-me-20180926.

17 Judicial Commission of Inquiry into Allegations of State Capture, Report: Part 1. Volume 3. Chapter 3: SARS.

18 Lackay and Van Loggerenberg, *Rogue.*

19 Exchange with the author, 17 March 2024.

20 Lackay and Van Loggerenberg, *Rogue.*

21 'Submission from Adrian Lackay, former South African Revenue Service spokesperson, to Yunus Carrim, Chairperson of the Standing Committee on Intelligence and Cornelia September, Chairperson of the Joint Standing Committee on Intelligence', 25 March 2015, https://www.politicsweb.co.za/news-and-analysis/sars-this-is-the-inside-story--adrian-lackay.

22 'Carrim: 'We did look at Lackay's SARS memo', News24, 4 October 2018, https://www.news24.com/fin24/carrim-we-did-look-at-lackays-sars-memo-20181004.

23 Judicial Commission of Inquiry into Allegations of State Capture, Report: Part 5. Volume 1: State Security Agency and Crime Intelligence.

24 Pauw, *The President's Keepers.*

Chapter 24: Democracy's worst year

1 Max du Preez, 'Zuma: SA's one-man wrecking ball', *Cape Times*, 30 December 2014, https://www.iol.co.za/pretoria-news/opinion/zuma-sas-one-man-wrecking-ball-1799819#.VLZmtyuUdFM.

2 Ibid.

3 Ibid.

4 Sitting of the National Assembly, extended public committee, Hansard, 26 May 2015, https://www.parliament.gov.za/ hansard?sorts[date]=-1&queries[search]=2015-05-26.

5 South Africa load shedding statistics, CSIR, 30 November 2021, https://www.csir.co.za/sites/default/files/Documents/Loadshedding%20plot.pdf.

6 Claire Bisseker, 'How load shedding hurts the economy', *Business Day*, 11 February 2015, https://www.businesslive.co.za/archive/2015-02-11-how-load-shedding-hurts-the-economy/.

7 Ariel Goldberg, 'The economic impact of load shedding: The case of South African retailers', research project, University of Pretoria, 9 November 2015, https://repository.up.ac.za/bitstream/ handle/2263/52398/Goldberg_Economic_2015.pdf? sequence=1&isAllowed=y.

8 Proceedings of the joint sitting of Parliament, Hansard, 17 February 2015, https://www.parliament.gov.za/storage/app/media/Docs/hansard/4719ad53-e1c4-42a6-bdaf-3c0e8c2fa598.pdf.

9 Ibid.

10 Ibid.

11 Basson and Du Toit, *Enemy of the People.*

12 Proceedings of the joint sitting of Parliament, Hansard, 12 February 2015.

13 Ibid.

14 Ibid.

15 Fiona Forde, 'McBride: I was axed because I was doing my job', *Business Day*, 3 October 2016, https://www.businesslive.co.za/bd/national/2016-10-03-mcbride-i-was-axed-because-i-was-doing-my-job/.

16 amaBhungane, 'Hawks boss Dramat quits after reaching settlement', *Mail & Guardian*, 22 April 2015, https://mg.co.za/article/2015-04-22-hawks-boss-dramat-quits-after-reaching-settlement/.

17 Basson and Du Toit, *Enemy of the People*.

18 Proceedings of the National Council of Provinces, Hansard, 2 September 2015, https://www.parliament.gov.za/storage/app/media/Docs/hansard/f40a46dc-7163-4e20-a5e0-42827899c90a.pdf (with acknowledgement to Gareth van Onselen).

Chapter 25: Zenith and nadir

1 Statement by Ismail Momoniat to the Judicial Commission of Inquiry into Allegations of State Capture, 1 February 2021.

2 Ibid.

3 The anecdote about Molefe is based on an informal conversation with a former cabinet minister who prefers to remain anonymous.

4 Judicial Commission of Inquiry into Allegations of State Capture, Report: Part 4. Volume 1, Part 1: National Treasury.

5 Genevieve Quintal, 'The ANC comes first, not the country – Zuma', News24, 8 November 2015, https://www.news24.com/news24/the- anc-comes-first-not-the-country- zuma-20151108.

6 Judicial Commission of Inquiry into Allegations of State Capture, Report: Part 4. Volume 1, Part 1: National Treasury.

7 Ibid.

8 Ibid.

9 Ibid.

10 Ibid.

11 Ibid.

12 Ibid.

13 Ibid.

14 Ibid.

15 Ibid.

16 Ibid.

17 Ibid.

18 Ibid.

Chapter 26: See no evil

1 Judicial Commission of Inquiry into Allegations of State Capture, Report: Part 4. Volume 2: President Ramaphosa as President.

2 Interview with the author, 24 April 2024.

3 Judicial Commission of Inquiry into Allegations of State Capture, Report: Part 4. Volume 2: President Ramaphosa as President.

4 Basson and Du Toit, *Enemy of the People*.

5 Interview with the author, 24 April 2024.

6 'Response to the rating actions by Fitch Ratings (Fitch) and Standard and Poor's (S&P)', Statement by National Treasury, 4 December 2015, https://www.treasury.gov.za/comm_media/press/2015/2015120403%20-%20NT%20Press%20Statement%20-%20Fitch%20and%20S&P.pdf.

7 'Moody's affirms South Africa's ratings at Baa2, revises outlook to

negative', Statement by National Treasury, 16 December 2015, https://www.treasury.gov.za/ comm_media/press/2015/ 2015121601%20-%20 Government%20Media%20Statement%20-%20Response%20to%20 Moody's %20Credit%20Opinion.pdf.

8   Lameez Omarjee, 'SA's credit rating journey since 1994', News24, 24 November 2019, https://www.news24.com/fin24/timeline-sas-credit-rating-journey-since-1994-20191124.

9   *Economic Freedom Fighters v Speaker of the National Assembly and Others; Democratic Alliance v Speaker of the National Assembly and Others* (CCT 143/15; CCT 171/15), 31 March 2016, https://www.saflii.org/za/cases/ZACC/2016/11.html.

10 *Democratic Alliance v Acting National Director of Public Prosecutions and Others* (High Court 19577/2009), 29 April 2016, https://www.corrup-tionwatch.org.za/wp-content/uploads/2016/05/DA-vs-NDPP-255.pdf.

11 Judicial Commission of Inquiry into Allegations of State Capture, Report: Part 4. Volume 2: President Ramaphosa as President.

12 'State of Capture', Report by the Public Protector, 14 October 2016.

13 Butler, *Cyril Ramaphosa*.

14 Ibid.

15 Judicial Commission of Inquiry into Allegations of State Capture, Report: Part 4. Volume 2: President Ramaphosa as President.

16 Ibid.

17 'Guptas & Jonas: Sunday Times article nothing but gossip masquerading as news', Statement by the ANC, 13 March 2016, https://www.politicsweb.co.za/politics/guptas--jonas-sunday-times- article-gossip-masquera.

Chapter 27: Victory for the axis

1   Interview with the author, 24 April 2024.

2   Natasha Marrian, 'Zuma says Van Rooyen was administration's "most qualified" finance minister', *Business Day*, 22 February 2016, https://www.businesslive.co.za/bd/national/2016-02-22-zuma-says-van- rooyen-was-administrations-most-qualified-finance-minister/.

3   Interview with the author, 24 April 2024.

4   Ibid.

5   Ibid.

6   Ibid.

7   Statement by the Minister of Finance, 26 February 2016, https://www.treasury.gov.za/comm_media/press/2016/2016022601%20-%20 Ministers%20Statement.pdf.

8   'Pravin Gordan's no-knowledge of letter is misleading', statement by the South African Police Service, 15 March 2016, https://www.gov.za/speeches/pravin-gordan%E2%80%99s-no-knowledge-letter-misleading-15-mar-2016-0000.

9   Interview with the author, 24 April 2024.

10 Ibid.

11 'Sitting of a joint session of Parliament', Hansard, 17 February 2016, https://www.parliament.gov.za/hansard?sorts[date]=- 1&queries[search]=2016-02-17.

12 'Sitting of a joint session of Parliament', Hansard, 16 February 2016, https://www.parliament.gov.za/

hansard?sorts[date]=- 1&queries
[search]=2016-02-16.

13 Proceedings of the National Assembly, Hansard, 1 March 2016.

14 Proceedings of the National Assembly, Hansard, 5 April 2016.

15 Ibid.

16 Judicial Commission of Inquiry into Allegations of State Capture, Report: Part 4. Volume 3 and Volume 4: Eskom.

17 Statement by Ismail Momoniat to the Judicial Commission of Inquiry into Allegations of State Capture, 1 February 2021.

18 Judicial Commission of Inquiry into Allegations of State Capture, Report: Part 6. Volume 3: Public funds to Gupta enterprises through state capture, dissipation of funds through money laundering networks and acquisition of Optimum coal mine.

19 Ibid.

20 Judicial Commission of Inquiry into Allegations of State Capture, Report: Part 4. Volume 2: President Ramaphosa as President.

21 Ibid.

22 Interview with the author, 24 April 2024.

23 Ibid, 24 April 2024.

24 Judicial Commission of Inquiry into Allegations of State Capture, Report: Part 4. Volume 1, Part 1: National Treasury.

25 Ibid.

26 Ibid.

27 Interview with the author, 24 April 2024.

28 Basson and Du Toit, *Enemy of the People*.

29 Judicial Commission of Inquiry into Allegations of State Capture, Report: Part 4. Volume 1, Part 1: National Treasury.

Chapter 28: Decline and collapse

1 'Closing address by ANC president Cyril Ramaphosa', 21 December 2017 (via Gareth van Onselen), https://inside-politics.org/2019/01/11/the-zumaphosa- monitor/.

2 Ibid.

3 Interview with the author, 11 April 2024.

4 'State of the Nation Address by President Cyril Ramaphosa', 16 February 2018 (via Gareth van Onselen), https://inside-politics.org/2019/01/11/the-zumaphosa-monitor/.

5 Statement by Ismail Momoniat to the Judicial Commission of Inquiry into Allegations of State Capture, 1 February 2021.

6 Interview with the author, 24 April 2024.

7 Ibid.

8 Interview with the author, 11 April 2024.

9 Interview with the author, 24 April 2024.

10 Interview with the author, 30 April 2024.

11 Ibid.

Conclusion

1 Pieter du Toit, 'The looters are on the run and the republic is holding firm', HuffPost South Africa, 17 February 2018, https://www.huffingtonpost. co.uk/entry/the-looters-are-on-the-run-and-the-republic-is-holding-firm_uk_5c7e83bfe4b06e0d4c22d-caa.

2 Ferial Haffajee, 'For the first time in a decade, I want to lend a hand', HuffPost South Africa, 16 February 2018, https://www.huffingtonpost.co.uk/entry/for-the-first-time-in-a-decade-i-want-to-lend-a-hand_uk_5c7e83b8e4b06e0d4c22dc40.

3 Justice Malala, 'Beyond a great speech, a bigger test awaits Ramaphosa', *The Times*, 19 February 2018.

4 Trevor Manuel, 'The ANC's deployment committee - end it now!' News24, 1 July 2022, https://www.news24.com/news24/Opinions/FridayBriefing/trevor-manuel-the-ancs-deployment-committee-end-it-now-20220630.

Acknowledgements

TO CONCEPTUALISE, RESEARCH, WRITE, edit and eventually publish a book is a large undertaking. This is my fourth book with Jonathan Ball Publishers, and as always it has been a pleasurable experience.

My thanks go to Eugene Ashton, the chief executive at Jonathan Ball, who is a firm friend and someone whose judgement and advice I appreciate and respect. Jeremy Boraine, my publisher, is unbending but fair and I benefit greatly from his insights and criticism. And to the rest of the team at Jonathan Ball – Jean-Marie Korff, Sharon Naidoo, Annie Olivier and Esmund Desai – you're a great bunch of people.

Dave Chambers, my editor, was crisp, clear and efficient. As was Vivien Wray, who transcribed my interviews. Thank you both.

Media24, under the leadership of Ishmet Davidson, is the standard bearer of journalism in this country. It remains a privilege to practise journalism in a company that continues to invest in the craft and understands the importance of the fourth estate's role. This book is an extension of my day job.

I also want to thank every journalist and author whose work I quote. Covering the tapestry of democratic South Africa's first three decades would not have been possible without their insightful and incisive writing. Thanks must also go to the individuals I was lucky enough to interview. All of them played a role over the last couple of decades and I greatly enjoyed our conversations.

And finally to my family, who again bore the brunt of my absenteeism. Allowing me to write this book entailed a significant sacrifice. Thank you to my wife, Janetha, and sons Schalk and Lukas.

Index

About the author

PIETER DU TOIT IS A JOURNALIST AT NEWS24, South Africa's foremost news publication. As assistant editor, he oversees the investigative team and writes a weekly column on politics and society. He has been a journalist for more than 20 years and worked as a sub-editor at *Volksblad* in Bloemfontein, a crime reporter at *Beeld* in Pretoria, and the latter newspaper's parliamentary correspondent in Cape Town for five years. After stints as news editor at *Beeld* and Netwerk24, he was appointed deputy editor and eventually editor of the now defunct Huffington Post South Africa. He has been with News24 since 2018.

His previous books with Jonathan Ball Publishers *are Enemy of the People: How Jacob Zuma Stole South Africa and How the People Fought Back* (2017, with Adriaan Basson), *The Stellenbosch Mafia: Inside the Billionaires' Club* (2019) and *The ANC Billionaires: Big Capital's Gambit and the Rise of the Few* (2022).

The Stellenbosch Mafia and *The ANC Billionaires* were bestsellers and occupied the number one position on the Nielsen BookScan sales charts. *The Stellenbosch Mafia* was voted the non-fiction book of the year by the South African Booksellers Association in 2020. *The ANC Billionaires* was included in the nonfiction longlist for the *Sunday Times* Literary Awards in 2023.

Du Toit went to school and university in Stellenbosch. He lives in Johannesburg with his wife and two sons.